Dr. Morris Cerullo is truly a legend among legends in the body of Christ. His teachings are inspired, his dedication undeniable, and his influence is global. His legacy will live for generations to come.

—Joel Osteen
Pastor, Lakewood Church in Houston, Texas

The Legend of Morris Cerullo is a life-changing journey through the legendary life of an American giant of faith. Everyone should get his or her hands on this book to experience the compelling story of Dr. Cerullo's journey with Christ. I recommend this fascinating story to everyone.

—Jentezen Franklin
New York Times Best-Selling Author
and Senior Pastor, Free Chapel

Jesus said many are called but few are chosen. Without doubt Morris Cerullo was chosen before his birth to become an apostle of Christ to the nations. Like Paul of old, Morris is a Jew ministering to both Jews and Gentiles. As a teenage minister my own life was impacted by his book *Proof Producers*, and he continues to impart to millions around the globe. This is his story, from the beginning; [it is] a fascinating journey into the life of a man whose ministry has impacted the world. From an orphan to an orator, from a doubter to a deliver, Morris Cerullo has proven that one man with God can change nations. This book will inspire every reader!

—Dr. Perry Stone, Jr.
Founder/President, Voice of Evangelism, Omega Center
International, and International School of the Word

God has always looked for a man. He found that man in Morris Cerullo, who has been used mightily to take the gospel around the world. Morris is a man of great faith, and the power of the Lord has been evidenced in his life. How wonderful that a book is now written to chronicle in part the miraculous life of one of the Lord's servants.

—Dr. M G Pat Robertson
Founder/Chairman, The Christian Broadcasting Network, Inc.

Dr. Cerullo is a general in the kingdom of God and a shining example of what it means to be a man after God's heart. He has impacted countless lives and ministries, and I am so thankful for him! He has truly paved the way for future generations.

—John Bevere
Author and Minister, Messenger International

Morris Cerullo is a friend of mine. I recommend this book because I know the righteous intent of this man's globe-encompassing ministry and his passion to assist in the training of church leaders: to preach the Word of God to win souls for Jesus Christ.

The tempo of his heartbeat for the world deserves your reading and feeling that vital concern.

—JACK W. HAYFORD
CHANCELLOR, THE KING'S UNIVERSITY IN SOUTHLAKE, TEXAS
PASTOR EMERITUS, THE CHURCH ON THE WAY
IN VAN NUYS, CALIFORNIA

Morris Cerullo is one of the great pioneers of the faith. There are few people who have had the courage that he has had to take incredible risks to advance the kingdom of God. This book will encourage you to do great things for God and live an extraordinary life!

—DR. CINDY JACOBS
PRESIDENT/FOUNDER, GENERALS INTERNATIONAL

For seven decades, Dr. Cerullo has touched the world like no other man I know. Not only has he preached to some of the largest crowds in history [and] seen incredible miracles, but also he has trained an army of millions of ministers world-wide, men who have built some of the great churches in their nation! This story is so miraculous one might find it unbelievable if they were not there to witness it firsthand. I have had a front-row seat to this extraordinary man and ministry. This book is a must read.

—TOMMY BARNETT
SENIOR PASTOR/FOUNDER, PHOENIX FIRST ASSEMBLY OF GOD
LOS ANGELES DREAM CENTER

The Lord Jesus, many years ago, planted the seed of His love in Gloria's and my heart for Theresa and Morris Cerullo that has steadily grown, grown for well over thirty, even closer to forty years ago. Those of us *blessed* to be in this generation are standing on the rock of God's grace laid for us by men like Morris Cerullo. Read and enjoy his life of faith. Jesus is Lord!

—KENNETH COPELAND

THE LEGEND

of

MORRIS CERULLO

THE LEGEND
of
MORRIS CERULLO

MORRIS CERULLO

CREATION
HOUSE

The Legend of Morris Cerullo by Dr. Morris Cerullo
Published by Creation House
A Charisma Media Company
600 Rinehart Road
Lake Mary, Florida 32746
www.charismamedia.com

Scripture quotations are from the King James Version of the Bible and the
Holy Bible, New Living Translation, copyright © 2007. Used by permission of
Tyndale House Publishers, Inc., Wheaton, IL 60189. All rights reserved.

Design Director: Justin Evans
Cover design by: Justin Evans

Visit the author's website: http://www.mcwe.com/

Library of Congress Control Number: 2016933819
International Standard Book Number: 978-1-62998-536-7
E-book International Standard Book Number: 978-1-62998-537-4

While the author has made every effort to provide accurate telephone numbers
and Internet addresses at the time of publication, neither the publisher nor the
author assumes any responsibility for errors or for changes that occur after
publication.

First edition

16 17 18 19 20 — 9 8 7 6 5 4 3 2 1
Printed in Canada

CONTENTS

———•———

ACKNOWLEDGMENTS

———◆———

THIS BOOK COVERING the details of my life, ministry, experiences, and extraordinary leading of the Holy Spirit would not have been possible without the help of my wife, Theresa, who has stood by my side and constantly supported me even when she may not have fully understood what God was speaking to my heart. She has faithfully undergirded me and our ministry with continual prayer for over sixty years. This book would never have been possible without her faithful contributions.

I also want to acknowledge Greg Mauro, a trusted and faithful co-laborer in the works of the Lord. For over thirty years Greg has gone with me into North America, England, Europe, and many other nations as together we have ministered the Word of God.

Both Theresa and Greg helped me co-author this book. I give special thanks for their long hours of sacrificial labor in recalling, organizing, structuring, and assisting me in writing these personal memoirs. (Please note that this book is written in third person even though Theresa and I both shared our firsthand experiences, which are captured in the following pages.)

There are a multitude of people over the years who have come alongside of me to fulfill the work the Lord laid before me. It has been an incredible journey. Thanks to Don Mandell, who has been my vice president of international ministries for over thirty years. He has pioneered the nations of the world, preparing the way so I might deliver training to now over four million foreign nationals who, after being trained, have ministered the gospel of Jesus Christ in their nations.

Thanks also to George Eckroth, Lowell Warner, Connie Broom, Pat Hulsey, and our ministerial staff, who have all played a major role in accomplishing what seemed to be an impossible task of reaching into areas of the world (such as Israel) that needed to hear and in turn share the gospel of Jesus Christ with others.

I want to give special thanks to my son David Cerullo, who through his contribution, his life, and as president of The Inspirational Networks shares the mandate God placed on my life and is a living portrayal of our legacy.

Most importantly I want to thank the Third Person of the Trinity, the Holy Spirit, for inspiration, insight, and for leading and guiding my steps since I left the orphanage in Patterson, New Jersey, when I was just fourteen years old. It is through His empowerment that what you read in the following pages was possible.

And to you, dear reader, I want to encourage you that what God has done through my life He can do through yours as well. God is no respecter of persons but is looking for hungry souls who are willing to surrender to the will of the Father and be obedient to His will in their lives.

I pray that this book will open up your spirit and that many of you will surrender to the calling God has placed on your life.

God bless you.

INTRODUCTION

————◆————

I
F THERE WERE such a thing as a Ministry Hall of Fame, who would be
inducted?

You can probably name a dozen people off the top of your head. Billy
Graham would be one of them, of course. Mother Teresa and Martin Luther
King, Jr., are shoo-ins. William Seymour, igniter of the Azusa Street revival,
and African missionary and evangelist William Wadé Harris would be
invited. Renowned teachers and disciplers like John Stott, Henrietta Mears,
and Francis Schaeffer deserve a place at the table. Desmond Tutu's work
in South Africa and Watchman Nee's efforts in China gain them entrance.
Less traditional but hugely influential servants like Bill Bright, Herbert
Taylor, and C S Lewis would certainly qualify. The names of other deserving
candidates are probably running through your mind right now.

Depending upon how far back in history you want to go, you couldn't go
wrong with the likes of Francis of Assisi, John Wesley, Augustine, George
Whitefield, and William Tyndale. That list would be lengthy as well.

One contemporary minister of the gospel who would indisputably receive
admission is Morris Cerullo. An American giant of the faith who is best
known in Africa, Asia, and South America, Dr. Cerullo has been a ministry
pacesetter for seven decades. Who else do you know who can claim to have
accomplished the following combination of exploits?

+ Personally trained more than four million Christian leaders around
  the world who have planted tens of thousands of churches and seen
  untold numbers of their countrymen—a figure certainly in the
  millions—embrace Jesus Christ as their Lord and Savior

+ Held evangelistic crusades in more than sixty nations of the world,
  which have been responsible for several million people coming forward to accept Jesus Christ as their Savior

+ Led more than a half-dozen presidents of nations to Christ

+ Performed literally thousands of physical miracles through the
  power of God

+ Raised money and provided leadership for building numerous
  orphanages, hospitals, schools, universities, and churches spread
  across six continents

+ Won awards for his outreach-oriented television and movie
  productions

+ Turned a failing television network into a successful broadcasting center
+ Pioneered the live call-in talk show television format
+ Operated his ministry debt-free for more than a half-century while personally living on income generated outside of his ministry (i.e., a "tentmaking" approach)
+ Accurately prophesied many world events
+ Personally mentored many of the Christian leaders across the world

Make no mistake, Morris Cerullo is an original; there has been no one quite like him. He was an orphan whom God raised up to be a prophet. He was born a Jew and emerged a Christian. He was raised in New Jersey but became an apostle to the world. He turned his back on God only to be transformed by the presence and anointing of God, shifting from doubting the power of God to experiencing and sharing the supernatural time after time.

Despite all these earthly accomplishments, he is invariably quick to remind people, "This is not the work of a man, but this is the work of the Holy Spirit of the living God!" It is not a false humility; it is a realistic assessment of his limited capabilities and an acknowledgement of the unlimited power of God flowing through him for kingdom purposes. He has long been sensitive to the supernatural power and guidance of God moving him to do the impossible, to see the invisible, and to understand the incomprehensible. He readily admits that his incredible life is solely attributable to his openness to allowing God to have His way with him.

Few have a legacy as rich and diversified as Morris Cerullo. The world is a better place for his decision to embrace the God of Abraham, Isaac, and John and to dedicate his life to serving his heavenly Father. It has been a remarkable ride—the kind that movies are made of. Perhaps one day his life will be the subject of such a film, but for now the miraculous works of God continue to be manifested through him.

But the life of Morris Cerullo has rarely been easy or predictable.

PART ONE:

———◆———

A TROUBLED
YOUTH

CHAPTER 1

———◆———

MORRIS CERULLO WAS a five year old with the mind and heart of a young adult. His difficult pre-school years only got harsher once his drunkard, widowed father dropped him and his four siblings off at their first foster home.

Morris was acutely aware of what was going on around him. He was growing up faster than any child should. He knew the pain of seeing his mother die when he was just two. He witnessed his father's love affair with the bottle. He grudgingly accepted the fact that he was a "ward of the state." For the time being he remained indifferent to the state of New Jersey's involvement in his life, though that would soon change.

But most of all, young Morris grasped the harshest lesson of all: nobody in this wicked world really loved him. He was just another hungry mouth to feed, another naked body to clothe, another empty mind to educate, another potential criminal to be contained.

Little Morris Cerullo, the youngest of the Cerullo brood, was a lot of things, but he was certainly no dummy. The little boy with the fire in his eyes knew that if he was going to make it in this world he was going to do it on his own—and on his own terms.

So, when his father dropped Morris, his brother, and three sisters off at a big house in a middle-class neighborhood in Teaneck Morris's adrenaline was flowing. It may have been late at night, but his system was on full alert. Morris knew that nothing good takes places in the shadows of the night.

Although he was too young to fully comprehend the implications of the exchange taking place, he sensed that something important was going down. Under hooded eyes he watched his father have a curt, whispered conversation with the owners of the big house, slam the door on his way out of the modestly furnished home, stride back to his car, and zoom away without a word to the children.

Instinctively, Dr. Cerullo knew his dad was gone for good. He was no longer a survivor in a single-parent home. He was now officially an orphan.

Morris stood among his brother and sisters as the apparent owners of the house, a poorly preserved, tired-looking couple in their late fifties, addressed the young Cerullos and blandly welcomed them to their new home.

Morris knew abandonment when he heard it. The anger inside him seethed to a new level. His mother was long deceased. His father might as well die too, the weasel. He wasn't much of a father, but how could he simply dump his children, his own flesh and blood, inside the house of some strangers and drive away scot free? What kind of man does that to his own children? What kind of loser would do that Morris?

After a brief time of getting acclimated and then settling into single beds strewn around the attic—their shared bedroom space—Morris lay alone on the bed in the dark room, staring vacantly at the ceiling. In his mind he replayed the rotten hand he had been dealt in life so far. From the early indications, this latest move wasn't going to make matters much better.

Like any child on the short end of the stick, he wondered what he had done wrong. Why didn't anyone love him? Why had his mother died and his father cast him aside like last week's newspaper? How much of this was his fault? Was he the loser that his circumstances suggested? He fell asleep void of answers but overflowing with hurt and indignation.

When he awoke the next morning he threw back the curtain covering the attic window and gazed down at the multi-acre yard that belonged to his new caretakers. He couldn't bring himself to think of them as parents, even foster parents. And he couldn't believe the travesty that sprawled before his eyes. A junkyard! He was now living in a house that was surrounded by a large lot littered with discarded tires, rusting auto parts, and a sea of other dilapidated items. As bad as things had been going in his life, he never saw this coming. He now lived in a home that was apparently funded by the proceeds garnered from other people's garbage.

Perhaps a five year old who still possessed hope would see the metal and rubber objects covering the yard as a magical wonderland—a property of discarded toys to play with. But Morris, wise beyond his years, knew better. He had been traded from an alcoholic to a junk dealer. As he turned from the window and approached his pile of clothes in the corner to get ready for his first day in a new school, a consuming sense of dread wrapped its hands around his heart.

CHAPTER 2

⸻•⸻

THE WOODEN PADDLE smacked Morris's rear end with a resounding *thwack*. The six year old craned his neck backward to see the satisfied look on the principal's face. He knew that he was the only student whom the principal hit with the paddle. He also realized it was because he had quickly earned the reputation as the worst-behaved student in the entire elementary school.

Morris had already learned the importance of mental toughness, so he began his mind games with the principal. He was not about to let her see the pain that the spanking caused him. He simply looked back at her and made the meanest face he could muster.

She swatted him again. And again.

When she was done she told the young boy to leave and learn to behave. He started his road to recovery by cursing at her.

With his anger running over, a new realization entered his mind.

"I don't have to take this," he thought. "They'll be glad to be rid of me. And I'll never miss them. I might as well run away from these jerks."

And so he did. He walked down the hallway from the main office, then turned right—out of the sight line of the principal—and continued all the way down that corridor. He marched past his classroom without looking in and continued straight out the exit door.

The sunlight momentarily blinded him as the heavy door thumped to a close. He stood there for a couple seconds to get his bearings and devise his escape route. A tingle of excitement made his day. He was once again free and in control, even if it might not last long.

He hurriedly marched off the school campus and made his way to the train tracks, which would lead to the woods and the swampland. He was determined not to get caught, even if he had no plan for survival.

⸻•⸻

He heard the footsteps of the police as they searched through the marshland. Morris tried to snuggle closer to the ground, buried in the dense but leafless branches of the bushes on the perimeter of the swamp. He could see one officer, bundled up in his black wool-and-nylon jacket with the police cap perched on his balding head, whacking some nearby shrubs with his nightstick, searching for him.

"Come on, Morris," the officer yelled. "You're going to freeze to death out here. Let's head back."

Morris had no intention of aiding their search. He couldn't understand why they didn't just leave him alone. Everyone else had.

Finally, one of the three officers saw the boy nestled in the bushes and stood over him. "Come on, son. Time to go." They stared at each other for a moment before Morris figured there was nothing to gain by making the cops get physical with him.

The quartet sullenly walked back to the police car. They drove directly to the station house and surrounded Morris as they entered the building. They marched him back to an interrogation room, where one officer entered with the youngster and began questioning him about his adventure. After a few minutes of silence from the disengaged boy the door opened and one of the investigating officers entered with a tray of food for Morris. It contained a bowl of steaming soup and some crackers. He placed in front of Morris, gave the seated policeman a look, and exited.

Unable to get much out of the child, the officer finally led him back to the car, putting him in a blanket to ward off the frigid evening air, and drove him back to the junkyard. His foster mother met him at the curb, apologized and thanked the officer, and silently led Morris back inside the big, dark house.

The moment the front door had shut behind them, the woman bent over, removed her shoe, and started to beat Morris with it. Again and again she slammed him with the shoe. Eventually the child surrendered and fell in a heap at her feet. His body throbbed everywhere, from his head down to his legs, where she had battered him.

"Get upstairs, you worthless snot," she growled at Morris. "Don't you dare come downstairs for dinner. That's the last time I want the police to have to deal with you. Do you understand?"

Morris laid there for a minute, waiting for her to leave. After she departed, he slowly got to his feet and slumped up the stairs to his attic room. He fell onto his mattress and sobbed quietly to himself. The fury and violence in his heart and mind throbbed. His determination to get back at the world had never been stronger.

CHAPTER 3

————•————

ORRIS SAT ON the edge of his bunk bed and watched the harried, middle-aged women try to wrangle the orphan boys. He despised every one of them—administrators, counselors, and peers. They knew nothing about him, his past, his feelings, his dreams. They were not allies.

Small for his age, the eight year old was already becoming hardened to the blows the world continued to deal him. After a difficult year with the German Jews who owned the junkyard, Morris wound up in what he thought of as a "Gentile orphanage." His Jewish heritage and traditions were nowhere to be found in this place and never acknowledged. Morris's mother had been an Orthodox Jew, and the state had determined that he and his siblings should be raised to be Jewish. But there were no viable options available at the time, so the Cerullo kids had been sent to interim residences. As the kids had proven to be a handful, they were eventually split up while waiting for openings in the desired quarters.

As isolated as he felt at the junkyard, Morris was truly alone now. His siblings were all in different locations. His oldest brother, Abraham, had become fed up with the junkyard scene and enlisted in the Army. The next eldest, sisters Frances and Pauline, launched out on their own as well, barely of legal age but eager to be done with the state's system of care. Frances soon got married, so Pauline was on her own again, moving in with some friends. That left him and his sister Bernice with the Gentiles. They were split up—the boys were in one part of the campus, the girls in another—and rarely had contact with each other.

Morris didn't care. His sister was not going to protect him or provide for him. He was on his own and intent upon determining his own path.

The small campus was inhabited by many other children, more than a hundred nobodies for whom the state was responsible. Like Morris, these were young people who were loved by no one. There was an unspoken understanding among them. They sure weren't family, but the collection of little people had common needs and experiences. And so life went on, with Dr. Cerullo learning to project himself as a little tough guy. Even at age eight, he had grasped the law of the street: rule or be ruled.

Morris made sure that everyone knew he was in charge. Height was irrelevant; it was the size of one's heart that mattered. Morris's heart, filled with rage, clearly eclipsed that of every other kid he encountered.

CHAPTER 4

B Y THE TIME he was ten, Morris Cerullo was a sad victim of life. Still short of stature, he possessed an oversized chip on his shoulder and challenged any and all forms of authority whenever opportunities arose. His palpable bitterness toward adults and institutions was unlimited and escalating.

Other young people who were on the same life trajectory gravitated toward Morris. He was accepted by other juvenile delinquents, having earned a reputation among the other hoodlums in the area as a tough kid.

He made no attempt to hide his disdain for authority. He defiantly drank alcohol, smoked cigarettes, stole merchandise from local shops, and cursed up a storm. Rare was the day when he was not involved in some type of physical scuffle. Fistfights were necessary to establish his place in the pecking order and to instill fear in the hearts of those who potentially stood in his way.

If there was one thing the young orphan had figured out, it was that life was a constant battle, and you had to be tough or be a victim. Although he had no plan for his future, he was determined that nobody was going to control him. He had memory after memory of authority figures whose decisions failed to advance his own best interests. If he was going to succeed, he'd have to orchestrate fruitful outcomes his way, in his timing.

As Morris bounced from one orphanage or foster home to another, he continued to fight the system. He ran away from his appointed housing, time after time, and cut classes in order to engage in illegal or immoral activities. Occasionally he was picked up by the police and threatened with fines and jail time. As he got older his defiance led to more serious consequences, including appearances in court. At each of his court hearings, however, the judges reviewed his life history and had mercy on him, hoping that he could be straightened out before the only alternative was prison time—and a life almost certainly defined by more crime and increasingly serious punishments.

Morris was naturally intelligent but congenitally disinterested in schoolwork. He never considered academia his road to riches and freedom. His classmates, aware that he was an orphan, didn't seem to mind. In northern New Jersey in the 1940s you made your reputation based on your skills and behavior, not your address. Morris gained a reputation for being a rebellious, hostile, tough guy. He trusted nobody: teachers, administrators, coaches, ministers, police, peers. In his mind, it was every man for himself.

CHAPTER 5

O NE DAY HE returned from school to discover that his possessions—which didn't amount to much, just a few pieces of simple clothing and the necessary toiletries—had been stuffed into a box that was sitting on his bed. A nondescript middle-aged man in a cheap suit was standing beside the bed staring down at the diminutive school boy.

"Morris Cerullo?" the man said with an air of superiority. "You are being relocated to another residence. Pick up your box and follow me."

He'd been through it before, but this reassignment process was both impersonal and humiliating. Who did these bureaucrats think they were? Was he just a piece of meat to be transferred from plate to plate? His resentment seethed inside as he silently picked up his box and followed the man.

He did not thank the orphanage personnel. He did not offer good-byes to his peers. He did not shed a tear over being moved again. Morris Cerullo was too angry to think about those things.

As they loaded his box in the man's state-issued automobile that was sitting in the front driveway, Morris figured he deserved better than this.

"Where are we going?" he demanded with a scowl.

"To another orphanage near here," came the reply.

"Why? What's so special about that place? You think they know how to handle kids like me?"

The man turned the key in the ignition and then twisted his body to look at the young boy in the backseat. "Morris," he said a bit more softly, "we have arranged for you to be in a Jewish orphanage. Your mother was an Orthodox Jew, and her request was that you be raised in that tradition. The state has not had the available beds to place you in such a facility. Now there is an opening, and so we are trying to honor your mother's request. It is a program with a good track record of success with its placements. I think you'll be happy there, and you'll be able to attend the same school, so you don't have to start over. OK?"

The man waited for an answer from the boy. Morris simply kept his squinting eyes on the man and refused to answer. "Another snow job," he thought to himself. "Something's up, and I'll find out what's going on soon enough. The system doesn't care about losers like me." He scowled at the man and turned his head to look out the side window.

The bureaucrat frowned and shook his head, righted his body, put the car in gear, and drove toward the next orphanage. He had yet to meet one of these orphans who seemed at peace with himself and the world. This kid certainly was not going to be the first.

CHAPTER 6

─────◆─────

S O, YOU ARE Morris Cerullo, huh? Welcome to the Daughters of Miriam," Mrs. Gold, the co-director of the orphanage, said sternly to the young boy standing in front of her. "I hear you are quite a handful, Morris. Well, I want you to know we don't tolerate bad behavior here. Come, follow me."

The two moved down the hallway as she continued over her shoulder. "To minimize your outbursts we have decided to place you in the wing with the older boys. You might think you're a real champion among the boys your age, but it would not be smart for you to take on the older boys. You would be smart to stop your fighting altogether."

Mrs. Gold showed him his new living space and then instructed him in the rules. The bed had to be made just right. He would have a job in the kitchen and a responsibility in the garden. He would be expected to complete his daily chores in a timely manner, and to be present at group meals at the designated time. The boys would all walk to the local school together, return home afterward to finish homework assignments, and attend the daily Hebrew class taught by Rabbi Gold, her husband.

She knew she had a ticking time bomb on her hands. She did her best to convey the zero-tolerance policies of the orphanage.

─────◆─────

Morris watched the woman carefully. He quickly grasped that this was a place that prided itself in its strict routines. He was neither impressed nor scared. In his mind, they hadn't yet built a facility that could contain the wrath of Morris Cerullo.

As far as he was concerned, the new residence was just another storehouse for unwanted kids. Yes, it had strict rules and a Jewish way of life, but that meant nothing to him. He considered himself to be Jewish only because his mother had been Jewish. So what? He still had to fend for himself on the playground, on the streets, in the classroom. Jewish, Italian, Catholic, black, Japanese—none of that mattered to him. You had to prove yourself every day no matter who or where you were.

Morris laid low during his first few weeks in the Daughters of Miriam orphanage, getting acquainted with the new rules and regulations and sizing up the security systems, the other kids, and the routines of the adult leaders. Even as a ten year old his mind was focused on independence, control, survival—and, of course, mischief.

As young Morris studied the ways of the world and reflected on his growing array of experiences, he began to dream about his future. One dream was to become a lawyer. That may seem like an odd choice for a thorn in the side of the criminal justice system, but his thinking was built on a perverse kind of logic. "If I become a lawyer," he reasoned, "that could lead to becoming a governor. As the leader of a state I would be able to live above the law and even create the rules that others have to live by. That would be the best!" He never gave a second thought to the extra years of advanced schooling his dream would require. In his mind, there had to be a way around all those years in the classroom, and he'd figure it out. Within a short time, Morris had established himself as a leader among the kids his age. He earned a reputation of being a kid you didn't want to mess with, a ruthless, no-holds-barred fighter, and someone who always got even with anyone who tried to take advantage of him. Your best bet was to be on his side. The easiest way to do that was to fall in line with his demands.

One day after another fight at school the kids were in their study area when one boy taunted Morris because of the bruised cheek and swollen nose he had sustained in the fight. Already smarting from the earlier battle, the taunting did not go down well with him. Morris jumped the fellow and badgered him relentlessly with his fists. Once he got the other kid on the ground he pummeled his face, his torso, and his arms. At one point the taunter attempted to get back on his feet. Morris hit the boy so hard that his head flew to the ground and bounced off the tile floor. It rebounded into Morris's mouth, breaking his front teeth.

Finally Rabbi Gold and a couple of other adults on staff at the home arrived to break up the fight. Despite the broken teeth and the blood pouring from his mouth, Morris struggled to free his arms so he could continue his attack. Rage was radiating from him as he eyed his vanquished opponent. It took a while for the fury to subside and for the adults in charge to drive Morris to the hospital so his mouth could be treated.

CHAPTER 7

————•————

THERE WERE TWO indisputable realities regarding Morris Cerullo.

He was a bully. Everyone knew it, and he was proud of it. In his mind, he had figured out the route to survival. Other bullies had tested him, and he emerged victorious—or, at least, with their grudging respect. He was physically small, but he had definitely proven himself to be a force to be reckoned with, a crazy kid not to be messed with. Spilling the blood of others did not bother him in the least. Those people meant nothing to him, just as he believed that his life meant nothing to the world that was trying to control him.

The other indisputable, if less well-known, truth was that Morris was consumed by hatred. He hated the orphanage. He hated school. He hated authority. He hated being Jewish. He hated his classmates.

Morris Cerullo hated being alive.

After returning from the hospital, Morris was lying in bed, unable to sleep, and made an important decision. He was tired of having to be constantly alert, having to prove himself day after day. He was sick of his lousy existence pursuing a life that was not working. As he gently rubbed his wounds and considered his options, he decided a major change was in order. He determined to hate no more.

Morris Cerullo decided to end his life.

Ten years of agony was more than enough. He could see the trajectory of his life, and it wasn't appealing.

He decided it was time to wipe the slate clean.

Morris reached that grand conclusion at two o'clock in the morning. Everyone else was sleeping soundly. He quietly tiptoed into the boys' bathroom and locked the door. He opened the second-story window and boosted himself from the edge of the tub up to the window sill and then out onto the cement ledge. He crawled a few feet from the window and looked down.

The black asphalt driveway beckoned him to come closer.

He moved into a squatting position and looked down again. It could all be over in just seconds. No more pain, no more struggles, no more inner rage and fury. The peace that had escaped him all his life was within reach. All it would take was a moment of courage.

Morris began to breathe deeply and slowly. He convinced himself this would be no more difficult than jumping off the diving board at the pool.

As he began to shift his weight for the jump, he was startled by a sound behind him. He turned toward the bathroom window and whispered, "Who's there?"

No reply.

Morris carefully slid a step closer to the window and glanced inside. The room was still empty. But he could sense a presence, an indescribable but undeniable presence of something, someone.

The boy shifted his weight again, balancing himself on the ledge looking across the parking lot. Then he turned his gaze upward as he exhaled and noticed the stars. They seemed more vivid and beautiful than they had ever been. The cold winter air was crisp and fresh as a stream of warm air escaped from his lungs. The whiff of the nearby evergreens filled his nostrils. The moon, the only light shining on him, illuminated the silhouette of the buildings and homes that lined the street.

Suddenly he was overcome with a sense of warmth. The sensation nearly caused him to topple off the ledge. The weight of rage that had pushed him onto his precarious perch was strangely gone. The throbbing of his teeth and gums ceased. And he felt that presence once again.

Morris Cerullo was not a religious child, but he realized that something supernatural was taking place. He couldn't explain it, and he didn't understand, but neither did he want it to end. He stayed frozen in position, absorbing the moment, embracing the presence. He felt at peace—a feeling he had never had before. The incredible rage, the hot anger, the gnawing emptiness—those intense emotions were gone. He simply felt release, calm, serene.

He gently shut his eyes and took a mental snapshot of the moment.

He slowly opened his eyes, cautiously and slowly moved back toward the bathroom, and lowered himself into the warm room. A glance at the clock on the wall showed that his encounter with destiny had lasted nearly an hour. He lay on his back and considered the experience.

He fell asleep still pondering the presence he had experienced on the ledge.

Little did he know that this first experience with the supernatural was not going to be the last. Not by a long shot.

CHAPTER 8

B Y THE NEXT morning, the presence was no longer strong and embracing; it was a fuzzy memory. Morris fell into his daily routine, still reflecting on his strange incident but maintaining his persona. Anger and rage had recaptured his heart.

His behavior in the weeks, months, and years that followed that special night gave no one an inkling of the supernatural encounter young Morris had experienced.

And so it was that by the time he reached his thirteenth birthday, he was ready for his bar mitzvah. While he had not bought into Judaism as a way of life, he suffered through Hebrew school every afternoon and figured this, his coming-out party, was part of the payoff he was due.

The Jewish tradition called for a thirteen year old to complete a ritual ceremony in which he demonstrated that he was an adult, a member of the Jewish community, and responsible to live according to the Scriptures.

Morris dutifully prepared for the ceremony and carried out his obligations without incident. He wore the phylacteries and the tefillin as prescribed by tradition. He delivered his Talmudic discourse from memory and carried the Torah down the aisle at the conclusion of his ceremony.

Mazel tov!

According to Jewish tradition, the newly bar mitzvahd Morris was now a man with all the rights, duties, and responsibilities that accompanied that standing. But in his own mind he had been a man for years, and he had the marks of survival to prove it. His self-image was unchanged by the ceremony. That was just a required religious performance.

Meanwhile, Rabbi Gold breathed a sigh of relief at the conclusion of the ceremony. Who knew that this young troublemaker would last long enough to successfully complete his bar mitzvah? Who would have wagered that the orphaned rabble-rouser would not have caused some type of commotion on the special day?

Rabbi Gold prayed, "May the good God of Israel continue to change the boy's heart, surround him with loving and understanding role models, and incorporate him into the community of the faithful to become a productive and commendable member of society."

On that day nobody could have imagined how the rabbi's prayer would be answered in unexpected but miraculous ways.

CHAPTER 9

N OT MANY WOMEN in the 1940s would have felt so at ease about being divorced and starting a new career in their fifties. But Ethel Kerr was not just any woman. She was a woman on a mission.

For many years she had been married to a gentleman who had become quite famous and wealthy, but during the course of their life together she discovered Jesus Christ and invited Him into her life—and that life was never the same. She tried for some time to get her husband to consider the claims of Christ, but to no avail. He eventually became infuriated with her spiritual intensity and gave her an ultimatum: "You can have this Jesus in your life or me in your life, but you cannot have both." She tried desperately to win her husband over, but it was not to be. She had to make a choice.

And she did. Her husband, enraged by her decision, threw her out. She left with just the clothes on her back and nothing else. She left behind the mansion, the good life, even her children—and while it broke her heart to do so, she knew she made the right choice.

In the 1940s, divorce was rare and attached a stigma to those involved, especially the women. Left on their own, life became an uphill journey for them. During that era women generally had limited employment options, so the new life Ethel suddenly faced was not an easy one. For the first time in years she had to think about being the breadwinner and how to make ends meet. It didn't take her long to realize that she was not qualified for much besides waitressing and unskilled jobs that did not pay subsistence wages, so she made arrangements to return to school to be trained in nursing and emerged as a practical nurse.

Even with that preparation and certification, though, her employment options were limited. She submitted applications in various places and eventually took a position at a Jewish orphanage working as a caregiver to all the people living in the expansive facility—the elderly, retired people as well as the young orphans being raised in their faith. When she applied the personnel director balked at hiring her—after all, she was not an Orthodox Jew like everyone else on staff and in residence—but they needed someone immediately, she was well-qualified, and her winsome ways persuaded the personnel manager to take a chance.

So Ethel Kerr continued her remarkable journey transitioning from a mansion in an upper-class neighborhood with maids and comfort to making a pittance of a salary while living in a single room in a staff dormitory. She spent her days making the beds of retired Jewish couples and widowers, tending to their infirmities, and addressing the needs of a bunch of young Jewish orphans.

Given her bright personality and kindness, she was a favorite of the residents, and she got along famously with the other staff members. But she became frustrated with her occupational situation. It wasn't the menial tasks or the lousy wages that disappointed her. She was convinced that God had led her to the Jewish enclave in order to be a light in the spiritual darkness, but the opportunities to be such a beacon of God's love were missing.

One day, while making yet another bed, she fell to her knees and wept. "Why, Lord, why?" she sobbed. "I believe you sent me here and that you opened the door for me to be hired, but you have never given me any meaningful opportunities to witness for you." As a good Baptist woman who regularly attended church services, read her Bible daily, and prayed constantly, she was distraught over her inability to serve the Lord in the manner she had expected. To a Baptist, the height of service was sharing the good news of Jesus Christ's offer of salvation with those who had not embraced Him as their Lord and Savior.

Baptists in the northeast in the 1940s may have been evangelistically motivated, but they were generally not people who were comfortable with what might have been called "Pentecostal experiences" such as physical healings or hearing the voice of God. But Ethel Kerr was less interested in being a good Baptist than she was in being a devoted disciple of Christ. Knowing her heart, God was about to shake her world up like it had never been shaken before.

Go to the window.

Although this was a unique spiritual experience for her, Ethel somehow discerned that she was hearing the voice of the Lord speaking to her. She immediately rose and stepped to the window.

Open the window.

Again, she obeyed.

Look outside.

She did.

What do you see?

Ethel saw nothing. In her head, she said as much. She saw the acres of wooded land that surrounded the orphanage, the buildings on the Daughters of Miriam campus, the cars parked on the adjacent street, and—

Look again.

Ethel dutifully looked at the same scene she had just examined. This time she noticed a little boy walking up the driveway below her window.

The Lord spoke to her again, more forcefully than before.

Don't ever say, "It's just a little boy." I have chosen that little boy. I see something in him that I will use for My glory. And I will use you in his life.

The discouragement that had been weighing so heavily on Ethel immediately evaporated. She closed the window and dropped to her knees to praise and thank the Lord. She never again questioned why God had sent her to that orphanage.

She knew the young boy by his reputation—a real troublemaker, that one. But she also knew with absolute certainty that her mission at that orphanage was to bring teenaged Morris Cerullo to the Messiah. Apparently He had significant plans for the little troublemaker.

CHAPTER 10

————•————

AFTER SCHOOL ONE day Morris encountered one of the nurses at the orphanage, lady named Mrs. Kerr. As Morris would eventually find out, she had many unusual qualities. For starters, she was the only Gentile who worked in the orphanage, and as Morris would later discover, she had a great love and respect for the Jewish people because of her Christian faith.

The most compelling aspect of Mrs. Kerr's life to Morris, though, was her demeanor. He would later reflect on the fact that he had never met anyone who had such a loving attitude and gentle spirit. Those qualities were a direct result of her faith in Jesus Christ, but at that point in his life Morris had no idea what "faith in Christ" meant. To him, *Jesus* and *Christ* were just common swear words.

Mrs. Kerr surprised Morris that day when she called him by name. "How does she know who I am?" he wondered. Cautiously, he stopped and fixed her with his customary glare and waited for her to explain herself.

"I have something I think you'll like," she said with a smile. "I was in the store today and was thinking about you. I bought this just for you." She handed him a candy bar, which was a delicacy for the young kids in the orphanage.

Morris was immediately on guard. Who would do such a thing? What was her game? He knew manipulation when he saw it. After all, he was a master manipulator, so he wasn't about to fall for this lady's tricks.

The rage monster within him reared up. His face turned scarlet as he snatched the candy from her hand and threw it on the floor with all his might.

"Don't you dare give me anything ever again," he snarled at her before stomping away in anger.

Mrs. Kerr smiled, picked up the candy bar and continued on her way.

"OK, Lord," she prayed to herself, "this is one person whose heart you'll have to melt. I can love him, but I can't transform him. I'm counting on you."

CHAPTER 11

O VER THE COURSE of the next two months Ethel Kerr seemed to run into Morris practically every day. Morris did not realize she went out of her way each day to ensure that they had contact. What he did notice was that the Gentile nurse always had a smile and a kind word for him, no matter how hostile he was toward her. Despite Morris's initial tantrum, she occasionally had a token gift to offer. She seemed oblivious to the young boy's bad temperament and overt animosity.

After two months, though, curiosity got the better of Morris. He was still suspicious of her motives, but he was also mystified by her graciousness. How could anyone be so genial and compassionate in response to his consistent demonstrations of animosity? Morris was determined to figure out her game. He was convinced that she had some hidden agenda—all adults did— and he was determined to reveal it.

Morris devised a plan to figure out what the nurse was up to. One night when he was sure that there would not be a surprise room inspection he slipped out of his bedroom and tiptoed down the fire escape. After surveilling the parking lot and surrounding area he ran across the property to the building in which staff lived, including Mrs. Kerr.

Morris grabbed the handle to the exit door and pulled—only to discover it was locked! Steam from his breath escaped as he quietly cursed his bad luck. Launching plan B, he stealthily duck-walked in the shadows to the cement wall directly beneath the second-floor window he had scoped out as Mrs. Kerr's. Getting footholds in the bricks of the wall, he carefully but confidently climbed the wall until he could grab hold of her window sill. He pulled himself up until both arms were resting on the outer sill and he was staring into the curtain covering the window from the inside. He drew a deep breath then knocked on the window.

No response.

Looking quickly over his shoulder to see if his knock had roused any response outside the building, and seeing nothing stirring, he returned to the business at hand. He knocked again.

Still no response.

He paused for a quick mental recalculation. It was dark inside the room, but it was too late for her to be out. His knocking was loud enough to awaken all but the heaviest sleeper. Was she on to him? Playing a game of cat and mouse? Had she freaked out at the knocking and called security?

Morris was on a mission. He was not going to be deterred. He knocked again, this time a more prolonged banging.

Nothing. Dead silence. No signs of stirring inside the room.

Now the fourteen year old was getting angry. He had no other plan. He had taken a big risk to leave his dorm room, break out of the building, sneak across the property, climb the wall, and attempt to rouse a grown woman from her sleep to answer his knocking at her bedroom window. Maybe the police would consider it attempted robbery or attempted breaking and entering. The orphanage would certainly discipline him harshly for this episode if he was caught.

Rage welled up in his mind and heart. How could this plan *not* work? He was not going to quit until that woman threw up the sash and came clean with him. Nobody got the best of Morris Cerullo!

He knocked again. And again. And again.

CHAPTER 12

T HE KNOCKING ON the window continued. It was after midnight. Her room was on the second floor. No bird could land on the window-sill and make such a racket. No person was tall enough to reach the window from the ground below. She would have heard a ladder being placed against the wall. What was going on?

Ethel Kerr lay in her bed clutching the covers and watching the window. She was terrified.

She could call the night staff across the property, but they'd probably sigh in disgust and tell her she was imagining things or that it was just the wind. She could call the police, but they'd take a good ten to fifteen minutes to get there. And then what if it was nothing? She would be embarrassed, feel like a fool, be looked down upon by her Jewish employer. Maybe she'd even lose her job.

Ethel mustered her courage, slowly climbed out of her bed, and approached the window.

As she stood directly in front of the pane, she pondered what to do. She finally moved to the side of the window and pulled back the edge of the curtain. What she saw did not make sense for a moment. Then she let out a big sigh of relief and opened the curtain all the way to be sure she saw things right.

It was that rascal Morris Cerullo!

She unconsciously smiled as she opened the window, grabbed his arms, and pulled him into her room.

"God," she thought to herself, "You have the oddest ways of answering my prayers. But thank You for caring enough to give me a chance to reach this child."

———•———

Ethel Kerr looked at Morris Cerullo standing there in her bedroom and shook her head.

"What are you doing here, Morris? You could have killed yourself climbing that wall. And what possessed you to climb a wall and bang on my window? It's the middle of the night!"

Morris noticed that even in this situation the lady did not seem angry—just surprised and confused.

"I want to know what you're up to," he said with his hands on his hips, going on the offensive immediately. "Why do you keep bugging me?"

Mrs. Kerr stood there for a moment looking intensely at the young man.

This was a make-it-or-break-it moment. She grinned and put a hand on his shoulder.

"God sent me here for you," she said softly.

Morris froze. He expected a list of demands or a denial, even a confrontation of some sort, but this—this was not in the realm of possibility. Did she think she was an angel from God? Morris had listened to Rabbi Gold drone on for an hour every day for several years about Moses, Abraham, and Joshua. God had spoken to them. But they were in the Tanakh, the Jewish Bible! They were the pillars of the Jewish people, the icons of a nation that had survived against the odds for thousands of years. They were special; of course God had spoken to them.

But those instances were also highly unusual. God did not just speak to normal people. God had never spoken to Rabbi Gold, who was as devout a Jew as Morris had ever met. Heck, God had never spoken to *anyone* that Morris knew. Why would He speak to this Gentile woman?

And this business about being sent for Morris? What in the world did that mean? What was this lady up to?

"What are you saying?" he demanded indignantly. "What do mean, God 'sent' you for me? That doesn't even make sense." He crossed his arms over his chest in defiance, glaring at her as he awaited an explanation.

Her grin became a full-blown smile as she moved toward the bedside table and took her well-worn Bible from it. She sat on the side of the bed, flipped toward the middle of the book, found a particular passage in Isaiah 16, and read it to the young boy who was staring at her. "Take counsel, execute judgment. Make thy shadow as the night in the midst of the noonday; hide the outcasts; betray not him that wandereth. Let mine outcasts dwell with thee."

When she finished, she looked directly at the boy and waited.

The intruder held his ground but scrunched up his face. "What's that supposed to mean? And what does it have to do with why you're always being nice to me and talking to me?" he asked. None of this was making sense to the boy. He felt as if she were talking in riddles. He wondered if she was making fun of him.

"Don't you see?" she said sweetly. "God sent me to the Daughters of Miriam to tell you about the Messiah." She beamed at him, as if waiting for a response.

Morris almost fell over backward. If there was one thing he was not prepared to hear about it was tales of the Messiah. He had heard Rabbi Gold speak on the topic many times. Israel was waiting for a Messiah to take His rightful place as the King of Israel, to bring political and spiritual redemption to the Jewish people. The Messiah would be a great military leader who would become the ruler of world governments, rebuild the temple in Jerusalem, and re-establish Jewish law for all mankind.

Yes, the Jews were waiting for the return of their King. In fact, Jews throughout the world were eager for that triumphant return and the restoration of their land of heritage. But nobody knew who the Messiah would be or when He would return. At least that's what Rabbi Gold had said. It made no sense that some Gentile lady working in a Jewish orphanage in New Jersey would have the answers. What kind of trick was she trying to pull?

"What are you taking about?" he blurted out, his voice and face conveying his obvious doubt. "What can you tell me, a Jew, about the Messiah?"

Mrs. Kerr paused as if preparing herself to launch into the discussion with the troubled juvenile standing before her.

"Morris, the Messiah has already come," she began.

"What?" he cried out, baffled. "What are you talking about? We have been waiting thousands of years for the Messiah. We're still waiting for him. Why are you telling me he has already come?"

"Because He has, Morris. This is so important to understand. Let me explain some things to you," she offered, patting the edge of the bed next to her inviting the boy to have a seat.

Bewildered but intrigued, Morris slowly moved to the far end of the bed and tentatively sat on the corner. This was either the greatest scam he'd ever witnessed or one of those life-changing moments. He wasn't sure which, but his distrust of this lady was unconsciously melting away.

Mrs. Kerr gently talked about the history of God's people, a story that Morris knew well, as history was the only subject at school that seemed to captivate his restless mind. He loved learning about the past because it was about power and control and action. The young man would sometimes daydream about the history lessons he'd heard, imagining himself in those situations. When Rabbi Gold spoke to the orphans, the religious rules he so painstakingly explained were of no interest to Morris. However, when the man described the historical battles, strategies, and consequences—well, that stuff was worth listening to and thinking about. Instinctively Morris knew that if you understood the past you could control the future.

But Mrs. Kerr was not simply reciting a history lesson to her intense guest. She explained how the Messiah had actually come to Israel almost two thousand years earlier and had surprised everyone by arriving as the Prince of Peace rather than a king of power or a traditional political ruler. Jesus showed His authority in many ways, including His refusal to be strictly a governing leader. Instead, He came to save humankind in an unexpected way by sacrificially dying for people's sins—even Morris's sins!

Morris was clearly uncomfortable as she described the mercy and unconditional love of Jesus Christ. In his world, everything came with conditions.

"That's enough," he proclaimed, jumping off the bed and marching back to the open window. "This is too much. I don't know about what you're talking about. It doesn't make sense. I'm going back to my room."

And before she could stop him, Morris was climbing out the window and retracing his steps to his dorm room.

CHAPTER 13

————◆————

ORRIS FOLLOWED HIS normal routine the next day, but it was anything but a normal or routine day. His head was swimming. To his peers, he seemed preoccupied. Indeed he was. The encounter with Mrs. Kerr had not gone as planned. He'd expected to turn the tables on her and get the scoop on what she was up to. Instead she'd turned his world upside down with all that talk about the Messiah.

While his instincts told him to resist her propaganda, he couldn't get her words out of his mind. God had *sent* her? God wanted her to speak to *Morris*? The Messiah had *already come*—and *died*? His death was to wipe away everyone's sins, even his own? It was crazy talk.

But there was something about Mrs. Kerr that kept Morris from just writing off her words as Gentile foolishness. She had been so relaxed and calm about him waking her up and breaking into her room like that. She almost seemed excited to tell him that story. She was always so kind and peaceful, different from all the other busy, brusque adults, especially at the orphanage.

He had climbed the wall and confronted her expecting to uncover her scam. But if this Jesus talk was a scam, what did she have to gain? Was she recruiting him for some secret crime group? He laughed out loud at the thought. Had Rabbi Gold sent her to test Morris's faith? It didn't seem likely. The rabbi wouldn't give him the time of day, so why would he go to such great lengths to evaluate the depth of Morris's faith?

Morris Cerullo did not get into any fights that day. In fact, he didn't get into any conversations that day. He was too preoccupied with his thinking about the mysterious conversation he'd had with the nurse the night before. Nobody got over on Morris, and he was determined that the Gentile nurse wouldn't be the first. He'd figure out her game and get back at her. Nobody made Morris Cerullo look like a fool, and those who tried always paid the price.

CHAPTER 14

ORRIS REPRISED HIS role as a night stalker, once again escaping his room and climbing the wall of the staff living quarters to get to Mrs. Kerr's room. He rapped on her window. This time it only took a single rap of his knuckles against the glass before the curtain parted and the window rose. And she did not seem at all surprised that he was back.

Morris began their conversation without hesitation. "I have some questions that you need to answer," he stated forcefully, getting right to the point. He swiftly made his way to the same corner of the bed he'd sat on in his previous excursion and eyed his host intently.

He was a boy on a mission. And his host was a very willing accessory to the adventure.

These meetings occurred several times over the course of the next few weeks. Each one resembled an interrogation more than a conversation. Everything Ethel Kerr said was challenged by her rapt audience.

Their discussions ranged from A to Z on matters of faith. They considered the lives of the great Bible heroes, like Moses, Abraham, Isaac, Jacob, Joshua, David, Samuel, Daniel, and more. The history of the Jewish people was examined. The nature of God and His purposes were batted back and forth. Everything was on the table. Nothing was taken for granted.

Morris Cerullo, the wannabe lawyer, was questioning his first suspect.

Meanwhile, Ethel Kerr was given a run for her money, theologically speaking. Everything she had ever learned at her church, from her personal Bible study, even the stories and commentary she had read in religious magazines and books over the years, was being brought into play by the hungry mind of Morris Cerullo. She discovered early on that this was no stupid street kid. When he applied himself to the task, Morris revealed a perceptive, analytical mind. The boy was rough around the edges, no doubt about it, but Ethel could begin to see why the Lord had chosen this one to do something special.

Toward the end of one evening's inquest the nurse handed her student a small, folded piece of paper. A single word was written on the facing.

Questions.

It was a Christian tract written by a well-respected lawyer from New York City, James Bennett. For many years, Bennett has been a leading Christian layman associated with the Presbyterian Church but known to and respected by pastors and other leaders throughout the region.

Morris didn't know what a tract was. He didn't even know what a Presbyterian was. In fact, he really didn't know what a Christian was apart from the insights he was receiving from Mrs. Kerr. But this was a paper written by a lawyer about a subject that now fascinated him. He delayed his departure that evening to read through the tiny handout.

He couldn't believe what he was reading. It asked and simply addressed various questions that had been brewing in his mind. As was customary with Morris, each answer raised another set of questions to wrestle with. He was digging deeper and deeper into this faith dimension than he ever thought possible.

Morris looked up from the tract. He carefully placed the tiny sheet in his pocket, nodded at his mentor, and made his way back to the window. He had plenty to think about until their next encounter.

CHAPTER 15

THE FOLLOWING NIGHT Morris showed up at Mrs. Kerr's room again. After secretly consulting the *Questions* tract throughout the day and pondering the content while his school teachers blabbed on about less consequential things, he was filled with new questions and concerns. The poor woman was overwhelmed by the sheer intellectual fury of her young protégé.

One thing that pleased her, though, was the fact that Morris no longer seemed to be getting into trouble. Since they had started their midnight meetings he had focused most of his energy on matters of faith. He was a smart kid, she realized. She also predicted that in no time flat his questions would transcend her own base of knowledge.

After Morris's obvious pleasure over receiving the little tract the previous night, she made a big decision that morning: it was time to give Morris the tools needed to foster his own spiritual development and confront the real issues related to the Messiah.

Soon after Morris began his nightly inquiry, assaulting her with thoughtful questions, Mrs. Kerr put up her hand in the midst of a barrage and looked at him sternly.

"Morris, this cannot continue every night. We have to make a change. It is too dangerous for you to be coming to my room all the time and even to be climbing that brick wall. The biggest danger of all is that someone is going to see you coming in here. I have a new plan."

Morris squinted at the nurse. He wondered if he was a fool after all. Maybe this was where she would try to pull the rug out from under him.

Mrs. Kerr took a small, black leather-bound book from her pocketbook. She smiled as she handed it to him.

"Take this. It's a gift for you." He stared at the cover of the book, reading the title in astonishment. "You don't have to take it if you don't want to, but I think the time is right. It's a New Testament. I think it's about time that you start reading it for yourself. The answers to your questions are all in there. What do you say? Do you want to read it for yourself?"

———◆———

Morris didn't know how to respond. He continued to stare at the book in his hands. Then, slowly, he raised his head and solemnly nodded. He knew she was right. This was the next step. He felt ready to continue the journey in control of his spiritual destiny.

"Absolutely," he replied. Then he got up to leave.

Mrs. Kerr put up her hand again to stop his exit.

"You have to be smart about this, Morris," she said seriously. "You know they don't allow those in Miriam," she explained, speaking of the orphanage and its strict policies about religious literature that was not written from an Orthodox Jewish perspective. "You'll need this," she intoned softly, handing the teen yet another gift, a palm-sized flashlight. "Be very careful reading that New Testament. It will be invaluable to you, but you have to treat it like contraband. Read it at night when everyone else is sleeping or in some secret place where you won't be discovered."

Morris looked at Mrs. Kerr with a newfound respect. He never would have thought she would break the rules—more than they already did each night—in order for him to grow spiritually. He nodded his grateful assent and quickly headed back to his dorm room. He couldn't wait to start diving into the pages of the rest of the story that the Jews never studied.

As soon as Morris got back to his room and assessed the security of his situation he immediately pulled the covers over his head, flicked on the tiny flashlight, and began reading from the opening chapter of the first book, the Gospel According to Matthew. He read and read until he couldn't keep his eyes open any longer.

For the first time in years, Morris fell asleep with a sense of hope.

CHAPTER 16

NIGHT AFTER NIGHT Morris would climb into bed at the appointed bedtime and feign sleep until the dorm supervisor left and he could take out his New Testament and flashlight. Those minutes seemed like an eternity to the anxious young man.

While his dorm mates lulled themselves into peaceful slumber by thinking about girls, sports, and other teen preoccupations, Morris feverishly ripped through the unanswered questions in his mind.

Were the tales in this New Testament really true? Why didn't Rabbi Gold ever teach these stories?

Was there historical proof of these events? If so, why would Jews reject such evidence?

How could a person be both divine and human, as Jesus was described? If God was in heaven, and Jesus was God, then how could Jesus have been on Earth?

Why was this new way of dealing with human sin better than the rules and personal effort that had characterized the basis of Jewish life for more than four thousand years?

Within a few short weeks Morris had read the entire New Testament from start to finish. Rather than discard the dangerous book he started over, re-reading the Gospels, then plunging back into Acts, then Paul's epistles, and so on. Each time he re-read the passages new insights were revealed to him as he built a more cohesive and sophisticated understanding of the narrative. He read through the book a third time, then a fourth.

With each new reading of the story, Morris gained a deeper appreciation for Jesus and His ways of handling tough situations. He was impressed that Jesus always had just the right answer for His critics and oppressors. He didn't fall for their tricks and traps but always offered them hope and truth. Just as Mrs. Kerr had said, He loved His enemies. Who could do such a thing? Dr. Cerullo marveled at the choices Jesus made.

Some of Jesus' teachings, though, stumped the young boy in New Jersey. A man had to be born again? How could that be? What did it take? Was it possible for a Jew, someone from Jesus' own people, to experience? If it was so important why wasn't Rabbi Gold teaching him these lessons?

Sitting in his high school classes during the day, Morris would daydream about what it must have been like to be in the presence of Jesus. He imagined watching the intellectual battles with the rabbis and the illegal physical beatings that Jesus endured. Morris felt his own rage swell as he thought about the unjust ridicule, persecution, and death Jesus experienced.

Morris could relate to Jesus. The Son of God had done nothing wrong, but He was exploited, mocked, tortured, and eventually murdered. Why? Because He was different. Morris understood the pain of being an outcast. He was an orphan. He was Jewish. He was small. He had no money. Like Jesus, he was ridiculed and rejected because he was different. He was spurned for simply being who he was. It wasn't fair.

Rabbi Gold lectured the orphanage students about the prophets. But as great as the prophets of the Old Testament were, their lives paled in comparison to that of Jesus. The miracles of Jesus blew Morris's mind. The faith of the disciples captivated his heart. The challenges in the writings of Paul were so practical and so perfectly integrated into a new way of thinking and behaving.

God had always been an abstraction for Morris, a deity who existed, if at all, more than an arm's length from humanity. But this Jesus guy—He was something entirely different. His life was moving and startling. His was clearly a better way to live.

In time, the ways of Jesus won over Morris. The young man became mesmerized by the power of love and forgiveness. His heart, previously fueled by rage and revenge, softened as he read and re-read Jesus's reaction to His tormentors. He decided that he, too, wanted to be like Jesus.

There was just one last problem. He couldn't tell anyone.

CHAPTER 17

—————•—————

Mrs. Kerr, perhaps affected by her exchanges with Morris, had been undergoing her own spiritual metamorphosis. Frustrated by the consistently low-key, controlled expressions of worship and joy at her Baptist church, one Sunday she ventured into an Assembly of God service in Paterson. She had never been in a Pentecostal church before and was not quite sure what to expect.

From the very beginning of the service she was bowled over by the exuberant, unrestrained experiences people there were having with God. It provided exactly the jolt of spiritual energy and intimacy that she was yearning for with God at that moment in her life.

Later that week she encountered Morris at the orphanage. She excitedly explained about her Sunday experience to the young man. He could tell what an impact the adventure had on her, with their lively music and shouts of praise, the hands waving toward the Lord, the exclamations of agreement throughout the sermon, and prayers beseeching God for miracles.

Morris listened in rapt attention trying to imagine what such an event must be like. After all, he had never set foot inside a Christian church of any type. It was all foreign to him—but mysterious and intriguing too.

It certainly was not like the boring services he attended at the synagogue each Saturday. This Pentecostal place sounded alive and connected to the living God. He got excited just thinking about it.

Before they parted company Mrs. Kerr handed Morris a magazine she had picked up at the church. It was called the *Pentecostal Evangel*. He couldn't wait to get back to his room to pour over its contents to find out more about these new ways of interacting with the God his older friend had been describing and to discover new insights from mature students of Jesus who attended such churches.

With the coolness of a diamond thief Morris smuggled the magazine into his dorm room and hid it under the mattress, where he stashed his treasured New Testament. He left the room to finish his chores, but he could hardly wait to read this new description of the spiritual life.

After impatiently completing his final tasks for the day, bedtime arrived. As usual, Morris played it safe, waiting for his roommates to fall asleep and for the nightly room check by one of the caretakers.

Finally, the coast was clear.

Morris silently withdrew the magazine from under his mattress. He began flipping through the pages. His frustration grew with each page he turned. Rather than finding stories of people enthusiastically celebrating the Lord and the miracles God was doing in the lives of His followers, it was packed with pages of print describing missionary reports, church attendance and financial statistics, and other religious trivia of no interest to a teenager intent upon tracking down God. He was hugely disappointed.

After his quick perusal of the magazine, Morris padded over to his locker and stuck it in the pocket of his robe. He'd dispose of the useless rag tomorrow. He returned to his bed and withdrew his New Testament to pick up where he had left off the night before. As usual, he read those pages until he could no longer keep his eyes open.

CHAPTER 18

————•————

"O H MY! OH! Mrs. Weinstein, please, come look at this right away!" exclaimed Mrs. Sternberg, one of the caretakers engaged in a routine inspection of the lockers in the boys' dorm. She was standing in front of Morris's locker.

"What is it?" asked the fellow caretaker who was on the opposite side of the room checking out other lockers, none too concerned about what could possibly be hidden in one of the lockers. They'd seen it all before: pocket knives, bottles of booze, girlie magazines. These lockers were, after all, the repository of all the worldly goods possessed by a group of testosterone-driven young boys.

Morris was aware that the hyperventilating woman was in front of his belongings. But he also knew his locker was in good order: all the clothing was hanging properly, his shoes were shined and lined up, and his school books were stacked neatly in the back corner. He felt no anxiety; he had nothing to worry about.

Then it struck him. What if one of his dorm mates had mischievously hidden some forbidden item in his locker? He knew that a couple of the kids in the house were still looking for ways to get back at him.

"It's a *Pentecostal Evangel!*" Mrs. Sternberg screamed. You'd have thought she was holding a hissing, rabid opossum.

"What? Where did *that* come from? Whose is it?" demanded Mrs. Weinstein, suddenly pumped with adrenaline as she charged across the room to get a closer look.

The blood drained from his face as Morris realized his blunder. He must have left that stupid, boring magazine from Mrs. Kerr in his robe. He had meant to dump it in the trash on the way to school.

But what was the big fuss over? It was just a boring religious magazine, certainly nothing to get all excited about.

CHAPTER 19

TEN MINUTES AFTER the discovery of the forbidden magazine, the two caretakers and Mrs. Kerr were all gathered in Rabbi Gold's office. A diminutive man with graying hair and always dressed in a dark suit, the rabbi's normally passive demeanor was in overdrive. He heatedly scolded Mrs. Kerr for breaking the rules by sharing such "garbage" with the students. The rabbi stayed on the offensive.

"What else have you been doing with that young man?" he demanded.

"We have talked about the teachings of the New Testament and—"

That's as far as she got. The rabbi, a serious and stern man, raised the decibel level.

"You are fired. You go straight to your room, pack your things, and get out. You have no right bringing these things in here. You know who we are and what we stand for, but you ignored the rules and took advantage of our kindness to you. You get your things and return here. I will call a cab, and you will leave immediately. You have done great damage, Mrs. Kerr. Do not use us for a reference. You must leave the premises immediately. Please hurry."

He put his right hand to his forehead and massaged his temple, as if dealing with a headache. Then he looked up and called out, "And do not talk to Morris on the way."

Mrs. Kerr had already slipped out of his office without further words, instantly resigned to her fate without a fight. But as she retreated from the angry rabbi's office the only thought running through her head was, "I wonder what will happen to Morris once I'm gone?"

CHAPTER 20

———•———

NOT MUCH HAD been said to Morris after the caretakers confiscated the magazine from his locker. They'd both gone running downstairs, probably to register their complaint with the rabbi or Mrs. Gold. He figured he'd get a stern warning from the rabbi later in the day. In the meantime he'd follow his usual daily routine and take extra care not to make any waves.

After completing his morning chores Morris headed downstairs toward the front door to head out to school. It was a brisk ten-minute walk. He had his books piled under one arm as he twisted his coat buttons into place before exiting the building and getting a face-full of winter gusts.

Just as he entered the main vestibule of the building, straight ahead of him, also in her coat and carrying a suitcase, was Mrs. Kerr. She was about to open the front door of the building. As the sound of his shoes against the linoleum floor reached her ears, she looked behind her and saw Morris approaching. A few feet to her right, at the entrance to the main office, stood the rabbi's wife, Mrs. Gold, who had been fully briefed by her husband of the unfolding tragedy.

"Go, now!" Mrs. Gold said to Nurse Kerr with a quiet urgency that did not reach Morris's ears.

Ethel Kerr grasped the door handle and quietly exited the Daughters of Miriam for the last time.

Morris had not seen her. He was still fussing with the buttons on his coat.

"Morris!" bellowed Mrs. Gold from the doorway of the main office. Her voice filled the vestibule and adjoining hallways. "Come in here, right now!"

At the sound of her voice, Morris's head snapped up. He had been unaware of her presence too, but he knew that the moment of reckoning was upon him. His mouth tightened as he strode to the office where the orphanage matron held the door open for him, glaring at him as he approached.

Inside the office Mrs. Gold moved to one end of the receptionist's desk as Morris moved toward the opposite end. She closed the office door, looked at the receptionist seated behind the desk, and then spoke.

"Morris, is this yours?" she asked, her eyes blazing while she held up the purloined copy of the *Pentecostal Evangel*.

"No," he said evenly, staring her in the eyes without fear, "but I was reading it."

An uncomfortable silence hung in the room for a couple of seconds. Mrs. Gold moved toward Morris to complete her admonition.

"Morris, you know better than to read garbage like this. That's all this is, trash. Lies, total lies. I know that you got this from Mrs. Kerr, and we have fired her. She is no longer here, Morris. She is gone. You are never to see her again. Do you understand?

"Everything that she was teaching you is untrue," the woman continued, her face flushed with anger. "It is all garbage, just like this magazine. Untruths, Morris, do you hear me? Do not believe what she was telling you. It may have sounded good, and many people believe those lies, but they are just lies. You put that rubbish out of your mind, Morris. Are we clear on this?"

Morris looked at her, unmoved by her piercing stare and the emotion in her shaking voice. The words that he spoke surprised him as much as they startled her.

"I don't understand everything I've been reading," he replied with a quiet but steady voice, returning the matron's glare with one of his own, "but the one thing I do know is that it is *real. You will never take that away from me.*"

With that, Morris broke eye contact with Mrs. Gold and walked out of the office. He had no explanation for the boldness he had just displayed to Mrs. Gold, but he knew in his heart that what he said and did was right.

There was no turning back now, he thought, as he mechanically walked toward school, fighting back tears.

CHAPTER 21

THE MONTHS THAT followed Mrs. Kerr's dismissal were difficult for Morris. She had been the first—and only—person he had ever been able to talk to about things that mattered. She was not so much a mother figure to him as a fellow traveler on a pilgrimage toward truth and purpose.

As he reflected on all that was happening he began to better understand that the Holy Spirit of God had been working on his mind and heart since his first conversation with the departed nurse. Morris took special care to read about the work of the Holy Spirit, a concept totally absent from his Jewish training, and considered what God seemed to be doing in his own life.

He thought about the changes in his behavior and demeanor and recognized the fingerprints of the Holy Spirit.

He replayed in his mind how Mrs. Kerr had entered his life, bringing with her the Good News of the gospel of Jesus Christ. He laughed at the absurdity of a Gentile nurse being placed in a Jewish orphanage specifically to introduce an orphan to the story and the reality of Jesus Christ. He was beginning to think that this was a sign from God of how much He loved Morris and the lengths to which He would go to incorporate the teenager into His plan.

The personnel at the orphanage found nothing ironic or heartwarming about Morris's journey. They were determined to ensure that the young man did not succumb to the religious brainwashing by the fired nurse. They talked to Morris about his beliefs. They beat him and threatened him unless he would recant any morsel of faith in Jesus. They withheld privileges from Morris, promising to restore them after he came to his senses.

Morris was still a high school kid, just fourteen years old. A lesser child might have simply said what the adults wanted to hear so that they would lighten up and his quality of life would return to normal.

But the more he pondered these things, the more convinced he was that none of this—the unlikely hiring of Mrs. Kerr, her befriending of Morris, his unique introduction to the gospel, his thirst for knowing the truth, and the persecution both of them experienced for their determination to follow what they believed to be true—was coincidence.

It just didn't add up in his mind.

The rabbi and other leaders of the orphanage were committed to forcing him to recant a faith he didn't understand and was not practicing.

God brought an older woman into his life to introduce him to a Savior he didn't know existed then allowed her to be removed from his life after the introduction was made.

The Orthodox Jews were deeply religious people, zealous about their faith, and highly educated about the Scriptures and Jewish history, yet they were so acutely threatened by a young orphan hearing an alternative faith narrative.

Morris read his New Testament and couldn't quite put it all together, yet Mrs. Kerr seemed the embodiment of the fruit of a relationship with God, just like the one that Paul described in Galatians 5, overflowing with love, joy, peace, patience, goodness, kindness, and the rest.

Morris, spiritually naïve as he was, accepted these events as part of God's plan to arrest the boy's attention and enlist his service to God. Morris had no idea what that meant, but he sensed that it was right.

And so the more the staff at the Daughters of Miriam challenged him or withheld material goods from him, the more determined he became to pursue the truth about Jesus and His claims to being the Messiah. Morris did not yet understand true spiritual conversion, but he knew, just *knew*, that something special was in process.

CHAPTER 22

————◆————

THE TWO MEN had Morris cornered in the basement of the orphanage. They offered him one more chance to unequivocally state that he did not believe that Jesus Christ is the Messiah, that he would not follow Jesus, and that he was fully committed to the teachings of Orthodox Judaism, as taught by Rabbi Gold.

The duo towered over Morris. Here he was, a physically tiny, fourteen-year-old boy. How could his belief system, as ill-defined and inarticulate as it was, threaten these people? Why did they hound him about these matters? How could they justify physically beating an orphan simply because he was attracted to the story of Jesus, a Jewish carpenter from two thousand years ago whose life exemplified love and grace?

"Listen to me," the young boy growled at the older men. "I'm sick of being mistreated over my religious beliefs. You people come at me time after time. If you dare lay your hands on me one more time I promise you I will walk out of this orphanage and never return. Now get out of my way and leave me alone."

As Morris moved toward the steps leading to the main floor, the two men jumped him and battered him yet again, assuring him that he would continue to get such treatment until he rejected Jesus Christ.

When the persuasion session was over, Morris slowly got to his feet and glared at the two men as they ran up the steps and disappeared into the building. His shirt tail was hanging out of his pants, his hair was disheveled, and his lip was bleeding. He felt nauseous from the repeated blows to his stomach. He was a tough kid and feared no one, but physically he was no match for two grown men with a religious vendetta.

Finally he, too, made his way up the stairway and into the vestibule of the main building.

Upon reaching the vestibule, he paused, looked around, and headed toward the front door. As his hand grabbed the door knob a voice called out from the main office, located directly opposite the door. It was the same door Mrs. Kerr had walked through, never to return.

Morris Cerullo, barely a teenager, with nothing but the flimsy clothing he was wearing, followed his mentor's lead. He slammed the door behind him and purposefully strode into the night. It was dark and windy, and a light snow had begun to float through the skies. He had no money, no friends, no plan, no alternatives.

All he knew as he invaded the unknown was that he was never going back the Daughters of Miriam.

CHAPTER 23

———◆———

CLIFTON, NEW JERSEY, had a population of about fifty-six thousand people in 1946. Outside of the people he knew at the orphanage, Morris could count the Cliftonians he knew on his fingers. And he could count those whose address he knew on one finger.

Peter Oostdyk.

One of the reasons why Morris knew where Peter lived was that they were friends from school. But the other was that the Oostdyk family lived practically next door to the orphanage on a large estate, thanks to the success of their trucking company.

Peter was a classmate of Morris's at school. Morris had never been to Peter's house, but as Morris stood in the frigid winter storm, suddenly homeless and penniless, it seemed like a good time to make his first appearance at their front door.

After traversing up the long, brick-lined driveway and knocking on the large, white front door, Morris waited, his circumstance running through his mind.

The lights in the house were on, but no one answered. Morris knocked again.

Hearing the noise of teen feet tramping down the stairs inside the house, Morris cleared his throat and stared at the door. It was thrown open, and there was Peter.

"Hey," Morris said evenly.

"Hey," Peter returned. As the chilly air enveloped him, Peter gave an involuntary shiver and then crisscrossed his arms across his chest to ward off the cold. "What's up?"

"I left the orphanage," Morris said matter-of-factly.

"Huh." Peter looked at Morris for a moment, then moved out of the doorway, revealing the entryway of the mansion. "Wanna come in?"

Morris nodded in thanks and moved inside. Peter threw the door shut, then nodded toward the stairs and took them two at a time, beckoning his friend to follow. They entered Peter's bedroom and shut the door so they could talk privately. Morris described his plight, happy to tell his tale to someone safe.

Peter thought it was a cool story. Teenagers love defying authority.

"What are you gonna do?" Peter asked casually, intrigued by the plight of his schoolmate.

Looking Peter in the eye, Morris leaned back in his chair, stuck his hand in one pocket, and pulled out a crumpled slip of paper. He carefully unfolded it and looked at the sheet.

"Can I use your phone?"

The teens jumped up and headed downstairs toward the kitchen, where a phone sat on the counter.

Peter's parents were in the kitchen. He introduced them to Morris, and they chatted for a few minutes. Morris felt accepted and welcomed in the Oostdyk home, but he had his immediate future on his mind. He waved the wrinkled paper at his buddy, who explained that Morris needed to make a call.

After she had been relieved of her duties at the orphanage, Mrs. Kerr landed another nursing job and would occasionally drop by the public high school in the morning or afternoon to meet Morris at the edge of the school grounds. She continued to encourage him spiritually and had given him the phone number with an invitation to call her if he ever needed her help.

Morris didn't think much of it at the time, though he carried the scrap of paper with him at all times just in case an emergency arose. He hadn't expected it to be like this, but it certainly qualified as an emergency. He desperately needed her help now.

To his immense relief, the nurse answered the phone. Morris explained his circumstance and let her know he was now destitute. Because she didn't own a car she was unable to pick him up. She asked if he could meet her at the Montauk Theater on the main street in downtown Passaic. Morris had no means of transportation other than walking, but he was willing to walk to wherever she agreed to be.

So Morris thanked the Oostdyks for their help and headed back into the storm that had picked up velocity since he'd entered their house.

The odyssey was about to enter a new level.

CHAPTER 24

————◆————

J EWS PRAY, BUT given his doubts about God's interest in his life, Morris had never been moved to ask for God's help. When he got in a tough situation, he had learned to turn inward rather than upward. By necessity, Morris was independent of outside interference. He had solved most of his problems with his wit, fists, and perseverance.

But on that blustery, snowy December night, as the tired youth trudged slowly toward the center of Clifton, uncertain of where he was or where he was heading, his determination moved his feet, but he felt something else moving his heart.

The more he thought about his predicament and what he was hoping to accomplish that night, the clearer it was that he was in over his head. He stopped for a moment, puffs of breath visible in the frigid winter air, as he tried to get a fix on his location.

It was a waste of time. Wherever he was, he knew he had never been there before, and he had just as little idea about where the Montauk Theater was.

If there was ever a time to pray to God, this was it.

Morris threw his hands into the air, and with his reddened face looking up into the snowflakes that were floating earthward he spoke a prayer unlike any he had ever read or heard—and surely unlike anything he had ever uttered.

"Dear God, if there is such a being as Jesus in heaven, please tell Him to come and live with me right now."

The prayer was neither long nor eloquent but certainly dramatic and heartfelt. Most people seeking refuge in the midst of a biting December snowstorm would pray for a ride or an instant change in the weather. They'd seek a means of survival.

True to form, Morris saw the world through a different lens. His prayer was indeed about being saved, but not just from the harsh weather or lack of adequate clothing. He wanted to be saved from himself and the world that seemed to have declared war on him more than a decade ago.

To his astonishment, the moment he finished that simple prayer, he felt as if a protective shield had been placed around him. The snow and sleet no longer seemed to be pelting his skin. Without explanation, he felt as if a warm breeze had blown his way, eliminating his shivering.

At the same time, as he resumed his walk he felt as if an invisible pair of hands had taken hold of his own and gently pulled him up one street and down the next toward his desired destination. He remembered reading about angels in the Bible, but was this what it was like? He couldn't see anything out of the ordinary, but he knew angels were invisible. Yet, what was happening had no plausible worldly explanation.

He had no idea how much time elapsed while he continued his trek, but his mood changed dramatically, so much so that he began to do something he rarely did in public.

Morris Cerullo, the fourteen-year-old runaway orphan, soaked to the skin and vulnerable to pneumonia, began to sing. He had no idea why he suddenly felt joy and peace. He simply accepted it. For nearly three miles he walked along oblivious to his location, wandering dangerously through the traffic and the elements, guided by the invisible Presence, nonchalantly shuffling toward the middle of Passaic. He could not explain it, but he knew—he *knew*—that God, or Jesus, or angels—*something* supernatural—was with him and that his journey would be successful.

To those driving by with their windows shut tight, the dashboard heater pushed to the max, and windshield wipers pulsing, Morris presented a most unusual sight.

En route to his destination Morris lost all track of time, but it seemed as if only a few minutes had passed when suddenly the Presence left him. With it went the physical warmth that had surrounded his body. Rattled by the change in his circumstances, Morris was on the edge of panic. He closed his eyes and desperately uttered another prayer.

"God, please don't leave me now."

When he opened his eyes, the need for panic dissipated. He looked upward at the bright, colorful lights of a theater marquee. At the top of the message board were the words he longed to see: Montauk Theater.

Standing beneath that marquee, just a few feet away and with her arms outstretched, was Mrs. Ethel Kerr.

Years later Morris would knowingly attribute his arrival at that place to the assistance of angels and another encounter with supernatural forces, but in that moment the fourteen year old was too dazed to understand what was happening. He simply ran to Mrs. Kerr and hugged her as she wrapped her arms around him and kissed the top of his snow-drenched head.

PART TWO:

—————◆—————

CALLED TO GREATNESS

CHAPTER 25

◆

THAT FIRST NIGHT of freedom from the orphanage found Morris staying with Ed Maurer, Ethel's brother, and his wife. They were new to the Christian faith themselves and welcomed Morris into their home until a more permanent solution could be identified.

Meanwhile, neither the orphanage nor the state ever sought to locate Morris Cerullo. The troublemaker apparently wanted to be on his own, and they were happy to accommodate that desire.

Morris attended a public high school near the Maurers' house for a few months. Once he reached his sixteenth birthday, though, he dropped out without any remorse. He had bigger and more important things on his mind.

Toward that end, Dr. Cerullo attended a Christian church for the first time, accompanying Mrs. Kerr and the Maurers to Bethany Assembly of God. It was the same church Mrs. Kerr had excitedly told him about that fateful morning when she had handed him the copy of the *Pentecostal Evangel*, the same magazine that eventually led to her firing and then to Morris's premature departure from the Daughters of Miriam.

The church blew his mind.

Morris had spent his entire spiritual life within the confines of the synagogue, with its rich traditions and earnest formality. The sense of freedom to connect with God that was a hallmark of the Pentecostal style of worship was a difficult concept for Morris to grasp. His first few times in attendance he watched in amazement as several hundred charismatic Christians sang songs of praise with great energy and emotion, many of them (mostly women) with eyes closed and waving their hands in the air as they sang. It was so different than the repetitious prayers and solemn incantations of the rabbi in the Jewish services.

Every week he watched in fascination as people prayed with a genuine belief that God was hearing their cries and would respond appropriately. After his miraculous journey to the Montauk Theater, Morris had a renewed sense that prayer really did matter, that there is a God who hears and responds. The intensity of the prayer life of the people around him left a deep impression.

To someone with an open and hungry mind, like Morris, the preaching was especially captivating. Each week the lengthy teachings intersected directly with the narratives he had been diligently reading day after day in the New Testament. As the teen tried to make sense of this new spiritual reality to which he was continually exposed, the lessons from the pulpit helped to fill in the blanks.

Other teens in the congregation were typically fidgety during the preaching. Morris was spellbound.

Bethany Assembly at that time was led by an elderly British preacher. Morris was drawn to the man's intellect and erudition. His teaching—the first Christian sermons Morris had ever heard—was a highlight, challenging Morris's thinking about God, his own life, and what the future held.

His head was swimming at the end of the first service he attended. But the most remarkable experience was yet to come that day.

Toward the end of the service the pastor said something that caught Morris off guard.

"If you would like to join me here at the altar to pray, please come down now. We serve a mighty God who hears and answers our prayers. Whatever your need or request may be, let's join together in asking Him."

People all over the building popped up from their seats and moved down the aisles toward the altar. Morris watched for a few moments then joined them. After his prayer experience when he left the Oostdyk house, walked through neighborhoods he didn't know, and wound up at the appointed spot where Mrs. Kerr was waiting for him, he had a child's naïve faith in prayer.

He knelt on the carpeted floor at the foot of the altar with people all around him and began to silently pray. He was not expecting anyone to pray for him or with him and had no expectations about the outcome of his prayer.

But neither did he expect what happened next.

Morris's eyes were closed as he concentrated on communicating with God. He was fully conscious, but at the same time it seemed as if his spirit had left his body behind and mysteriously arrived in an unknown place, which he assumed was part of heaven. That place was filled with people—so many that he could never count them all. Everywhere he looked his field of vision was packed with people.

Looking around at the masses, Morris focused on the front of the crowd and saw himself in the very front row of the throng. As he considered his place in that multitude, a blinding light appeared before them all. Somehow he knew without a doubt that it was the presence of the glory of God. He just knew it.

Without warning a ray of brilliance shot out of the central light toward Morris. It actually hit him like a wave of the ocean overtaking him, and his entire body shook. Then, like a strong undertow of the ocean current, he felt himself being irresistibly pulled toward the primary light source. Morris had no sense of control; it was as if he were a robot and had been programmed to move at a predetermined time toward a designated spot. Without any sense of time lapsing he found himself standing at the foot of the light with the crowd hovering all around. The light had a mesmerizing beauty and sense of power. It was riveting and majestic. He could not take his eyes off it.

In the next instant the light moved away from Morris. Immobilized, he immediately felt keen disappointment, almost like the loss one feels when a loved one dies. Morris wondered why the light—a manifestation of God—moved farther from him. Had he done something wrong? Was there a way he could get closer to the light again?

Morris looked back at the place where the light had moved from. That's when he noticed two large footprints.

He knew at once that God had communicated to him that it was his choice, Morris's choice, of what to do with his life. As Morris stared intensely at those footprints, he realized that they revealed a manifestation of the pit of hell. Peering down into the space beneath those footprints he saw a sea of people aflame, physically engulfed in fire but not being consumed by it, twisting in pain and yelling for relief. Their agonized suffering conveyed the hopelessness of man without the saving presence and forgiving love of God. He could hear bloodcurdling, tortured screams coming from within the pit.

Morris felt distraught, desperate to do something to help them. Without further hesitation, he placed his own feet in those footprints.

In that next moment his life changed. Morris felt engulfed by the presence of God. He felt as if God had wrapped His arms around him. He felt secure, powerful, and loved like never before. His entire body was warmed, with a slight tingling sensation, and he had an indescribable sense of pleasure and rightness.

God then startled Morris by speaking to him: "Arise and shine, for your light has come. The glory of the Lord is upon you. When you feel this presence, know that I am there in your midst to do great things for My people."

Morris was overwhelmed by the love and power of God. He committed his life to serving the Lord God from that instant forward.

CHAPTER 26

-------◆-------

AFTER MORRIS'S SUPERNATURAL experience, he was picked up from the floor at the altar by his friends and brought back to their house. They knew something dramatic had taken place but had to wait for Morris to recover before he was able to describe his adventure.

Hearing the details of his encounter with God amazed and humbled the four people sitting around the table at the Maurer home. They were so moved by it that they spontaneously returned to their knees in the living room and prayed non-stop into the early morning hours asking God for further revelation and guidance.

Not too much time had passed when, to his own shock, Morris prayed aloud in a language he had never heard or spoken. While Pentecostals are familiar with praying in tongues, this was more new territory for the Jewish teenager.

Although his prayer language did not seem to faze his older prayer partners, Morris was baffled by the experience. At one point he asked to use the phone and excused himself to do so.

After looking up the church's number in the phone directory, Morris called the pastor. He described what was happening and asked the pastor for an explanation.

"Don't be alarmed," the Brit calmly reassured him. "That is completely normal. You had an encounter with the Lord, and now you are experiencing another manifestation of the power of the Holy Spirit. Your experience is a bit different than that of other people, but you must allow the Holy Spirit to have control of your life. You have a special calling, Morris, and God has sent His Spirit to empower you to fulfill that calling."

Satisfied for the moment, Morris returned to the prayer meeting with the Maurers and Mrs. Kerr. Before the night was over they too had received the indwelling of God's Spirit and were speaking in tongues alongside Morris. As longtime Baptists they knew little about such things but were fully devoted to following the leading of God, no matter how He chose to empower and direct them.

Everyone in the house that evening was filled with a swirl of emotions: gratitude, joy, excitement, confusion, anticipation, and hope.

This was a game changer for each of them, but especially for Morris. God had not only initiated him into the family of God but had also ushered him into a life of ministry—even though he still had only the vaguest idea of what was happening and what lay in store for him.

But one thing was clear beyond question to the teenager: the supernatural dimension was as real as anything in the visible world. This God whom he was seeking to understand was much grander and more powerful than he had ever imagined—and He seemed intent upon sharing supernatural experiences with the born-again Jewish orphan.

CHAPTER 27

———◆———

A FTER A FEW hours of sleep subsequent to the extended prayer time, Morris awoke and immediately began to replay in his mind everything that had happened over the past forty-eight hours. It seemed as if a lifetime of seminal events had been packed into the blink of an eye.

Before his experience with God, Morris had been a self-focused young man. He had always had to fend for himself and had few close friends because he didn't trust anyone. He lived in the moment, and his primary purpose in life was to survive another day until something better came his way.

And now, something better—*much* better—had come his way.

He had never spent much time thinking about the future, much less an afterlife or religious concepts like heaven, hell, sin, and salvation. But now it seemed as if his foundational purpose for existence was wrapped up in those concepts.

As a result, instead of continuing to focus solely on himself, as had been his habit, he now harbored a sense of urgency about sharing what he had discovered of God's love with other people. The fact that he now felt eternally secure and knew that most other people did not have that same security was deeply upsetting to him.

Further, for a guy who had spent his life calling the shots of his existence and striving to produce outcomes based on his strength, intimidation, and street smarts, none of that seemed to matter anymore. He now understood that he was virtually powerless. He had encountered the true Power of the universe and willingly submitted himself to that Power.

It was the first time in his life that he felt fully understood and genuinely and completely loved. That love redefined him and his life. And it made him desperate to share that same experience with others.

What a forty-eight hours it had been! Morris was totally shaken by the presence of God, the vision he'd been given, the power and love of God, the working of the Holy Spirit within him, and the calling that the Lord had delivered for his life.

He was well on his way to being wholly renewed by the love of God. That new life, as promised in the Scriptures, inspired him to reestablish his life priorities. It also motivated him to understand more about the heavenly Father who had pursued him and bought his future for such an outrageous price. The reborn Jew was determined to comprehend the life calling he had received and to fulfill it to the utmost of his ability.

Morris Cerullo was ready to become the man that God was calling him to be.

CHAPTER 28

T HE TRANSFORMATION OF Morris Cerullo was immediate. Even to the most casual observer it was obvious that Morris was a miraculously changed person. Gone was the foul-mouthed, cigarette-smoking tough guy who looked for opportunities to defy authority or to make peers fear him. That angry young man was replaced with a reflective, purposeful teenager who was now focused on sensing the leading of God and doing something about the woeful, oblivious spiritual plight of humankind. The vision and calling he had received at the altar had shaken him to the core and recalibrated both his sense of self and his dreams for the future.

Becoming a lawyer and then the governor was no longer his goal.

Mrs. Kerr and her kin had been deeply moved by Morris's encounter with the Holy Spirit too, as much as their own special moment with God. The stirring of God in their lives was a constant topic of conversation at the dinner table each night.

"I think we should find a messianic congregation for Morris to lead," Ed announced one night. He had been thinking for several days about how to best facilitate Morris's call to ministry and concluded that providing leadership to other Jews who had become born again was the optimal course of action.

"That makes sense," chimed in Ethel, smiling at the prospect of her young friend doing a great work for God. "What do you think about that idea, Morris? We could help find or even start such a church."

Morris's Gentile friends were blown away by his conversion and had high hopes for how God would use the young boy. But as new believers themselves with little spiritual background and experience, their capacity to dream big about ministry opportunities was rather limited.

As they—and other believers—would discover, Morris had no such limitations on his dreams. He did not share their enthusiasm for the idea of leading a small band of reborn Jews in a dingy storefront setting in northern New Jersey. There was nothing wrong with that, but the Lord had displayed the nations of the world before him and provided an unspoken sense that he would be ministering to that entire world, not to a small sliver of it.

So when his benefactors became excited about helping him find a messianic congregation to lead, he did not share their exhilaration.

"No," he replied simply. "That's not for me. God has a much bigger plan for me, and I'm going to pursue it. Someday I will be standing in front of hundreds of thousands of people in countries all over the world. I'm not meant to be in a storefront church in New Jersey," he responded with a finality that shocked his dinner partners.

Who was this fifteen-year old who seemed to think he was God's unique gift to the world? He had no Bible training, no leadership development, no contacts with anyone in the ministry field. He couldn't describe how a church worked if you put a gun to his head. He didn't have any idea how to preach a sermon or baptize a new believer. He had been to exactly one church in his whole life, and now he was proclaiming that churches everywhere would recognize his authority to teach the multitudes! He was a new believer in Christ—one who didn't even fully comprehend what that meant. How arrogant could an individual be to reject the privilege of leading people from his own heritage group? This kid thought he was going to be a household name, a spiritual influence on millions of people around the globe.

They passed it off as the arrogance of youth but were disappointed by what appeared to be an inflated ego behind his pronouncement. Discouraged by what they perceived to be a character flaw, the adults did not raise the topic again.

Although they could not know it at the time, they simply misunderstood the dynamic of the situation. It's true that Morris had no idea of the enormity or absurdity of what he was saying. But none of this was his idea. In his own heart he felt he was simply being obedient to God's calling, much as David and Joseph had suffered ridicule from friends and family for faithfully pursuing God's incredible calling.

The young boy had not attended that unforgettable church service with the expectation that God would meet him supernaturally and unveil a breathtaking vision of an implausible future, yet that is exactly what God did. Morris's sketchy description of his own future seemed out of line, but it was not arrogance on his part; it was a simple reflection of how God was preparing him for the future.

In the months and years to come many people would hear Morris Cerullo's vision and be turned off by the inane claims by this uneducated orphan that he would be used by God in such expansive and trailblazing ways. To his credit, Dr. Cerullo never sought the approval of other people. In fact, he remained deaf to their protestations. In his heart, he knew that his mission was a calling from God.

Morris knew that if God did not bless that audacious mission, it didn't matter how he described it, because his efforts would be doomed to failure.

CHAPTER 29

————•————

OR THE NEXT few months word of what had happened to Morris spread among Christians throughout the area. He was invited to numerous churches to give his testimony. He had never spoken in public but had no fear of doing so. He instinctively realized that this was his introduction to ministry.

Once he turned sixteen, Morris dropped out of school. He wasn't interested in the things they were teaching. He had a burning passion to help people find the love and forgiveness of Jesus Christ, to avoid the hopelessness and torment in hell that God had shown him.

Word soon spread over the state border and into nearby New York City about the young Jewish kid who had a fabulous conversion experience. As a result, Dr. Cerullo was invited to speak at various places in the big city. One of his recurring appearances was on a popular radio program with a well-known black pastor, Ed Roberts, who was a former gangster turned soul-winner. Pastor Roberts loved Ed Roberts's story, and the two ministered on air together on numerous Saturday nights.

Other Christian leaders in the city invited him to speak as well. Jack Wyrtzen, an internationally known youth evangelist and founder of Word of Life Ministries invited Morris to address the city's kids. These experiences enabled him to eventually influence the start of Youth for Christ. The big Assembly of God congregation across the street from Madison Square Garden gave him the platform. Many other churches and ministries from a diverse group of denominations invited him to serve under their banners as well.

While Dr. Cerullo made the most of the ministry opportunities that were presented to him, there were life realities to be addressed, such as making a living. He continued to live in the Maurers' home, but he needed to pay his living expenses. Without school to fill his days, Dr. Cerullo took on jobs as a laborer in factories and warehouses. He even managed a diner at one point. He was young but willing to work hard.

But his heart was inexorably drawn to ministry, and he eagerly devoted all his free time to any form of outreach that was available. When there were no such openings, he created them. If he did not have an invitation from an existing church or parachurch ministry he would hit the streets and attract a small group of people to speak to. If he was unable to gather a group together he'd hitchhike down to the central square in downtown Paterson and preach on the steps of the government center. He refused to take rides from Mrs. Kerr or the Maurers because hitching a ride gave him a captive audience. Many of his drivers wound up accepting Christ. One of his proudest moments was leading a Catholic priest who had picked him up to the Lord!

On the street corners Morris always drew a crowd. He was fearless. Between his unusual story and his ever-improving speaking ability, he never failed to provide passersby with a memorable encounter. He often worked with a group of young people who shared his passion for proclaiming Christ. It was an unusual day when nobody received Christ as their Savior in response to Morris's exhortations.

He tried creative approaches too. He worked with one group that used to go into bars, ask for permission to sing to the patrons, and then sing about family. One particular song they crooned about a child's commitments to their mother never failed to bring tears to the eyes of the crowd as the listeners thought about the broken promises they'd made to their moms. After the songs the group would circulate throughout the bar talking to the patrons, giving out evangelistic tracts, and occasionally praying with someone to receive Christ.

During the summer Morris asked the Assembly church to allow him and his friends to put on a Vacation Bible School for the local kids. As soon as permission was granted, Morris and his group wasted no time hitting the streets, knocking on doors all over town, talking to parents, and inviting their children to attend. To the astonishment of the church's leaders Morris and his cohorts had nearly five hundred kids show up, the overwhelming majority of whom were black! For five consecutive days they spent all day playing games, singing Christian songs, and teaching the Bible. Not surprisingly, many of those children accepted Christ as their Savior.

Through his ministry at the church he met an older man who would become a very dear friend and mentor, Dr. Nickolas Nikoloff. He was the president of Metropolitan Bible Institute. As an educator who constantly worked with young ministers from across the nation, Dr. Nikoloff saw something special in Morris and became both a father figure and ministry mentor to the boy. He was confident that God would do a great work through the boy.

Dr. Nikoloff had no idea what he was getting himself into.

CHAPTER 30

———◆———

MORRIS NEVER CARED much for the classroom. As he spent time ministering in churches and other settings and as he thought about how he could make the greatest headway for God, he concluded that attending a Bible college might provide a big boost to his ministry efforts.

But how could be accepted at a college if he hadn't even completed high school?

Fortunately, Dr. Nikoloff's Bible college was located right in the heart of Morris's ministry area—in North Bergen, New Jersey. Given his personal passion for ministry and his ever-deepening relationship with the president of the school, Morris figured that if he applied to attend the college he'd be granted admission.

He was dead wrong.

The rejection letter set Morris on his heels—for an hour or so. He quickly realized that the school was simply following its own regulations regarding ministry education. After all, Morris had no high school diploma, no formal Bible training, a very brief church relationship, and limited skills. The rejection made logical sense. But he knew in his heart that somehow he'd wind up getting the training he needed to better serve God.

In the meantime, Morris continued to spend time with Dr. Nikoloff, peppering the man with questions and ideas every chance he got. Each word out of the college president's mouth was like a sacred text to Morris. He listened carefully and spent hours contemplating the wisdom gleaned from his mentor. They shared the same love of Christ and intense desire to save souls. Morris was bowled over by the man's humility, intelligence, integrity, Bible knowledge, and zeal for people. Spending time with Dr. Nikoloff was Morris's alternative seminary exposure.

But like so many schools, the little Bible college was having a tough go of it financially. To keep the school solvent Dr. Nikoloff had to either cut expenses or close the doors. Sensing that God was not yet done with the school, he developed a new strategy, one which included moving from the expensive downtown space the school rented into much cheaper space within a large, Bible-training-friendly church—the same church that Morris attended!

The move opened up additional spaces for new students. Morris applied immediately and was accepted. It didn't surprise him one bit. He knew God would provide a way for him to get the training he needed to serve more effectively. God's hand remained on Morris's life in very tangible ways.

CHAPTER 31

————•————

THANKS TO HIS appetite for learning about ministry, Morris's checkered educational pedigree didn't hinder his progress. But a significant obstacle emerged soon enough.

After Morris completed his first year of the program, a miracle happened for the school. Dr. Nikoloff swung a deal to purchase a beautiful old estate in upstate New York. The new grounds were big enough to house all the school's classes and administration, providing a sprawling campus in a sedate location. It was an ideal setting for theological reflection and discourse.

Unfortunately, it was also a couple of hours away from Morris's home.

Meanwhile, Morris became disenchanted with some of the Christians he knew. As a "completed Jew" called to serve God in a very special way, he was far from perfect, but he was all in when it came to his faith. He knew he had a lot to learn, that he was rough around the edges, and that it would take much time and experience for him to have the kind of impact that God had shown him through the vision.

Still, the double-mindedness of some Christians he encountered blew his mind. It was so distressing to him that he decided he needed to make some major changes in his life's plan. He made the mental transition away from preparing for a life of full-time ministry to going into the secular world, getting a "regular job" like most people.

After some soul searching and practical reflection he decided to abandon his plans to go into the professional ministry and instead get a job in a new location. Florida appealed to him. Everything he had heard about the Sunshine State made it sound like an exciting place. Many people from the New York metropolitan area raved about the weather and the relaxed lifestyle in the southern hot spot. It sounded like an ideal location to begin the next chapter of his young life.

After tying up his loose ends in New Jersey he set about to hitchhike to Miami. On a brisk morning he trudged down to the edge of Route 1 and stood on the curb with his thumb out, waiting for someone to offer a ride. It wasn't too long before a shiny black Cadillac pulled off the highway and rolled to a stop a few feet beyond Morris. He picked up his suitcase, ran up to the car, and put his head through the open passenger-side window.

"Where are you heading?" the driver, an older man, asked.

"Florida," was all the young man said, and he was invited into the car. He threw his bag in the back seat and jumped in the front passenger seat.

"I'll take you there if you'll help me drive," the man said.

"No problem," Morris confidently responded, and he settled in for the next hour. He neglected to inform the kindly driver that he did not have a driver's license. Oh, and that he had never driven a car.

CHAPTER 32

ORRIS MADE IT to Florida without any problems. The more miles he drove, the more his anxiety diminished and his driving improved. The first hour or so was a little uneven, but he had watched adults drive for years and figured it couldn't be that hard. It turned out it wasn't, thanks partially to driving on a highway that had been built to go from Maine to Florida, a straight shot, albeit with a lot of traffic lights along the way. Thankfully, his host didn't seem concerned about the young man's lack of familiarity with some of the nuances of driving.

After arriving in Miami the two men parted ways, and Morris was all alone in a bustling city where he knew nobody and had no place to live. His first job was to figure out how to make it in his new hometown—but then, he was a survivor.

After walking around a while to get a sense of the territory, Morris wound up being hired as a busboy and dishwasher in the restaurant at the Eden Roc Hotel. It was a gorgeous, relatively new hotel just down the block from the prestigious Fontainebleau Hotel. The pay was lousy, and the tasks were not challenging, but it provided him the money he needed to rent a room nearby and begin his new life.

The menial tasks he performed provided lots of time to reflect on how he had been burned by a few Christians in New Jersey whom he had trusted and on his severe disappointment that so many people who passed themselves off as followers of Christ were not living the life that they pretended to lead. He did not want to be judgmental, but his naiveté about the clash between the ways of the world and the ways of Christ sent him into a tailspin.

Within a few weeks of beginning his tenure at the hotel, Morris was promoted to the job of waiter. It was a swanky restaurant, so he made good money, receiving generous tips from the gamblers, gangsters, and other characters who liked to display their wealth and power in public. Previously unbeknownst to Morris, Miami Beach in those days was a haven for people whose wealth came from dubious sources.

While getting established, Morris mostly kept to himself. Along the way he met a girl with whom he became good friends. She was not a love interest but a genuinely nice girl to whom he could talk openly and honestly. She turned out to be a born-again Christian. Given his disappointing experience with Christians in New Jersey, Morris had mixed feelings about her faith, but it turned out to be a major blessing. Their talks helped him sort things out in his mind and make sense of the disparity between Christian talk and the Christian walk.

Those conversations proved to be the kind of soul healing that Morris needed. He embraced a more mature understanding of the role of faith, the challenges of biblical living, and the role of the evangelist and disciple in a religious but not always Christian society. Those insights would have a profound effect on his future life choices.

As the months flew by, his disillusionment with Christians dissipated. Each day, waiting on tables and interacting with a diverse base of customers, Morris gained deeper insight into the human condition and people's desperate need for God's love and grace.

After nine months in Florida, Morris Cerullo made peace with the moral and spiritual weaknesses and inconsistencies of humankind. Maybe that's what God had intended his detour to the south to provide: a chance to further grasp the frailties of people and churches. Tired of his humdrum life in Miami, Morris decided it was time for another change. He packed up his suitcase and returned to New Jersey.

He was not yet eighteen years old.

CHAPTER 33

————◆————

THERE WAS NOBODY waiting for him when he pulled back into the central square in downtown Paterson, New Jersey. Thanks to his marketplace adventure and personal soul-searching he had changed, but Paterson was just as he remembered it.

Back in familiar territory, Morris rented a room and quickly picked up a laborer job in a garment factory. While he had developed a deeper understanding of the frailties of humanity, he was not in a hurry to jump back into full-time ministry. However, he did re-establish contact with Dr. Nikoloff, hoping to continue his reflection upon the gap between professed faith and practiced faith. His mentor, now presiding over the Bible school in its new upstate location, was happy to have the young dynamo return to the northeast.

One day he received a call from Dr. Nikoloff. "Morris, I want you to come and join us on the campus," the school's president said. "I would like the students to hear your testimony. And then I'd like you to preach for them. They will be moved by your passion for Jesus and some of the incredible experiences you have had."

Morris was excited to have a chance to spend time with his mentor, check out the school's new campus, and to have an exchange with the students. But he retained mixed feelings about the educational experience itself. Sure, he missed the exposure to the biblical knowledge and theological reflection that he had experienced during his year in the school, but he was not a student at heart and did not envy the academic pressures that students had to bear.

After taking the two-hour bus ride to Suffern, he was picked up at the station by Dr. Nikoloff and driven to the sprawling, wooded estate. The city kid was not used to such spacious, uncluttered beauty. He fell in love with the grounds.

Following a tour of the educational facilities, they got down to business. Morris had a wonderful time sharing his testimony, preaching, and interacting with the students, a few of whom he knew from his time enrolled in the school. It was a satisfying day, and Morris felt an unexpected yearning to be back in an environment where he too could be discovering truths that would help him grow spiritually.

But the best was yet to come. After the day's events were completed the students gathered with the faculty in the massive dining room for lunch. They arrayed themselves along the outer edges of the elongated table, seating all fifty of the students plus another dozen professors and administrators.

Dr. Nikoloff sat at the head of the table with their honored guest, Morris, next to him.

Seated next to Morris was quiet girl whose name Morris didn't catch. He noticed she wasn't eating much. As he watched her push food from one spot to another on her plate, he realized how attractive she was. The more he observed her, the more taken he was by her beauty and serenity. She did not speak to Morris and seemed very self-contained. He was intrigued.

As soon as the meal ended and everyone scattered to their next class or appointment, Morris stood in front of the girl, blocking her exit. He looked her in the eye and smiled.

"Would you do me a favor," he began earnestly, "and step into the vestibule for a minute? I just want to tell you something."

She remained silent, staring at the visitor, but gently nodded her head. They walked out of the dining hall and over to a corner of the adjoining ante-room in the mansion.

"Listen, lady, I just want to let you know something," Morris said once they were facing each other. "One day I'm gonna come back here and attend this school again. And I'm going to marry you."

The city kid stood there and smiled in triumph. The shy girl faced him, staring in disbelief at the brazen stranger. Before he could add any more crazy comments she put up her hand in front of his face like a traffic cop halting the rush of cars and then screamed at the top of her lungs and ran to the stairway at the far end of the room. She bounded up the stairs past a dozen startled students who were left in her wake.

After watching her hasty and dramatic exit, a handful of students made a beeline toward Morris and demanded to know what he had said that had upset their classmate.

"Hey, it's no big deal," he replied with calm confidence. "I just told her I am going to marry her."

With that, he headed off to see about getting a ride back to the bus station. His journey upstate had been more eventful than he had expected. For the first time in a long while he could feel the excitement about life return to his being.

Game on!

CHAPTER 34

————◆————

W ITH A NEW set of goals in mind Morris began a running dialogue with Dr. Nikoloff, who eventually arranged for Morris to be readmitted to the school with some financial assistance to cover his expenses. Morris would have been hard pressed to identify exactly which was his greater motivation: obtaining a ministry degree from the Bible college or marrying Theresa, the girl he was so taken with during his visit to the school.

Upon his arrival in Suffern, though, an immediate dilemma emerged. Morris was given his student ID, his class assignments, a meal schedule, and his room assignment. It was his housing situation that produced a serious issue.

Morris had been used to living on his own. The fact that he now had to share a room with someone he'd never met took some time to accept. He was assigned to a room with Danny, a well-liked student. What nobody told Morris was that Danny also liked Theresa.

In fact, Danny was engaged to her!

As soon as this situation came to his attention, Morris knew he had to devise a plan to break them up. He was certain that he was supposed to marry Theresa, but he had to facilitate the breakup very carefully and delicately.

CHAPTER 35

————◆————

As time went on Morris got into the rhythm of the Bible school. He was not the most diligent of students—he was bored most of the time—but he did enough to get by.

Theresa was on his mind more than the complicated biblical arguments of old German theologians.

As the months passed Morris got to know Theresa's parents. They lived a short distance from the school and would visit her often. Morris developed a special relationship with her mother. The older woman took a liking to him.

"Why don't you go out with Morris?" her mother occasionally asked Theresa. "He's such a nice boy. He'd make a good boyfriend."

"Mom, I'm already engaged to Danny. I'm not looking for another boyfriend. Don't you want me to be a loyal wife? Isn't that what you taught me? Isn't that how a Christian wife should be?" she fumed at her mother.

"That's good, yes, but Morris is such a nice boy. I think you'd like him."

Theresa would usually walk away in a snit, upset at her mother's meddling—and at what she perceived to be Morris's manipulation of her parent.

Morris was invited over to the family's house every once in a while, which left Theresa emotionally perplexed. On one hand, she liked Morris. On the other hand, it felt disloyal to have another boy visiting her in her own house—with her parents obviously approving of and enjoying his company.

Morris made little progress trying to come up with a stealthy means of undermining Theresa's relationship with Danny. In the end, it didn't matter; God took matters into His own hands and produced a solution that nobody saw coming.

CHAPTER 36

THERESA WAS A very godly young lady. She worked hard at her Bible courses, and she was a real prayer warrior. Before every significant decision she sought the Lord's guidance through prayer.

One of her most significant decisions was what to do about Danny.

As their relationship progressed Theresa was having some doubts about their future together. It didn't have much to do with the presence of Morris; that was a different issue altogether. Her concern was more spiritual in nature. Not sure what else to do, she prayed about the relationship, asking God to give her some kind of sign or experience that would clarify if Danny was the right man for her.

Meanwhile, Danny was going through some emotional jitters of his own regarding marriage. Like many young men, he had an occasional moment of doubt as to whether Theresa was the right girl for him—or even if he was ready to get married.

One morning during one of his bouts of indecision he sat at his desk in the room he shared with Morris and penned his fiancée a very personal letter. He explained that he thought she was very special but that they should stop seeing each other for a while to help determine how much they really meant to each other. He read it over, sighed, then sealed it and deposited it in the campus postal box.

The next day he realized what a stupid idea that had been! Of course he wanted to marry Theresa. Who wouldn't? As soon as his classes were finished for the day he raced over to her house to retrieve the letter before she could read it.

To his horror, once he arrived he discovered that the mail had already been delivered and distributed. He stammered his way through an explanation to Theresa.

"You shouldn't have read that letter," he began nonsensically. "I didn't mean what it says. It was a crazy idea, and we should just go on as if you never saw it. It was a stupid idea. Can you just forget that you ever saw that dumb note, Theresa?"

Gracious as always, she took his hand in hers. "Danny, I can't forget what I've read. Even so, your suggestion was an answer to my own prayers. You're a great guy, and I appreciate your second thoughts about, well, your second thoughts, but you're right. We need to break up. We both need to move on."

CHAPTER 37

I N ADDITION TO his pursuit of Theresa and his education, Morris enjoyed some of the leisure activities that the students engaged in. One of his favorites was softball. He became the pitcher on the school's softball team and had a good time being in the center of the action.

During one game, however, Morris's pitching career came to a quick halt. On the mound, he focused on the catcher's mitt, wound up, and hurled a fastball at a larger-than-average batter. The pitch crossed the center of the plate and was smacked back at Morris so fast that he didn't have time to react. The ball made a sickening crunch as it pounded into Morris's jaw. He fell to the ground immediately, unconscious.

Play came to an instant stop as the players from both teams rushed to the mound to check out the fallen pitcher. Some of his teammates immediately began to organize for emergency assistance. After a few minutes, with female students crying and his teammates and opponents watching in a daze, he was carried off the field and rushed to the hospital.

The doctors who examined Morris spoke to each other in hushed tones before standing directly over him to deliver the prognosis.

"The good news, Mr. Cerullo, is that you are alive," one doctor explained with a grim look. "Unfortunately, you have sustained some very serious damage. Your jaw is broken in two places, and you cheekbone is splintered. We will do the best we can to enable your face to heal properly, but I can pretty much assure you that there will be lasting damage."

The doctor paused, as if waiting for Morris to ask about the damage. Realizing that Morris was unable to speak, he continued. "We are waiting for a special brace to arrive from another hospital in New Jersey that will help your bones stabilize. I am sorry to say, though, that you will probably never have normal movement of your jaw. That will permanently affect your speaking."

Morris's eyes involuntarily closed as he listened to the damage report, thinking about what the recovery process would be like. Oblivious, the doctor delivered the rest of his report.

"In the meantime we will set and bandage your jaw. This is going to be a bit uncomfortable, even with the sedation you have received. You won't be able to eat or drink normally for a few months, and speaking will be very difficult. But we'll do everything we can to restore basic functions."

A thousand thoughts seemed to race through Morris's mind at once. Foremost among them was the excruciating pain that throbbed throughout his entire head. He had been in numerous street brawls during his lifetime, but he had never experienced such intense pain. Yet he felt equally as much agony from the realization that his courting of Theresa would grind to halt while he recovered. Just as the coast had cleared for him to move forward in their relationship with Danny falling by the wayside, this accident had to happen. He was absolutely heartbroken. At the same time, he was confident that God would heal him and allow him to do things the doctors couldn't even imagine.

But in the hospital that night, the thought that dominated Morris's mind was a simple one.

"Please, dear God, just make the pain stop."

For weeks the pain continued, occasionally forcing an involuntary tear out of his eyes. His head was wrapped in a white bandage to hold everything secure while the healing slowly took place.

After several weeks in the hospital he was allowed to return to school and attend classes and school functions, his head bandaged like the skull of a mummy. As he carefully walked around campus he was embarrassed for Theresa to see him like this, but he would not avoid her. He'd mumble sweet words to her, which she could not understand, but she never disregarded or mocked him. She paid careful attention, hoping to make out a word or two and offering kind thoughts and comforting words.

Morris constantly prayed that God would miraculously heal him. As time went on, though, his expectation of supernatural intervention waned.

CHAPTER 38

———◆———

PRIOR TO THE softball incident Morris had received an invitation to speak at a small Pentecostal church that was not too far from the school. He had enthusiastically accepted the invitation and had been earnestly praying about and preparing for the event.

The broken jaw, however, changed everything.

Morris's teachers and fellow students naturally expected him to cancel the appearance. What good was a speaker who couldn't speak? Even though Morris had been so excited about the opportunity to minister to the tiny congregation, his passion couldn't make up for his inability to communicate.

As the date of the event approached, Morris was laying on his bed in his dorm room one afternoon praying for souls and wondering how he would explain the news of his accident to the pastor of the church. While seeking God's wisdom he felt an overwhelming and clear sense of God's voice.

"Son, if you will keep the commitment you have made to minister to My people at that church, I will heal you."

Improbable as it seemed, Morris immediately rejoiced, believing that God would do exactly as He had just promised. During Morris's short life as a follower of Christ, God had never led him astray or broken a promise. He was ecstatic that he would be healed and that he would be able to speak to the people at that local church.

But Morris's joy was challenged by the doubts expressed by many of his teachers and classmates. They applauded his desire to believe in God but felt that their "realistic feedback" would ultimately save him from a major letdown and public embarrassment. They claimed to believe in miracles but assured Morris that God was not about to heal his jaw and enable him to speak to the congregation. Some tried to shame him into backing out of the event, noting that his failure would disgrace their school as well.

Their words of discouragement never penetrated his mind or heart. It was a brutal lesson in people's lack of faith—especially among those who were preparing to represent God to the world! He listened to their exhortations to abandon his plan to show up and speak but remained unmoved by their arguments and their emotion.

When that Sunday morning arrived the whole school was buzzing with curiosity about Morris. Would he really have the nerve to show up at the church with his broken jaw and bandaged head thinking that God would suddenly heal him and allow him to speak? Had something else in his head been jarred loose by the softball?

The tiny country church was built to accommodate just a few families, maybe thirty people in total. Having never been inside the building, Morris did not realize how compact it was. When he arrived prior to the service, he saw dozens of people milling about outside the front of the building. Assuming they were waiting to enter and take their seats, he made his way to the entrance. After he opened the door and tried to take a step inside, he realized that the inside of the building was already crammed with people. Every seat was taken, and there was an overflow crowd standing along the walls. The people waiting outside were those who had arrived too late to get a seat! More than one hundred people had shown up at a church that normally attracted fifteen or twenty people.

Morris took a moment to study the people waiting outside the front door. It wasn't until then that he noticed they were mostly students and faculty from his school.

They wanted to see what God was going to do—or not do.

Grasping the possibilities for building people's faith, Morris seized the moment. As he stood in the doorway, the crowd had gone silent, watching the young man with the bandaged head. He looked inside, then outside, then inside again and outside one last time. He said a silent prayer and then began to pull off the bandage.

Morris's jaw immediately fell open. His eyes closed. Drool slopped over his lips.

Everyone continued to stare in disbelief at Morris.

Some probably thought he had closed his eyes to pray. In reality, he closed them in response to the stabbing pain that wracked his body as his jaw fell open. Immediately after the accident the searing pain had caused him to pass out. He was determined not to succumb to the pain this time. He remained conscious at the entrance of the church but was sure that the pain was even greater than that he had experienced on the ball field.

He slowly opened his eyes and found every eye in the church bearing down on him. Determined to trust God, he started moving toward the pulpit at the front of the sanctuary. He felt as if everything was moving in slow motion—except the pain that seemed to escalate with each step. In fact, any movement of his body heightened the suffering.

As he moved down the center aisle to the pulpit, his jaw was hanging, swaying from side to side with each step. By the time he reached the front of the sanctuary it looked to him as if everyone else's jaw had dropped too.

As soon as he reached his seat on the platform, the music director whipped the audience into a frenzy of song.

Morris watched the congregants sing. Much as wanted to, he was unable to join them. His face felt ready to explode in pain.

After the singing came the weekly announcements and then the offering. The pace of the service slowed down. Was the music leader, who orchestrated the flow of the service, stalling? Was he trying to figure out what to do with the apparently crippled young man who was sitting on the stage?

Upon completion of the offering the congregation was led into a few more songs.

After the final hymn, the music leader glanced at Morris for a few seconds, then took the microphone again. He introduced Morris and slowly made his way back to his seat and joined everyone else in staring at the guest preacher.

Morris had been expecting a miraculous moment to remove the pain and strengthen his jaw, but no such moment arrived.

Confused, he slowly rose from his chair and gingerly shuffled to the podium. He carefully mounted the three steps to the pulpit and placed his Bible in the center of the podium, flipping to the page he wanted. He then raised his head and looked out at the congregation.

Every eye was glued to the young man whose jaw was hanging limp. They seemed fascinated by the spectacle they were witnessing. Nobody was moving. It was silent as a morgue—which seemed appropriate to Morris, as he prepared for what may have seemed like the death of his nascent ministry career.

Morris lowered his eyes to the text he wanted to read. He took a deep breath.

Suddenly his jaw snapped into place. In his head, he heard a raucous noise, a pop and crack as his bones realigned and the muscles tightened around them. His cheekbone smoothed out as the fragmented bones became smooth and normal once again. The very shape of his face shifted before their eyes.

A gasp of disbelief filled the air. A couple of people jumped to their feet, awed by the miracle they were experiencing. The students and faculty craning their necks outside the front door of the church began excitedly twisting and turning to share the news of what those in front had seen. The hum of their exclamations sounded like a sonorous rumble up on the platform.

Morris was slightly shaking with the nervous energy that was racing through his body. He did it! God did it!

Cool as an ice cube, Morris nonchalantly proceeded to read the passage he had chosen as his primary text. He then preached his sermon as if nothing special had happened. He smiled, shouted, pounded the pulpit, and waved his arms in all the appropriate places. He was pain-free and full of the power of the Holy Spirit. Internally, he was celebrating the fulfilled promise of God to heal him and then speak through him.

The results of his presentation were beyond his control—and they were also beyond expectations. Not only had God visibly and indisputably healed the student preacher, but He swept the congregation off its feet as well. A mini-revival broke out in the church and among the Bible college students!

The students realized that they were not to worship any person, but after that event they looked at Morris with a newfound respect.

CHAPTER 39

ORRIS'S REMAINING TIME at Bible college flew by. With Theresa no longer betrothed to Danny, he and Theresa spent more time together and developed an ever-deepening relationship. They graduated and planned to get married a few months after receiving their diplomas. To Morris, it was yet another in an unending string of instances in which God moved the mountains and he obediently followed the available path.

That didn't mean that his life was bed of roses, though. Shortly after graduating, while he and Theresa were getting ready for their marriage, he arranged to lead a series of evangelistic meetings in Maine and was preparing to drive there to meet with the group of locals who would facilitate the events. Before leaving for the meeting, though, he received a phone call from the district superintendent of the Assemblies of God churches in the six New England states. Technically, he was Morris's boss, since the young preacher was ordained by the Assemblies of God denomination and he was part of the denomination's New England region.

"Morris, on your way north, why don't you stop by my house and stay overnight," Dr. Smuland, the regional leader, offered. He lived just outside of Boston, which was along the route that Morris would take on his drive to Maine. "There are a few things I'd like to speak to you about."

His manner was friendly, not the least bit ominous or threatening, and Morris had a good relationship with him, so the new graduate agreed to drop in. But when he arrived at the older man's house the conversation took an unexpected turn.

"Here's the thing, Morris," Smuland began haltingly. "People don't know this yet, but my doctor recently informed me that my heart condition has gotten worse. The doctors don't want me traveling or exerting myself, but I had already obligated myself to speak at our church in Claremont, New Hampshire, this coming Sunday morning and evening. Would you do me a big favor and cover that obligation for me?"

They talked through the challenges of making such a switch and finally worked out a way for Morris to take on the opportunity. He left the superintendent's house early Sunday morning in plenty of time to get to the little country church to fill in for Dr. Smuland.

Upon arriving in Claremont Morris was delighted to find a picturesque, colonial-style church building in good repair. He parked and went inside the church, ready to do his guest sermon. The sanctuary was cozy and inviting with seats for about two hundred people.

But there was something that was not so inviting about the environment. Morris could sense something was wrong.

Soon enough he discovered the problem. The church's regular pastor had been caught in adultery earlier that week with one of the young girls from town. Apparently it had been more than just a one-night stand, and there was talk that maybe the pastor had been involved with more than just one girl in the recent past. Upon finding out, the congregants were furious and immediately fired the pastor. The local newspaper had been running a series of articles about the scandal.

As the time for the service rolled around, there were only forty people sitting in the pews. Already nervous because he did not consider himself a preacher as much as an evangelist, Morris took the platform and did his best. The parishioners said nice things to him while he shook their hands as they exited after the completion of the service.

As nerve-wracking as the morning service had been for him, the evening service was even worse. The paltry crowd that had shown up in the morning dwindled to less than a dozen for the evening celebration! It was not much of a confidence-builder for the young speaker. Again, he gave it his best shot. As soon as the final words of the last hymn were finished, he hurriedly grabbed his Bible and ran to his car.

By his calculations, he had managed to reduce an already tiny congregation to a micro-church thanks to his powerful preaching and magnetic leadership! This was not how he had envisioned his ministry launching.

Morris didn't let the disappointing experience get to him though. He drove up to Maine for his scheduled meetings, then motored all the way back to Theresa's parents' house. He had already put the Claremont experience out of his mind. He was fresh out of school, about to get married, and had a series of evangelistic events lined up in Assembly of God churches throughout the region. He was focused on those opportunities.

Upon arriving back in Newburgh he received a call from Dr. Smuland. Morris suspected that his boss might call. It was a conversation he was not looking forward to having.

"Well, Morris, I hear you had quite a day on Sunday," the senior minister began, sounding surprisingly upbeat. "What did you do to those people?"

A sullen Morris quietly offered his defense. "I did the best I could. You asked me to preach for you, and I did. It was really last minute. What else could I do?"

"Well, let me tell you, son, the phone has been ringing off the hook since Sunday night. I certainly didn't expect this kind of reaction."

No reply came to Morris's mind. Was an apology in order? Maybe a different excuse? Perhaps shift the blame to his boss for not thinking through the plan more carefully? It didn't warrant his resignation, did it?

But before Morris spoke again, Smuland continued.

"It must have been one unforgettable day of ministry," he said with a chuckle. "Yessir, apparently the church board got together after the Sunday evening service and unanimously voted you in as their new pastor. A unanimous vote! Congratulations, Morris. That's tremendous. God must have really been moving that night."

Morris held the phone to his ear and stared straight ahead, his eyes narrowing in disbelief. He was speechless as he tried to make sense of what he had just heard. Was this a joke?

But as the district superintendent continued to describe some of the compliments he had received from Claremont congregants, the young preacher realized it was not a put-on. This news was for real; apparently the folks in Claremont found Morris to their liking. As the superintendent passed along more of the positive feedback he had received Morris's brain quickly shifted into gear, and the horror of the situation dawned on him.

"Wait a minute," he stammered after Dr. Smuland paused. "You don't think I'm going back there, do you? You don't really think that I'd take that position?"

"Why not?" Smuland asked with a laugh. "You're fresh out of Bible school and don't have a full-time position. You're getting married soon, and you and your wife will want to settle down and start a family. These people want you. It's a chance to take a congregation that is going nowhere and inject some life into it, Morris. This is your chance to let God work through you to build up a hurting church. It's a chance to make your mark for the kingdom. What more could you ask for, Morris? At least give them a call and talk to them. Their elders are waiting to hear from you."

He gave Morris the phone number to call, wished him the best, and hung up.

The prospect staggered him. God had called him to a global, world-changing ministry, not some out-of-the-way, dying congregation in the midst of turmoil and public humiliation. Some eager beaver preachers might have jumped at the opportunity. All Morris could ask himself was why this was happening to him.

So, as requested by his superior, Morris telephoned the lay leaders in Claremont, thanked them for their vote of confidence, and told them in no uncertain terms that he would not be returning to Claremont as their pastor. Satisfied that he had nailed that door shut, he hung up the phone and sat in the chair for a moment.

Morris was trying to sort things out in his mind when he suddenly sensed the Spirit of God speaking to him.

"Morris, go back to New Hampshire. Pastor the church. Call them back and tell them you will be coming as their pastor."

It was not what he wanted to hear.

Humanly speaking, it made little sense. The church had no money. The congregation was emotionally devastated by the moral failure of their previous pastor. Morris's personal ministry plan did not include pastoring a church, much less a tiny congregation of old-timers who probably had little interest in a serious outreach ministry.

But God had spoken. He remained in his chair and prayed.

Indeed, the longer he thought and prayed about it, the more convinced he was that the Lord had opened this door for him and that it was God's will, for whatever reason, that he return to Claremont with Theresa.

Dutifully, he picked up the phone and made the call.

Then he sat in the quiet house for a long time trying to wrap his mind around God's plan for his life. His reverie was shattered by the ringing of the telephone. He answered the call, hearing Dr. Smuland's voice again.

"Brother," he began, exuding excitement, "I just got off the phone with the elders in Claremont. Those people are beside themselves with excitement. God will do great things through this partnership, Morris."

Oddly enough, that's exactly what Morris was starting to believe, even though it made little sense to him.

CHAPTER 40

————◆————

BEFORE BEGINNING HIS new pastorate, Morris had one other little detail to iron out: his wedding.

He and Theresa worked hard at putting the finishing touches on everything before the big day. Finally, the wedding day arrived. Everything went smoothly. Close to three hundred friends and relatives attended the wedding—almost all of them from Theresa's side of the family. Morris had no relatives and just a few friends from school. The ceremony was beautiful, Theresa was beautiful, and the reception was a big Italian celebration. It couldn't have gone better.

When it was over, Morris and Theresa Cerullo were one.

One broke couple, that is.

Morris had never owned a car, so he had no means of getting from upstate New York to his new job in New Hampshire. In his closet hung the few clothes he had. There was no bank account. All he had was the money in his pocket. The day after the wedding, Morris got right to the point with his new bride.

"Honey," he stated quietly, facing her as she sat serenely on the bed, "I'd love to take you on a fabulous honeymoon trip, but you know I have no money. This is all we have."

With that, he turned the pockets of his pants inside out, and thirty-five crumbled dollars bounced onto the floor.

Ever the upbeat, no-worries woman of faith who trusted God to take care of things in His own timing, she laughed and put Morris at ease.

"Oh, don't worry about that, honey," she said. Lifting a little white satchel from the bed stand, she unzipped the case. "Come here," she instructed him, patting an empty spot on the bed next to her. "Let's see how much money we got as wedding gifts."

The satchel contained all the monetary gifts that Theresa's Italian relatives had brought for the newlyweds. Their eyes got big as they opened envelope after envelope and finally counted up three hundred and fifty dollars in cash. That was a substantial sum in 1952. They laughed in joy together when they tallied the full amount.

Excited about their newfound treasure, Theresa suggested that they go to New York City. However, knowing that hotels in the big city cost a fortune, she insisted that they stay with one of her friends from Bible college who lived across the river in North Bergen, New Jersey. Having grown up near there Morris had no objections. They arranged with Theresa's father to borrow his car—Morris had a driver's license by now—and made arrangements to stay with Theresa's friend.

Loaning Morris and Theresa his gleaming Chevy was no small matter. It was a beautiful car, and Mr. LePari was a man who always kept his vehicles in pristine condition. Allowing two young kids to drive his car into the traffic and craziness of New York City and its surroundings was a major sign of trust.

"Morris, I'm counting on you to take good care of my baby," he said, handing the keys to Morris and then hugging Theresa. "Oh, and take good care of Theresa, too," he said with a laugh.

CHAPTER 41

NEW YORK WAS a virtual playground of leisure options, but neither of the twenty-somethings cruising toward the Big Apple on their honeymoon had ever been to a major league baseball game. After a bit of discussion they decided to attend a game at Yankee Stadium, in the Bronx.

Everything went well. They found the stadium without too much trouble, gawked at the price of parking, and enjoyed the game. Theresa didn't know too much about the Yankees, but the hot dogs, popcorn, hot pretzels with mustard, and other junk food helped make the experience pleasant and memorable.

After the Yankees squeaked out a victory the young couple braved the post-game traffic and made it back to North Bergen in good spirits. Morris parked the car alongside the curb up at the top of the hilly street and locked it up. He and Theresa walked arm in arm across the street and had just hopped onto the sidewalk when they jumped at the sound of a huge crash.

Together, they turned around to see what had caused the loud noise. What they saw made Morris want to vomit.

The beautiful Chevy they had borrowed from Theresa's dad was crunched into a big tree in the middle of a neighbor's lawn! The windshield was shattered, the hood was crumbled into a V-shape, and the front bumper was lying on the ground.

When Morris had parked the car, being a novice at such things, he had failed to turn the wheels toward the curb or to put on the emergency brake. Because they were on a steep hill, the car's transmission dislodged and slid into neutral, which enabled the vehicle to begin rolling. It jumped the curb and picked up speed, stopping when it met an object of resistance—the huge tree, which left the front end of the car crinkled like an accordion.

A cold sweat broke out on Morris's forehead. Here he was, staying with guests on the first night of his honeymoon, and he had caused an accident in the neighborhood and wrecked the precious luxury car owed by his new wife's father.

Suddenly the Yankees having won the game didn't seem so special.

To make matters worse, the mother of the girl with whom they were staying ran into the front yard and starting yelling at Morris—half in Russian, half in her version of English! An emotional and religious immigrant, the woman kept raging that this was the judgment of God against Morris. She had been upset about them going to a ballgame—she had ranted about the kind of people you meet there, the vulgar language people use in stadiums, the scandalous outfits some of the women wear, and so forth—and now felt vindicated that this newly married young man was not trustworthy. She left no doubt that she was upset with her own daughter for inviting them into her home.

It was not how Morris envisioned spending his honeymoon evening.

CHAPTER 42

———◆———

I F THERESA FELT like marrying Morris Cerullo destined her for a life of adventure, the honeymoon was just the start. After a night spent enduring a Russian monologue about how evil he was, Morris spent the next day arranging for the car to be repaired. The collision experts made quick work of it, and the young couple returned to upstate New York as soon as the paint was dry on the rehabilitated auto.

Upon returning to Theresa's parents' house, it was time for the couple to head to New Hampshire to commence their life in pastoral ministry.

But there were obstacles they had to overcome.

They had no transportation to get from New York to New Hampshire. They had no money left after visiting Yankee Stadium and then paying the auto repair bill in New Jersey. Morris had leased an apartment that was waiting for them in the center of Claremont, but they had no belongings to move into their new home.

Moved by their situation, Theresa's brother agreed to drive them to the apartment. Upon arrival, they entered the empty rooms and placed their luggage and few wedding gifts on the floor. They silently walked the empty rooms, peered out the windows into the town's streets below, and then stared at each other. They had no bed, no chairs, no table, no silverware. Their modest collection of clothing was hanging in the bedroom closet. They had a few blankets and a pillow they had received as presents.

Morris stood by a window and stared vacantly at the lawn outside. He daydreamed about how people would eventually be drawn to the Assemblies of God church that he and Theresa would lead and how God would eventually expand their influence to touch thousands of lives around the nation and, someday, around the world. He could see the smiles on faces as people gratefully accepted God's grace or cried in appreciation for God's healing touch. Morris knew it would happen. The flame of passion for souls still burned hot in his soul, and the vision of people tormented in hell remained vivid and moving.

Slowly he refocused on the street scene below and then turned to see Theresa contentedly sitting on a blanket she had spread on the floor, silently watching her husband. He smiled broadly and went to his suitcase. He withdrew their one item of food—a can of Franco-American spaghetti. He went through the drawers in the kitchen, searching for any means of opening the can, and found a wooden ruler, a few pieces of silverware, and a rusted, rickety can opener that had been left behind by the prior tenants. Giving thanks to God for such a small but important gift, he patiently manipulated the can opener until the lid was sliced off. He slowly rinsed a couple of forks under the hot water in the kitchen sink and returned to the living room, where his bride was patiently waiting.

"I love you, Theresa," Morris said in a soft tone. "Remember this day and these humble beginnings. The Lord will use us to bless many people, just as we are blessed. This is the start of a new day for us. We will never be the same. And neither will those whom God touches through our ministry to them."

As the sun set outside their bare windows, they sat and passed the can of spaghetti back and forth, uncertain of what the future held but confident that it would be a great adventure. Their circumstances were challenging, but they both felt a kind of excited anticipation to see what God had in store for them. It was exactly the kind of challenge that Morris had always had to face on his own as a child. Now he felt fortified by the love of his wife and the power of God.

Soon thereafter they fell asleep on the blanket covering the floor sharing the pillow they owned, eager for the next chapter of their life to begin.

PART THREE:

———— ◆ ————

THE EARLY DAYS
OF MINISTRY

CHAPTER 43

————•————

Pastor Cerullo quickly learned that Bible school had not fully trained him for the kinds of challenges he immediately faced in the church. Barely twenty years old, he started his pastoral career addressing the damage of his predecessor's affair. Meanwhile, his tiny congregation was pleased to have him aboard—and quickly dumped its endless demands on their new spiritual leader.

Using his natural leadership gifts, Morris was able to get the ship pointed in the right direction and sailing a smoother course toward spiritual health. With nothing to lose, he made bold statements and took strong steps toward reshaping the church and its ministry. He challenged the people to step up and reflect their membership in the kingdom of God. He eliminated the membership rolls of the church and dared people to live the life of Christ within the community, being a living testimony to an observant but doubting town.

"If you ask people in this town about our church, they all know it. They speak of it as the church where the pastor shacks up with young girls. That's a disgrace. The only way we will gain back respect and have a positive influence in this town is for you and me to prove them wrong," he bellowed as he stood on the platform and tore up the church's membership cards. "As of this moment, First Assembly has no members. If you'd like to be one, earn it by being a living example of the life of Jesus Christ."

The two dozen remaining members of the church looked at the young man with the New York accent like he was an escapee from a psychiatric hospital. Who did he think he was? What preacher in his right mind would toss out the membership roster during his first week in the job? What first-time pastor would be so brash? Was this kid serious?

"Here's how it's going to be," he continued. "If you live like Christ and give a good testimony in the community, I'll reinstate your membership. But this is no country club. I know some of you come from families who have belonged to this church for generations. But there is no inherited membership here. This is a church, which means it is made up of people who live for Christ because He died for us. You cannot earn your salvation, but you must show me that you deserve your membership here through righteous living. I challenge you to be part of the real church—the church that Jesus died to save, the church described in the Bible!"

Theresa sat in her pew wondering how people would react to the bold challenge her husband had just hurled at them. She was proud of his courage and his conviction. She knew that he was simply doing what he felt God had called him to do.

But she wondered if they would be moving back in with her parents the next day.

One new family had ventured into the sanctuary that first weekend curious to find out what the new pastor would be like. It was not what they expected—and they loved it. They not only chose to keep coming to the little Assemblies church, but the entire family came forward at the end of that first service to dedicate their lives to Christ.

Morris beamed as he prayed over the family members. God was at work!

To Morris and Theresa's relief, the former members who had been blistered by his challenge to prove they deserved to be members embraced both the challenge and the new couple who were leading them. Proof of the congregation's enthusiastic adoption of their new pastor came when no less than eight families invited them home for a post-service meal.

Having run out of canned spaghetti, Morris and Theresa gratefully accepted the first offer that came their way.

CHAPTER 44

THE CONGREGATION SLOWLY started to shape up. The number of attenders grew, hitting triple figures before the end of Morris's first quarter at the helm. Locals had been hoping for a gutsy spiritual leader. Morris filled that need, and the public responded.

Of course, it wasn't all about preparing sermons and imagining great outreach events. Pastoring the equivalent of a one-room schoolhouse meant that Morris had to be a jack-of-all-trades. He spent his time every week mowing and watering the church yard, repairing the roof and windows, cleaning the floors, painting the walls, repairing the pews, and so forth. The odd jobs that Morris had held during his school years were coming in handy in his first professional position.

Not content to be growing a local congregation in a small town by just a few people per month, Morris felt led to hold an evangelistic event to escalate the growth curve. He explained his plan to the elders, who bought in to the aggressive strategy. With their approval Morris went to City Hall, rented out the town's public auditorium for a week, and began laying the groundwork for the event.

As often happens to those who step out in faith to do a great evangelistic work, though, Morris's life immediately went into a tailspin. His health took a sudden dive, and at one point his doctor told Theresa, "Make sure you keep this man in bed. He is on the edge, and we cannot take a chance of him dying because he wants to work. Tie him down if you have to. Just keep him in bed so he can rest and his body can fight back."

As the time for the event approached, Morris was desperate to get the word out and ensure that crowds would show up for the week of ministry, which he was certain God had called him to undertake. But with him in bed—most of the time—and with a limited budget, how could he get the word out?

Fortunately, a week before the start of the crusade, Ohio senator Howard Taft was campaigning throughout New Hampshire seeking the Republican presidential nomination. Taft was a highly regarded legislator, but he was running against General Eisenhower, a war hero and the favorite to gain the party's support. When Taft came through Claremont all of the local and regional media turned out to cover his appearance. After his private meetings with city officials he emerged with a big smile and stood on the steps of City Hall to address the assembled media.

Morris was too ill to join the crowd at the foot of the steps at City Hall, but he could hear the commotion on the streets from the bed in his apartment. It wasn't until the day after Taft's appearance that Morris praised God for what took place during Taft's visit.

The wire photo carried in newspapers around New England showed Taft speaking on the steps of City Hall—with a huge banner over his head proclaiming "Morris Cerullo Evangelistic Crusade. Salvation, signs, wonders, and miracles. August 10–17, City Hall. Don't miss it!" That banner had been stretched across the front of the city building for a couple of weeks. Suddenly it was visible on the front page of newspapers and in television newscasts all over the state. It was even highlighted in the newsreel accounts shown in movie theaters throughout New Hampshire that week.

In Morris's mind, that unforeseeable publicity was the first miracle of the crusade!

When the date rolled around Morris gathered up his strength and led the crusade. They had good turnouts, growing from a small initial gathering to up to three hundred people filling the auditorium by the end of the week. As a result the church doubled in size that week, adding nearly one hundred new people to the congregation! Just as importantly, several hundred more heard the gospel proclaimed, dozens accepted Christ as their Savior, and others experienced supernatural healings from God.

God had given him the strength to carry out the event and had produced an unimaginable spiritual return on that investment. And as exhilarating as the outcome was, it was just a hint of the things to come.

CHAPTER 45

W HILE MORRIS LABORED to grow the church, he and Theresa existed on a meager salary of forty dollars a week. It was not enough to keep them going.

To make ends meet—and give him more evangelistic opportunities— Morris took a part-time job selling pots and pans. He went from house to house knocking on doors and demonstrating the benefits of steel cookware versus the cheaper and more common aluminum varieties. He proved to be an effective salesman, but it also gave him a chance to meet more people in the community and to invite them to attend the church.

Morris used to visit the area's Russian farmers every Monday night. Claremont had a large population of Russian immigrants, and many of them worked all day on the farm. Morris would visit them and serve as their pastor since many of them felt they could not attend church services on Sunday mornings; the farm demanded their attention, they argued. Morris bene-fitted from those visits because many of the farmers would give him some of their produce.

The Russian farmers relied on Morris for their spiritual guidance. They would call him in emergencies, hoping that the man of God would help them.

One night, about three o'clock in the morning, an urgent phone call woke up Morris and Theresa. A frantic woman with a heavy Russian accent explained that they needed him to come to their barn right away. It was an emergency. Groggily, Morris dressed and walked to the farm. Upon arriving, he found a group of people yelling and crying. When he got to the center of things he discovered that the problem was that a cow was unable to finish giving birth. At first he was flustered, but then he realized that these were the central needs in the lives of these hard-working, God-fearing people. He should feel honored that they called him in their moment of crisis.

So Morris gently moved alongside the burly Russian men and placed both hands on the cow's rear. In a loud voice he began praying to God. As soon as he finished his first sentence, the cow's water broke—showering Morris. Minutes later, the calf was born.

He walked home, drenched and stinky, as the sun was rising. But he also had the makings of a good breakfast—some eggs, bacon, and butter that the farm ladies shared out of gratitude for his spiritual house call.

CHAPTER 46

————◦————

FOLLOWING THE SUCCESS of the evangelistic crusade, the church maintained a healthier pace of growth. Within a few months the church had blossomed to become the sixth-largest Charismatic church in the six New England states!

While pastors around the country were seeking the latest and greatest ways to increase church membership, Morris's superiors knew that the young preacher saw such dramatic gains in attendance because he waited to take the pulpit each Sunday until he was certain that God was present and ready to minister to the people in the sanctuary.

Pastors from other churches occasionally visited on a Sunday morning hoping to capture the secret to the young pastor's undeniable success. One Sunday, after the completion of the service, a visiting leader asked Morris about his approach.

"I don't watch the clock to see if it's time for me to preach," he explained without any arrogance or boast. "I wait until I sense the glory of God to be in our midst, and then I approach the pulpit. There is nothing special about me, and I have nothing special to say to these people. But when God's glory is in this place, and I remain sensitive to His leading, incredible things happen that only He can do. It's all about waiting on Him to show up."

Anchored to that practice, the church continued to grow, enabling an expansion of the programs and facilities. He had been there barely a year, and the church was now filled each Sunday. Morris began to feel comfortable and secure at the church.

That's when God intervened.

Once again God spoke clearly to Morris. "Son, your work here is done. I want you to return to full-time evangelistic work."

Knowing that no one wins an argument with God, and suddenly feeling a sense of discomfort at being able to reach just a small corner of the world, Dr. Cerullo set his mind and heart to the larger mission field. It meant giving up the security that he and Theresa had been building in Claremont, but a transition also brought the thrill of being on the edge of worldwide ministry, seeking to do things no one else was doing.

The vision God had given Morris just a few years earlier—the vision of people dying and suffering across the globe because they had never heard about Jesus and the gift of eternal life—continued to burn inside of him.

Morris felt the excitement start to build within his being. The more he thought about it, the more excited he became.

That enthusiasm diminished, however, when he realized that he had to break the news to Theresa, his congregation, and the denominational leaders.

CHAPTER 47

———◆———

THERESA, WHO HAD been in her new home not quite a year, was now seven months pregnant. Before the marriage she had been all-in regarding the evangelist lifestyle—traveling constantly, living in hotels and pastors' homes, eating in restaurants and people's homes, unable to accumulate possessions because of the nomadic lifestyle. When the pastoral position came along and changed their trajectory, she was all-in regarding the more stable and confined ministry setting of a local church. She just wanted to serve God and empower her husband to do the same, whatever form that took.

But being pregnant, waiting for your first child, changes a woman's needs and expectations. Morris still didn't grasp all the subtleties and needs of a young woman entering motherhood, but he was aware enough to know that informing her of a pending transition in their lifestyle was no simple announcement.

At dinner in their apartment, Morris broke the news to Theresa. She could sense that he was nervous about telling here and uncomfortable with the circumstances. He watched her countenance change after he dropped the bomb. She dropped her head and her eyes closed for a few seconds. He held his breath.

Theresa lifted her head and gave a forlorn smile to Morris. She spoke softly.

"When we were engaged, we talked about this, didn't we? We agreed that we would be obedient to God's call, whatever it was, wherever it would take us, whatever would be required. Things have been going so well in Claremont. We have been so blessed. I guess I thought we might be able to finish what we started here. But it sounds as if that's not God's will. And you know I'd rather be faithful to God's will for our lives than to try to tell God how to do things.

"When do we leave?" she asked Morris, placing her hand on top of his on their dinner table.

It was a great question—and one for which Morris had no answer. Being immersed in ministry to his church for nearly a year had left him without any speaking engagements lined up. As far as other pastors were concerned, Morris Cerullo was no longer part of the evangelistic circuit.

He was uncertain how his denomination's leaders would respond to the young preacher leaving a rapidly-growing church after less than a year in place. Would they question his stability? Wonder about his ego? Balk at helping him advance his evangelistic dream in lieu of the job they had hired him to fulfill?

And what about other church leaders? Would the word spread that the twenty-one-year-old pastor was simply out to make a name for himself? Would inviting him to hold an event in their town truly be something that honored God?

Morris had no answers, but he was confident that he was doing the right thing. When God speaks, you either obey or disobey. He was determined to obey no matter what the cost and regardless of public perception.

What he did not know at the time—but recognized as time went on— was that God was establishing a precedent in Morris's life. This was just one of numerous times when God would uproot Morris just as he was beginning to get comfortable in ministry. The Lord knew that a servant who felt like he had everything under control was not a servant at all but an individual who felt in charge and capable of calling the shots. God uses those who are dependent upon Him, not the self-reliant. He saw in Morris the makings of an obedient servant who would do what was required to fulfill a God-given call and vision. Such servants are rare.

God continued to test Morris's will to obey.

CHAPTER 48

————◆————

MORRIS CONTACTED THE denomination's regional leaders and told them he was resigning. At first they were stunned. But as he quietly and respectfully reminded them of the circumstances of his hiring—the surprise congregational vote after his day of ministry filling in for Dr. Smuland—and then explained his desire to be obedient to God's calling, they were sympathetic and supportive.

To affect an orderly and timely transition, everyone agreed that there should be a special meeting with Morris, district officials, and the entire congregation. After they explained the transition that would take place, the district would have "temporary custody" of the congregation as they searched for a new pastor.

The church building was filled to capacity on the night of the meeting. As Morris and the denominational officials talked about how the church would be restructured and people's membership would be restored, one crusty old farmer kept interrupting and bad-mouthing the outgoing pastor. Morris several times stood and scolded the man—Mr. Rudowski—and warned him that he was out of order and such outbursts could not be tolerated.

But the Russian farmer was in no mood to be silenced. After his final warning from Morris, Rudowski stood up again and launched more insults and criticisms at Morris. The atmosphere was getting tense.

Morris was still just a young man—only twenty-one years old at that point—but one who had certainly lived a more robust and difficult life than the average person his age. Infuriated by the older man's lack of respect and decorum, Morris finally stormed off the platform, his face grim and his eyes locked on to his critic's face. He left the three elderly denominational officials sitting on the stage watching the drama unfold with a mixture of fascination, trepidation, and anger.

Morris reached the pew where Rudowski sat and lowered his face until it was just a couple of inches from the face of his seated tormentor.

"Mr. Rudowski, do you see my hands?" he shouted, dramatically lifting them above his head. "If you dare open your mouth one more time and disrupt this meeting again I will lay my hands on you and command you to give up the ghost!"

Rudowski's eyes got as big as grapefruits, and he broke out into a sweat. As Morris turned his back on the man and stomped back to the platform, the Russian dropped his head and closed his eyes. He was aware of how God had used those hands as instruments of miracles that had changed people's lives.

The meeting proceeded without any further interruptions.

As Morris and a very pregnant Theresa accepted people's applause at the end of the meeting and walked down the center aisle to depart, Rudowski suddenly jumped out of his pew and clasped his hands around Morris's. Tears were streaming down his face.

"Here, pastor," he wailed in his heavily-accented English, "please take this. I hope it will help you," he sobbed, thrusting a crumpled ball of cash into Morris's hands.

As it turned out, that was all the severance pay Morris received from the church.

CHAPTER 49

A FTER THE MEMORABLE congregational meeting Morris and Theresa moved back in with her parents. They lived in Newburgh until she gave birth to their first child in late 1952. Everyone got along well, and her parents were happy to have their little girl back home for a while, realizing that it might be the last extended opportunity they'd have to see her once Morris's worldwide ministry plans took shape.

But that was all theory at that point. After leaving New Hampshire Morris was certain that God was going to place him on a bigger ministry stage, but as he sat in Newburgh he had no invitations and no meetings booked. He had left his first pastorate after a year, had no worldly possessions of value, was living in his in-laws' home, and was about to become a father.

Most people would feel uncomfortable in such a situation. But Morris was sure that God had called him to leave the church in Claremont to be available for the next stage of his ministry adventure. He had no idea what God had in mind but was willing to wait for the Lord to move.

A week after arriving in Newburgh, He did.

A well-known pastor from the largest Assembly of God church on Long Island called Morris and asked about his departure from Claremont. After confirming his departure and his plan to engage in outreach events, the pastor invited Morris to join them at the church in Long Island for exactly such an event. Without hesitation, Morris agreed to partner in the event. It was scheduled to last for a full week. Theresa would stay behind, as she was getting close to the baby's due date and would be well cared for by her parents.

The event took place as scheduled and went better than expected. A couple dozen people came forward to accept Christ as their Savior every night. After the first week the church extended the event for a second week. And then a third.

Toward the end of the third week Morris received a call informing him that his wife was in labor at the hospital back in Newburgh, about to have their first child. After discussions with the pastor who had invited him to hold the crusades, Morris immediately drove back to Newburgh. Unfortunately, he arrived after the baby's birth.

When the nurse ushered him in to see Theresa, she asked if he'd seen the baby.

"Of course," he said. "But he's so small," he noted earnestly.

Theresa, tired as she was, smacked him on the head with her hand. "Small?" she exclaimed. "He came from inside of me. He's eight pounds, ten ounces, Morris. Believe me; that is not small. Maybe next time you can give birth instead."

He was twenty-one, unemployed, and a father for the first time. He had a vision to save the souls of millions, but he had lot to learn about the fundamentals of life.

CHAPTER 50

S HORTLY AFTER HE got home from Long Island and his son David had been born, other churches in the Northeast again started inviting Morris to hold revival meetings in their areas. The word was spreading quickly that the young Jewish boy who loved Jesus seemed to have a special anointing and was effective at leading people to Christ.

Indeed, the hand of God was clearly on Morris.

After finishing a revival event on a Sunday night in upstate New York, Theresa, baby David—not quite two months old at the time—and Morris were driving through the night to get to his next meeting. It was scheduled to take place on Monday in Canada, near Toronto, which was about a six-hour drive away.

When they began the journey it started to snow, and within a short time it had turned into a full-scale blizzard. Snow was rapidly accumulating on the highway, and the snow was blowing so hard that Morris could barely find the road. Although he'd grown up in the northeast and was accustomed to the rugged winters, he didn't have much experience driving in snow storms. Even though he was physically drained from the crusade, he had to get to Toronto by morning. He was intent upon staying tightly focused on the road.

Suddenly, at about three o'clock in the morning, the car glided to a stop. Morris tried to start it up again to no avail. He looked at the instrument panel for any clues and quickly got his answer.

The car was out of gas.

Between replaying that night's evangelistic event in his mind and concentrating on the blizzard-obscured road, Morris had totally ignored the gas gage. He felt like a fool.

Disgusted with himself, he got out of the vehicle and waved down an approaching car. He explained his dilemma and asked for advice.

"You realize you're in Canada now, don't you?" the driver asked. "Our laws prohibit stores and gas stations from being open Sunday nights. Nothing will be open again for a few more hours. A policeman will probably pass through soon. Maybe you can ask him what to do."

Disheartened by the news, Morris shuffled through the snow, back to his car, and told Theresa the bad news. The young couple looked at each other and then at their newborn son, concerned about how the frigid temperatures would affect their baby.

Morris smiled at his bundled-up wife and said simply, "Let's pray." And they did. They could see their breath in the air as they cried out to God with young David crying in Theresa's lap and Morris's hands on the dashboard. They asked God to get them through this circumstance and to protect their baby against the elements.

As soon as they finished, Morris twisted the car key in the ignition. After a couple of sputters and coughs the engine turned over and started! Morris shouted an exclamation of joy and thanks and began making his way toward Toronto.

Just before they reached the city limits, with the sun rising, they saw a neon light flicker in the distance. It was a gas station opening for business on Monday morning. As they turned in to the station and pulled up to the first pump, the car died.

Morris laughed at God's sense of humor, got out of the car, and filled the tank. "What a God we serve!" he chuckled to himself. As gasoline coursed into the car's tank, he prayed words of praise and thanks to His heavenly Father, once again cognizant of God's presence and supernatural guidance of his life.

CHAPTER 51

A COUPLE OF MONTHS later the young Cerullo family was traveling to Wisconsin for an evangelistic event. To draw a crowd, newspaper ads had been run informing the public that a "Spirit-filled Jew" would be preaching the gospel in their area.

Nobody was more stirred up by the ad than the owner of the newspaper—an atheistic, avid communist named John Chappel. In his eyes it was disgraceful that his newspaper was promoting what he deemed to be a double threat: a religious advocate and a Jew.

Chappel held the classic Karl Marx philosophy that religion is nothing more than the "opiate of the masses," a drug that relieves people of their senses and places them in a deluded frame of mind. Communists contend that religion enslaves people.

Although it was too late to block the advertisement by the time he found out about it, Chappel took action. He showed up at the meeting where Morris was scheduled to speak. He was red with rage by the time the meeting started and prepared to disrupt the evening.

But even before Morris took the stage, the Holy Spirit began working on Chappel's heart and soul. By the time Morris began preaching about salvation, Chappel knew he was spiritually lost and was seeking a way to rectify his condition. When Morris called for sinners to repent and come forward to receive Jesus Christ as their Savior, Chappel couldn't get to the front fast enough.

Some people in the crowd, aware of Chappel's radical views, figured he was mocking the process. But they watched in awe as the newspaper owner made his profession of faith. It was a miracle that nobody could have expected.

The next day newspapers throughout Wisconsin carried stories about the conversion of the atheistic communist leader. The public was amazed at the turnabout. Thousands of people who had never heard of Morris—or never heard of a Jew who proclaimed the glory of Christ—took note of the name.

The legend of Morris Cerullo was gaining a foothold.

CHAPTER 52

———◆———

T HE PUBLIC SAW Morris on stage during the outreach events but often had no idea of the spiritual challenges he and his family faced behind the scenes.

While they were in Wisconsin the Cerullo family stayed in a tourist home. Theresa remained in the bedroom with young David while Morris was out teaching and meeting with people. One day Theresa developed excruciating stomach pains. She was not able to reach Morris by telephone. Realizing she could not take care of the baby, she temporarily left her son with the woman who owned the boarding house and unsteadily walked a few blocks to the home of one of the local pastors who was facilitating Morris's events in the area. Finding the pastor's wife there, she explained her condition.

After assessing the situation, the pastor's wife concluded that Theresa was having a gallbladder attack and needed to get to the hospital right away. She offered to drive Theresa there, but Theresa instead insisted on being driven back to the boarding house, where she would wait with David for Morris to return.

When Morris arrived at the boarding home a few hours later, he was deeply worried about his wife. He immediately got on his knees and sought the Lord's guidance. He sensed the Lord saying that he was to fast and pray for her for three days, and then she would be well.

And so he did. When he wasn't leading crusade events he was in the boarding room taking care of David and praying for his wife. When he had to leave for an event he placed David in bed with her and went off to minister. Morris had a serenity about the unusual situation because he believed that God had promised him that his wife would be fine if he was faithful to pray and fast.

The events continued to bear tremendous spiritual fruit—such as the conversion of the communist leader, John Chappell—even as the spiritual battle against his family raged on. He never mentioned Theresa's condition in the meetings or to his ministry colleagues. He was focused on the assignments God had given him and fully confident that God would do as He promised.

A tired Morris returned from a crusade meeting on the third night after Theresa's gallbladder attack and resumed his place on the floor praying for his wife's health. When he could no longer keep his eyes open he climbed into bed next to her.

When morning came the couple awoke. Morris got out of bed to tend to the baby. He was surprised when he heard Theresa getting up as well.

He turned to watch her, showing his surprise as she began gathering their belongings and preparing to leave for home.

Theresa noticed Morris staring at her. She stopped packing, put her hands on her hips, and frowned at her husband.

"Why are you looking at me that way?" she asked, in mock anger. "Didn't you say that God told you I'd be healed after three days of fasting and praying? Well, you fasted and prayed for three days, and God did just what He said He'd do. I'm feeling good as new. Now, let's get packed up and go."

Unable to suppress a smile, Morris shook his head, said, "Well, thank you, Lord," and joined her in packing their belongings.

Theresa never had any further problems with her gallbladder.

Morris had more evidence of God's love and faithfulness toward him and his family as they did whatever they could to serve Him. Challenges would come, but Morris knew he could trust God to do what was right and necessary.

CHAPTER 53

————•————

WITH A GROWING reputation, and with God doing miracles through him on a regular basis, Morris's speaking calendar filled up. As public awareness of his ministry expanded he needed the capacity to seat larger and larger crowds—more than the typical church could hold. The solution that Morris and Theresa settled on was to begin traveling with his own trailers and tents. By using his specially designed tent it became possible to set up in large fields and have ten-day crusades, reaching bigger crowds than could fit into church halls.

While tent crusades have been part of evangelistic folklore for a long time, not many evangelists were using them in the latter half of the 1950s and during the 1960s. Oral Roberts was perhaps the best-known of the tent preachers at the time, along with regional favorites like Bob Shamrock. Morris quickly rose through the ranks to join them as an accomplished revival preacher.

The process itself looked more glamorous from than outside than was actually the case. Once a church (or group of churches) invited Morris to visit their town for an evangelistic rally, the onus was on him to handle virtually everything. It was his responsibility to conceive the event, coordinate with all the churches in the area, raise the funds for the crusade, create and distribute all the marketing and advertising materials, prepare the facility (e.g., event licenses, parking, seating, sound, lighting), train volunteers to handle the crowds and set-up, capture the names of attenders, provide trained counselors, and so forth.

Each event was a substantial undertaking. Managing them from afar, working largely with volunteers, and juggling all the events simultaneously while each was at a different stage of development was a challenging task for the young man and his wife.

Perhaps such a Herculean endeavor was not humanly possible, but Morris and Theresa had a secret weapon: prayer.

Following the fundamental principle that catapulted his church in New Hampshire to explosive growth, Morris refused to pursue any potential events until he felt he had God's guidance. Before he would accept any invitation to conduct a ministry event, Morris and Theresa spent hours and hours in prayer to discern God's will. Sometimes he could sense God's approval in a matter of hours; other times it took the couple days or even weeks of intense prayer to know what God wanted of them.

Occasionally Morris had to inform a church that he could not come to their area for a crusade because he did not sense God's leading to conduct the event at that time. Those calls were never enjoyable to make, but taking such a stand was part of his obedience to God and serving people as effectively as possible. He knew that if God was not in it, the event would be a meaningless disaster—a man-driven show that lacked the heart and soul of God at the center. In the vast majority of cases, however, there was a unity of spirit between Morris and the host churches that led to a crusade being presented.

Morris created an organization to support his outreach work: Morris Cerullo World Evangelism (MCWE). From the start of that support system Morris knew that his calling was to preach the gospel and serve as God's conduit for signs and wonders. Often those miracles involved some type of physical healing. Some people may have looked down at the youthful man with an organization claiming to reach the world, but Morris never doubted that God's calling was to touch as many people as possible everywhere on the planet with the good news of Jesus Christ and the opportunity to know and serve God.

Morris and his team created a template for their outreach efforts. In addition to the myriad organizational details that had to be addressed, they put on ten-day events starting on a Friday and continuing every day until Sunday of the following week. Depending on his sense of how the Spirit of God was leading him, there were often sessions during the morning and afternoon, as well as evenings. Morris would be joined on stage by other Bible teachers and preachers, along with a music team and a variety of people giving testimonies of God's supernatural work in their life.

Even though he was the new kid on the block, God packed Morris's tent with people week after week. That was no small feat since the tent was more than one hundred feet long and in excess of two hundred feet wide. The seating capacity exceeded three thousand people! Filling such a venue more than a dozen times in every community he visited was nothing short of the hand of God assisting him. And from the first moment, Morris knew it.

One of the distinctive qualities of Morris's ministry was that God regularly performed miracles through the young man during those meetings. Not many evangelists could make that same claim. In fact, making the claim at all was an act of faith on Morris's part since those miracles were beyond his control. Even the usually skeptical media were generally accepting of Morris and his efforts, perhaps because he never took any credit for what God chose to do in the events.

Morris retained his passion for these tiring and challenging ministry ventures by constantly returning in his heart and mind to God's calling to save souls from eternal despair. He would vividly recall the vision God had given him of people suffering in hell. When he began feeling fatigue, that vision would recharge his batteries and enable him to keep moving forward.

As spiritually victorious as the meetings continually proved to be, they were physically and mentally exhausting for the growing Cerullo family. Theresa usually accompanied her husband on these journeys. They stayed in countless motels and boarding houses, occasionally in their car or trailers, and raised their children—which expanded to include two sons and a daughter—on the road. But they had lots of time together and plenty of fun and excitement along the way.

The tent-based ministry went on for four years. Maybe it was a period designed not only to minister to tens of thousands of people but to test Morris's motives. He must have passed the test, because after four years God had something huge in store for him.

CHAPTER 54

—◆—

Four years of successful events—preaching the gospel, seeing lost souls saved, people healed, signs and wonders supernaturally provided by God—could easily have led to a ministry formula.

But it didn't. In fact, to the surprise and occasional dismay of the experts who expressed their opinions about the validity and sophistication of his work, Morris's ministry essentially ignored the best practices of the day.

Morris did not have a strategic plan that laid out how the ministry would grow.

There was no map of the United States covering an office wall with push-pins harpooning desirable future event locations.

He did not have a chart specifying the number of people they would seek to reach by certain dates or targets for the number of miracles or saved souls to achieve.

Consultants were not hired to craft an exhaustive SWOT analysis, the tool used by cutting-edge organizations to identify and quantify the strengths, weaknesses, opportunities, and threats facing MCWE.

Morris's plan was much simpler: wait on God and do what He says.

Anyone who knew much about his ministry would agree that life with Morris was always an adventure. God was undeniably using him in grand and unexpected ways, and he was holding on for dear life. It was a ride unlike any other.

Theresa was his cherished and irreplaceable partner in every facet of life and ministry. She learned to cope with the challenges of such a footloose, obey-in-the-moment ministry. Two years after giving birth to their first son, David, she delivered a daughter, Susan. The family drove here, there, and everywhere throughout the nation living frugally on the limited funds that the ministry raised through love offerings collected at the events. They often stayed in a tiny motel room for a week or more while Morris led a crusade. It was common for Theresa to remove a pair of the bureau drawers and line them with extra blankets to provide snug sleeping areas for the children.

During the daytime Theresa would carefully manage the children's sched-ules to allow Morris time to study the Bible and to pray. They both recog-nized that God could not work through Morris unless he was completely surrendered and focused on God. Throughout the day Theresa would pray for wisdom, strength, protection, power, and discernment for her husband. They worked together creatively to balance family and ministry.

The compelling impact of their ministry enabled them to stay busy year-round. Morris was preaching somewhere most days of the year, sometimes speaking both in the morning and evening. Occasionally he would have a chance to minister to people for extended hours throughout the day too. It was a bruising schedule, but the Lord kept Morris and his family healthy, enthusiastic, and energized.

By worldly standards, some outsiders concluded that the Cerullo family was getting nowhere. They did not own a house or even have an apartment they could call home. They had little to no savings; they poured as much as they could back into growing the ministry.

There were days when they wondered how they would get enough food to feed themselves and the children. Getting by from day to day was often an act of pure faith. But God always provided what they needed when they needed it—and it was usually no more than they needed, and not a minute before they needed it!

Their joy came from the privilege of serving God on the front lines of the spiritual battle and seeing victory after victory in people's lives. Morris told those who asked that his goal was to store up treasures in heaven rather than to live like a king on Earth. They learned to be content with what they had and to trust that God would take care of them.

And to their relief, He always did.

CHAPTER 55

———◆———

B Y THE TIME 1955 came around Morris and Theresa decided that it made sense to have a home that would provide some stability for the children and perhaps even for the ministry operation.

After discussing the options they chose to seek a home in Theresa's hometown, Newburgh, New York. They searched high and low before finding a home still under construction that would meet their needs. It was not a large home, but it was affordable—a modest eleven thousand five hundred dollars. They scraped together the six-hundred-dollar deposit and intermittently checked on the progress of their future home while they lived with Theresa's parents (again).

In the meantime they continued to accept speaking invitations, which took either Morris alone or the entire family on the road while the house was slowly being finished.

On one such trip in Pennsylvania, Morris received a word from the Lord: "Son, get ready to go to Athens, Greece."

At last, the Lord was about the initiate the international phase of the ministry He had promised Morris. The young father couldn't have been more excited. Athens! Morris had no idea where in the world it was, but he knew it was overseas somewhere, and that was good enough for him.

Of course, the Lord had not told him how the trip would unfold, but Morris and Theresa waited expectantly, certain that a trip to Greece was coming in the near future. The Lord had given them countless promises over the years and had never failed to deliver on one of them. They had no reason to expect anything different now.

A few weeks after the initial revelation a letter was delivered to Morris that had a foreign-looking stamp on it. He excitedly tore open the envelope and pulled out the letter inside. Sure enough, it was from a Reverend Koustis, the leader of the Church of God denomination in Greece.

Rev. Koustis wrote that he had been praying for guidance when God responded by telling him to invite Morris to Greece to hold an event. As soon as he finished reading the letter Morris sat down and composed an acceptance letter describing how God had revealed the coming invitation two weeks earlier. As he finished the note Morris shook his head in wonder at how God works. Here God was, orchestrating a ministry that was so reminiscent of what had happened nearly two thousand years earlier when God sent another Jew (the apostle Paul) to minister to the Greeks.

He sighed with hope, counting on God to allow him to have even a sliver of the spiritual impact that Paul had experienced on the historic island nation.

With the acceptance letter en route to his host, Morris and Theresa excitedly set about preparing for his first overseas ministry opportunity. There was a passport to apply for. He had never traveled outside the US and Canada, so he had never needed one, and he found the application process to be slow and frustrating. He also had to get the required shots and take care of all the other matters that had to be done in advance of such a trip.

In fact, when he looked up Greece on a globe and saw its location, he was ecstatic. It was just a short flight over the Mediterranean Sea from Israel, the homeland of his ancestors. In his heart he knew that God was preparing him to reach into the Jewish culture and present the gospel of Jesus Christ to his people. After talking it over with Theresa, Morris decided that it would be an ideal time to hop over to Israel for a bit of reconnaissance—a chance to experience the nation so that he could pray and prepare himself more intelligently for an eventual ministry trip there.

When the couple spoke to a travel agent to lay out the trip and get an idea of the financial needs for this undertaking, Morris almost passed out. The least expensive round-trip airfare they could get was $961.80. (For the sake of context, an airplane ticket costing $962 in 1956 would be the equivalent of about $8,428 in 2015.) That was out of the question! Given the size of their ministry's operational expenses, the cost of raising their family, and the yet-to-be-paid expense of their soon-to-be-completed home there was no way Morris had the funds to purchase that air ticket.

But they knew God had orchestrated the trip and was expecting Morris to be in Greece in August 1956. The cost of the airfare alone—$961.80— might as well have been $1 million; it was beyond anything Morris could hope to scrape together in the coming months. He laughed and shook his head as he thought about it; that was more than the deposit they had placed on their house! But God had never let them down yet, and Morris was confident that He would come through in some unexpected way yet again—and probably at the last minute. Morris put the matter on the back burner and waited expectantly for God to take care of the details.

All he had to supply was the faith to keep moving toward the goal.

Because the trip was still a number of months in the future, Morris had to keep up with his busy schedule in the meantime. But in the back of his mind, no matter where he was, there was a growing sense of excitement about the forthcoming trip overseas.

CHAPTER 56

URING THE INTERIM period prior to his journey to Greece one of the events Morris led was in Pennsylvania. It was a very well-attended series of meetings: crowds two to three times the size of those jammed inside the tent were standing outside its canvas walls each night, straining to hear and be part of the incredible things that were happening.

Most importantly, not only did an abundance of people show up, but God was palpably present in a big way doing miracle after miracle among those who came day after day and night after night.

During one of the evening meetings Morris was led to step from the elevated platform to pray for a farmer woman whose backbone was so twisted and deformed that she could not come close to standing upright. She was hunched over in what had become her normal, albeit painful, posture. The Holy Spirit drew Morris's attention to her, so he descended the steps to come next to her on the main floor. As he approached her, his heart went out to her. She was so misshapen that she looked like the letter L.

From her bent position she craned her head and saw Morris approaching her. Tears began to drop from her eyes, and she painstakingly raised her right hand toward him. Morris grasped her hand and felt the warm and electrifying sensation that often overtook him when God's power coursed through him to heal someone.

God had been working overtime that night, and this was yet another spectacular moment in an evening that thousands of people would never forget. People who had never thought much about the power of God and those who arrived at the event comfortable in their disbelief in miracles were blown away by the supernatural acts God was performing through Morris at that crusade.

One of those who would treasure that night forever was the suffering farmer. The second Morris's hand clasped hers, the woman was healed! She immediately stood up, erect as a steel beam. The flow of tears got stronger as she lifted her arms toward heaven. Morris smiled broadly and slapped his knee in excitement, raising his other fist in victory and shouting to God with joy and praise. He loved being used by God so intensely in changing people's lives.

The Pennsylvania meetings continued on night after night, with the crowds growing bigger with each passing day.

Several days after Morris had ministered to the crippled farm woman, he saw her again. She had come to another evening meeting, and this time she was standing tall and proud, smiling broadly. She whispered something in the ear of a security member at the foot of the stairs leading to the platform, then made a beeline for Morris. He was happy to see her again but was trying to focus on the night's event. The service was in progress, and they were just a few minutes from him taking the microphone again, so he was trying to focus his mind and heart on what Lord wanted him to do.

When the farmer woman reached Morris he smiled at her and shook her hand. She smiled back and handed him an envelope. Without looking at it, he thanked her, and she headed back to the main floor. Morris stuffed the envelope into the back of his Bible and turned his full attention back to the service.

As the woman reached the top of the steps before starting her descent she turned around to look at Morris. Noticing that he had not opened the envelope, she frowned and immediately turned around and headed back in Morris's direction. Seeing the movement out of the corner of his eye, Morris glanced her way and then turned his body toward her. She, in turn, stopped and shouted above the din, "Prophet of God, you really need to open that envelope." She then furiously motioned with her hand.

Anxious to refocus on the service, he nodded and quickly pulled out the envelope.

Inside the slim package was a beautifully crafted note thanking Morris for his part in her healing and praising God for His love to her. The letter described the pain she had been in, the duration of her agony, and her blind faith in God's willingness to heal her. Morris momentarily forgot everything that was going on around him, he was so moved.

The final paragraph of the note really caught his attention.

"In memorial to the Lord for healing my body, I enclose this gift. I sold my farm a little while before you arrived in town. This is some of the money I received from the sale. I want you to have it for your ministry."

Morris had not even noticed the other piece of paper inside the envelope: a cashier's check. He removed it and gazed at the donation. His jaw dropped when he saw the amount: $961.80.

God had been working miracles for the people in rural Pennsylvania. Now He produced one for Morris.

Next stop: Greece!

CHAPTER 57

L EAVING HOME TURNED out to be harder for Morris than he had anticipated.

As the family waited in the airport for his flight to board, Theresa was squeezing one hand. David, who was just old enough to understand that his dad was leaving the family to go someplace far away for an extended time, had a death grip on the other hand. Young Susan just watched everything with big eyes, sensing that something significant was taking place but not comprehending what it was.

Even though Morris knew beyond a doubt that this was the start of the next stage of his ministry career and that God had called him to this trip, he was choked up all day. Here he was, just a young father, leaving his family for parts of the world he barely knew anything about to minister in partnership with a church he'd never heard of and whose leaders he had never met. He had domestic financial obligations to meet, and he had no idea how the foreign trip would work out money-wise.

But he had made a commitment to God. And God had made one to him. There was no turning back, no matter how scary or heartbreaking the process was.

Once the airplane took off, Morris turned his thoughts to the upcoming challenges. He spent his time alternately napping and silently praying about the forthcoming meetings—except during the prolonged times of extreme turbulence as they crossed the Atlantic Ocean. During those episodes his prayer focus switched to their safety, the pilot's skill, and the weather conditions.

After finally landing in Athens Morris was eager to deplane and start preparations for the outreach meetings. The first face he saw as he emerged from the airplane was that of his host, Pastor Koustis. As excited as Morris was to embark on his first international ministry event, the Greek churchman seemed equally dispirited. The man looked tired and dejected.

They greeted each other warmly, then moved toward the exit so they could board the bus that would take them into town. During the ride Pastor Koustis said nothing more to Morris. He seemed sad and distant. His body language—head down, slow movement, shoulder sagging, a forlorn look—suggested despair.

Morris was disappointed and perplexed but held his tongue. There was plenty to see during the bus ride. As he watched the neighborhoods pass by he started to get a feel for Greek culture. He was mesmerized by the mixture of ancient buildings, historic statues, and cobblestone streets standing alongside the modern glass and steel buildings that were introducing a new way of life for the lively city.

As they neared their destination, Morris forced himself to stop gaping at the passing sights and asked Pastor Koustis for an update.

"And I'd like to see a copy of the handbill you printed for the event," he mentioned to his older colleague. Evangelistic meetings in those days depended on posting and passing out promotional materials, especially half-page announcements known as handbills.

Koustis slowly raised his face to look Morris in the eye. "Well, we have a little problem there."

That was not what Morris was expecting to hear. What kind of "little problem" could they have? Maybe they had none left to show Morris because they had distributed all of them to the target population? Perhaps the words were in a language Morris would not understand? In his haste to meet Morris, perhaps the pastor had forgotten to bring one to the airport, so they'd have to retrieve one from his office later?

"What's the little problem?" Morris innocently asked.

"I have not printed any handbills." Seeing the look of astonishment on Morris's face, he explained. "It is against the law to print or pass out religious literature in Greece."

"You're telling me this now?" thought Morris. Confused but remaining calm and polite, he continued to work through his mental checklist of critical event preparation items.

"How about the event team? When can I meet the organizing committee?" he asked brightly. "It will be very helpful for me to speak with all the other preachers and missionaries and city leaders who have been helping to put together ideas and resources for the meetings. Their insight on how to best approach the events will be invaluable to me."

Again, the hangdog face slowly raised to meet Morris's gaze.

"Actually, we have a little problem there too."

Morris's eyes narrowed as he got a sinking feeling in his gut. "What kind of little problem?"

The Greek's head dropped again as he answered. "I did not tell anybody that you were coming."

That reply hit Morris like a sledgehammer. In the United States, early and consistent promotional activities were crucial to drawing a crowd. And getting as many prominent and competent leaders behind the event as early as possible was another necessary ingredient to successful events. Those individuals raised the funds, attracted the volunteers, spearheaded the organizational details, arranged for media coverage, and so forth. These were all things that Morris had copiously described to Pastor Koustis in the numerous letters he had sent to Greece during the intervening months.

As he pondered what he had been told, Morris considered the possibility that maybe they did things differently in Greece. After all, the pastor had described these things as "little" problems.

"What about the auditorium we will be meeting in?" he pressed. "Where is it located? Are we close enough to it to go take a look at it right now?"

Pastor Koustis let out a big sigh and uttered his now-familiar refrain. "We have a little problem there."

Wary of the reply, Morris coaxed it out of his host. "We have not rented a site yet."

"Any particular reason?" the American asked.

"It is against the law in Greece to rent a building or auditorium for religious events."

Suddenly Morris felt dizzy. He was in a country four thousand miles from his home and family with a man who appeared to have accomplished nothing during the months needed to prepare for a crusade. As far as Morris could discern, nothing had been done to pave the way for a successful work of God in Athens.

There was no advertising or promotion to inform people of the event. There were no leaders or helpers. There was no strategy or plan in place. No money had been raised to fund the venture. Morris felt like an alien who had unexpectedly dropped in on a planet of inhabitants who had no idea he existed—or cared.

Something had to change—quickly.

CHAPTER 58

————•————

THE NEXT FIFTEEN minutes were an eye-opener for Morris as Pastor Koustis sheepishly explained why his arrival in Greece was a better kept secret than America's nuclear launch code.

"In Greece, Brother Cerullo, we do not have religious freedom like you have in America. Here, only one church, the Greek Orthodox Church, is able to do whatever it wishes. Every other church, like ours, has heavy restrictions. Doing evangelistic events—the state does not allow this. If you print handbills, distribute them, pay for newspaper advertising, rent an auditorium for an event, evenly openly speak about the gospel—these things are all punishable by law.

"On my body I bear the marks of disobeying the state in order to preach the gospel," Koustis continued sullenly. "I have been in prison. I have been banished from the mainland and sent to an island. I have spent many weeks, even months at a time, in dungeons because I violated the law by spreading the good news of Jesus Christ. Brother, this is not like America, I am sorry to say."

Morris was dumbfounded. Not only had he not known where Greece was located, but he knew virtually nothing about their limitations on sharing the gospel. He expected such antagonism toward Christianity in communist countries like Russia or China. But Greece? His mind reeled as he listened to not only the circumstances but what this brave brother had been through for the sake of the gospel. Growing up in America Morris had taken religious freedom for granted and innocently assumed that most people around the world experienced the same privilege.

After a few moments of silent reflection on Koustis's sobering words, Morris pressed further.

"Sir, if you knew all of this, why did you invite me? And why did you let me come here?"

The eyes of the Greek pastor came to life. "I invited you because God told me to," he smiled. "And I allowed you to make plans and come here because in your letter you said that God had spoken to you about coming here too. It is not my responsibility to try to keep you away when God has instructed you to come."

The gnawing disenchantment that had started to build up in Morris's mind evaporated at that point. This was a godly man doing his best in a difficult situation, and Morris happened to be in the middle of it. It wasn't the pastor's fault; after all, it was God who had commanded each of them to move forward. All that made sense at that point was to assume that God was still in it until they had evidence otherwise.

What had seemed like hopeless incompetence and a huge waste of limited resources just a few minutes ago now became more intriguing to Morris. God had never yet sent him down a path only to abandon him before there was a positive conclusion. Clearly, God knew something significant about Athens that his two servants didn't.

As the bus rolled to a stop outside the boarding house where Pastor Koustis had reserved a room for Morris, the American evangelist decided he was going to find out what God had up His sleeve.

CHAPTER 59

ORRIS WROTE DOWN Rev. Koustis's phone number and address and asked him to sit tight until Morris called. He then mounted a one-man intelligence operation to grasp the lay of the land and to discern God's desires in the strange situation.

The more he poked around trying to understand what was happening, the clearer it became to Morris that the enemy had been having his way in Greece for a long time. Freedom of religion was severely limited and had placed a damper on people's spirit. Public evangelism was uncommon. Worship had become routine and formulaic with worshipers displaying little life or enthusiasm in their tributes to God. The Greek people seemed to have little interest in the Bible. Church services were not very compelling, and most of those who attended seem to do so out of habit more than joy and gratitude. Pastors seemed to be operating on automatic pilot, demonstrating little creativity and determination and living in fear of government reprisal.

Although he had spent months planning for this crusade, it appeared that it was over before it began, but Morris could not believe it was God's intention that he travel four thousand miles and spend a large amount of money only to be separated from his family, spiritually contained, and emotionally deflated. He realized that something beyond his understanding and control was in progress, which meant he had only one choice.

It was time to fervently pray and worship God.

Yet even that well-practiced discipline was a bit of a challenge for Morris. The boarding room he was given was on the fourth floor of the building—and there was no elevator to get him there. After dragging his luggage up several flights of stairs he unlocked the rotting wooden door and stared in disbelief. He was appalled by the room. He was used to living in modest quarters, but this room stood out as perhaps the least appealing accommodation he had yet experienced. The tiny room had a dirty window, a wobbly wooden chair, and a single bed—a lumpy old mattress laying on a rusty iron frame with no sheets or pillowcases to be found. The room itself smelled. The walls were dirty and dark, and the floor looked as if it hadn't been swept since the apostle Paul had spoken at nearby Mars Hill.

As he arranged his belongings in the room he did a mental review of the rooms he had lived in over his decade on the road. He could not remember one that was worse than this.

But he was not here for a vacation. The oppressive conditions simply reinforced the fact that he was at war against God's enemy, and sticking him in subpar housing was just one salvo from that enemy. Morris was determined not to let his circumstances dictate his thoughts or actions. He was there to serve God and His people, and he would do whatever it took to acquit himself well in that undertaking.

He paced back and forth in the tiny room praying out loud to God and recalling the many glorious miracles the Lord had performed in his own life and through him for the benefit of others. He recited passages of Scripture, raising instances where God intervened on behalf of His servants to give them victory. He sang songs of praise to God, reveling in the privilege of speaking to Him, of knowing Him, of being eternally saved by Him, and of having the chance to serve Him in a spiritually dark culture. He reaffirmed his own willingness to do as God saw fit in order to spread the gospel and bring hope and healing to a spiritually oppressed nation.

As his time with God went on for hour after hour he felt his own spirits lifting and the joy of the Lord filling his mind and heart. He was convinced that what the enemy had intended for evil God would turn around and use for a glorious outcome. Morris's hope was in the almighty God. Nothing could defeat him if he simply remained in the Lord's will and devoted to pursuing God's purpose.

When he fell asleep just before dawn he was ready for the coming day. God would show him what to do and how to do it.

Morris knew that his first international ministry adventure would be one to remember.

CHAPTER 60

WHEN HE WOKE a few hours later Morris decided that his first order of business was to relocate. He dressed, packed, and checked out of the boarding house. He marveled at the historic city while lugging his bags through the streets of Athens. His relocation mission turned into a partial reconnaissance mission at the same time, as he studied how the people lived and interacted. He was struck by the marriage of the old and new in the buildings that littered the streets. It was certainly a city of contrasts, with the ancient edifices vying for attention with the more modern homes and offices that were strewn among them. To his eyes it was beautiful and confusing at the same time—and probably a clue to the minds and hearts of the people he hoped to reach.

After a few hours of wandering around without any idea of where he was or exactly what he was looking for Morris found a promising hotel on Constitution Square and booked a room there. It was economical and basic but pleasant enough. At least it had clean sheets and pillow cases! Unfortunately, it consumed a large share of the spending money he and Theresa had put aside for the trip. Once embedded in his new quarters he contacted Rev. Koustis and informed him of the housing change.

"What can I do for you, Brother Cerullo?" the Greek churchman asked expectantly.

"Please wait patiently," Morris replied. "God will reveal what we should do next. All we need to do is obey once He makes His will clear to us. You should pray as well."

After he hung up the phone Morris continued to pray out loud and with passion. As he continually reminded God, he was a man in dire need of a miracle.

In fact, Morris spent ten days in the room praying and waiting for God's guidance. He did not eat during that time and drank only water. Desperate times call for biblical measures; seeking God's intervention was plan A for Morris.

There was no plan B.

On his tenth day in Athens Morris was continuing his regimen of prayer and fasting when there was a forceful knock on the door. The only person who knew he was in that hotel was Pastor Koustis, so he assumed it was his Greek contact coming to make sure he was OK—and still there. He strode to the door and threw it open.

What he saw was not what he expected.

A carefully coiffed woman in expensive clothing stood in the doorway. Her jewelry probably cost more than Morris's airplane ticket to and from Greece. She stared at him. He stared back, taken by surprise at the unknown visitor's presence.

"Good morning, Brother Cerullo. My name is Mrs. Torakes. My husband is the vice president of the Bank of Athens. I am here to help you," she said as if it was the most normal thing in the world.

Morris was shocked. Here to help him do what? Where was her husband? What could she do? What did she think he was in Greece to accomplish?

If her opening words were not exactly what Morris had anticipated, his initial response was probably not what she expected either.

"I'm sorry," he stammered. "I really cannot invite you into my room. As a servant of God I have to follow the Scriptures, which teach that I must abstain from all appearances of evil. Having a married woman in my bedroom—or any woman in my room—could easily be misinterpreted by people who don't know any better. Please do not be offended.

"Now, can you tell me more about how you think you can help me?"

The banker's wife went on to explain that two weeks earlier she had been walking down a street in the city and heard music and other sounds coming from a second-floor room overlooking the street. Her curiosity had gotten the best of her, so she made her way up to the room and discovered it was the mid-week service of a Foursquare church.

Like many Pentecostal churches, that congregation was highly expressive. The woman had never experienced any religious event quite like it and was drawn to the unusual mixture of teaching, music, and congregational response. She stayed around for the rest of the service, during which she was so moved that she surrendered her life to Jesus.

Eager to immerse herself in her new faith, she had spent a lot of time during the past two weeks with other members of the tiny congregation. She then revealed what she knew of Morris's plight.

"Some of the church members told me that you were supposed to come to Athens to help share the gospel and perform miracles," she said softly. "But they said it seemed that you would not be allowed to hold the events because it would be impossible to get the necessary permits. Is this correct?"

Morris shook his head in affirmation.

"Then I must tell you not to worry. We will get you the permits you need to hold the services you flew to Greece to offer. I will ask my husband to use all of his influence to make sure the crusade happens."

Excited by the news, Morris clasped her hands and thanked her.

After she left Morris returned to his knees, thanking God for His incredible intervention and seeking His wisdom for what to do next. God was arranging for the permits to legally hold the crusade, but that was just one step in a long list of things that needed to fall into place very quickly. It was encouraging, but that was only the beginning.

He stayed locked in his room continuing in prayer, praise, and meditation. Mrs. Torakes was the first sign that God was going to make it happen. He was committed to do his part.

During those days the hotel maids smiled at each other as they passed by room 42, where the crazy man had again locked himself inside and could be heard praying at all hours of the day and night. For almost two weeks now he had refused their daily offers of service. They shared stories of hearing the man yelling at the devil or clapping while singing to God.

"Americans!" one maid giggled, and rolled her eyes as she pushed her cart down the corridor to another room.

CHAPTER 61

—◦—

TWO DAYS LATER Rev. Koustis pounded on Morris's door until the evangelist opened it.

"Brother Cerullo," the harried Greek pastor excited proclaimed, "you will not believe what happened." Without waiting for Morris to speak, the older man continued. "The premier of Greece, George Papadopoulos himself, approved the permits for your event. The premiere did this! He heard that a man of God had come to our country who is going to pray for the sick and heal the disabled, and he immediately ordered that the permits be issued. This is a miracle!

"I cannot believe that the bank executive was able to get the premier to do such a thing."

Morris stood tall and locked eyes with the pastor. "No!" he said firmly. "It was not because of a powerful businessman, and it was not because of the premier. It happened because we serve a powerful and compassionate God who has determined that this event will take place. God wants the people of Greece to be saved and to be set free from bondage. This is just the first of many miracles you will see, my friend. But none of them are because of any power that the elites or leaders have, or that I have. It is the power of God on display for us to meet His purposes."

With that, the two men began working on the slew of details that needed to be addressed in the next few days. They worked feverishly to complete all the tasks that were supposed to have been done during the previous eight months.

During those next forty-eight hours the pair accomplished much. They found a suitable building—the Kentragon Theater—and rented it for the desired dates. They designed and then printed the handbills to publicize the event. Advertising space in the local newspapers was purchased. Musicians were secured, lay counselors were enlisted, and the facilities were appropriately prepared. It was a flurry of focused activity.

As handbills appeared on walls throughout the city and were handed by volunteers to people in public places, people's interest was piqued. It had been so many decades since public evangelism was allowed that spiritually indifferent Greeks paid attention to this sudden offer of a unique religious experience.

With just hours to go before the first meeting was scheduled to take place, everything seemed to be ready—except for one important element.

Morris needed an interpreter.

The people of Athens spoke Greek. Unless Morris could find someone to translate his words into Greek his Herculean effort would go to waste.

After all that God had done to get the event to this point, not to mention the countless miracles that God had performed for and through Morris over the years, Morris was not the least bit worried about the need for an interpreter. He mentioned it to Rev. Koustis, prayed for God's provision, and continued to prepare for the event, which meant praying without ceasing until he sensed the presence and power of God.

Meanwhile the theater seats were quickly filling up. People were curious to find out what the big deal was about the American preacher and to see if there really would be miracles, signs, healings, and other evidence of the supernatural, as had been promised on the handbills and newspaper advertisements.

With less than an hour to go before the meeting was scheduled to start, the phone rang in Morris's hotel room, where he was deep in prayer. Reluctantly, he answered the call. He was glad he did.

"You don't know me," said the voice on the other end of the line, "but I am your interpreter."

Morris's eyes widened a bit. "That's great," he said, expressing some of the natural relief that even someone who expected God to come through would feel. "By the way, who are you?"

"My name is Reverend Nicholas Frangus. I am the general superintendent of the Assemblies of God in Greece. I had not planned to be here today, but my plans were rearranged and, well, here I am. I have been visiting our missionary here, and she just informed me of your need for an interpreter, so I will leave now for your hotel. And, by the way, I will rearrange my schedule again to stay with you for the duration of the meetings if you desire."

Morris hung up the phone, smiled, and looked heavenward. The miracles just kept coming.

CHAPTER 62

———◆———

THE OPENING NIGHT of the evangelistic meetings in Greece was unforgettable.

Morris took the stage and began with the words, "I greet you tonight in the name that is above all names, the name of Jesus Christ."

The people applauded loudly. Then Morris noticed that as he started to speak again dozens of people who were crippled or too sick to stand were being carried to the front of the auditorium in anticipation of being healed by God.

In his mind Morris envisioned a similar scene when the apostles, led by Paul, had also ministered in Philippi in the northeastern corner of Greece. No evangelist had preached openly in Greece in many years. No Christians had come forward to do miracles in the name and power of Christ. This was a momentous occasion for Greece.

"The greatest healing is not the restoration of sight to blind eyes," he preached as the Greeks listened intently. "It is not the fixing of crippled legs. It is not the opening of deaf ears. Those miracles will happen tonight through the power of Jesus Christ. The greatest miracle of all is when Jesus saves a sinner's soul from the ravages of hell. That is the miracle of salvation, and you can experience that miracle tonight."

As the night went on the atmosphere was electric. When Morris finished preaching he asked who wanted to receive Christ as their Savior. Fully ninety percent of the people in the auditorium stood. It was by far the largest percentage he had ever seen respond to a call for salvation.

God's presence was thick in the auditorium. Morris moved from one sick person to another healing people of all sorts of maladies that evening. Cries of excitement could be heard all over the venue as loved ones hugged and praised God for their healing. Grown men and women who had come just to see a spectacle were kneeling on the floor weeping, their lives changed forever.

The service went on for hours but nobody left. It was unlike anything anyone in the massive theater had ever witnessed. They were experiencing a whole new concept of the living God of Israel. They were entering a new era of their life.

Revival had come to Greece.

CHAPTER 63

———◆———

I T WAS WELL past midnight when Morris left the auditorium and returned to his hotel room. What a night it had been! Not only had the event taken place despite all the red tape and political obstacles, but a big crowd had taken a chance to attend an event unlike any that had been held in Greece for hundreds of years. In fact, someone informed Morris during the evening that it was the first public evangelistic event that had been allowed in modern times.

Word spread like wildfire throughout Athens about the incredible happenings at the theater. Morris wondered how they would handle the crowds. They had filled the large auditorium the first night; surely there would be overflow crowds on subsequent nights. As usual, he did not worry about such matters knowing that God had everything under control. He had proven that beyond question.

Sure enough, each succeeding night drew larger and larger crowds, and people lined the streets outside the theater, hoping to wiggle their way inside. Morris needed special assistance to get into the theater each night. Families who brought crippled or disabled loved ones tried to get close enough to him that perhaps his shadow would fall on their relative and heal the one in need. It was not unlike the depiction in Acts 5 of how the people of Israel carried their sick into the streets in the hope that Peter's shadow might pass over them and heal their infirmities. Morris was treated the same way.

Everywhere he went people flocked toward him, hoping to touch him. In one instance a crippled man did his best to amble alongside Morris and managed to touch the American on the arm. He immediately cast down his cane and began walking without assistance, fully healed by the power of God. A few minutes later Morris encountered a woman who had been coughing violently for some time. She too pursued Morris on the street, caught up to him, and touched his sleeve. Immediately her lungs cleared, and she was healthy again.

This was all new to Morris. He understood that it was God working through him to change people's lives, but it was still a bit freaky to the twenty-four year old. God was always blowing his mind.

As God worked through him Morris realized that no matter how many times God might do something you never get tired of seeing His glorious power and unfailing love revealed. Without fail, seeing God intervene in the natural world with supernatural acts was breathtaking every time.

The outreach events continued to be a staggering ministry success. Each night the packed house resulted in at least 90 percent of the people committing their lives to Christ. Healings were rampant. The streets outside the theater were clogged with people hoping to push their way inside or to encounter the miracle-working evangelist on his way to or from the event.

After the next to last night of the crusade, the local ministry leaders and event organizers met with Morris.

"You cannot leave after tomorrow night's meeting," one of them stated flatly. "You see the need. You know God is at work in this place like we haven't seen in hundreds of years. We are so grateful that you are here. We appreciate that you are away from family and other duties you have. But you simply cannot go. God is at work, and we dare not abandon what He is doing," he said, pounding the table in front of him. The others in the room murmured their agreement.

It was a moving expression of both their passion for people's souls and their gratitude for Morris's partnership with them. But what could he do?

"Friends, I share your awe at what God has been doing. I have never had an experience like this—and I may never have another one. I do not want to see this end either." He paused as his colleagues voiced their agreement. "But we have to be realistic. I poured all of my money into this event, and now I am broke. Your laws have prevented us from taking offerings at the meetings. Your churches have no money. Reverend Frangus tells me that even if his denomination agreed to provide more funding it would not arrive in time to keep the meetings going. To continue, we need to rent the theater and cover all the other expenses. This is not an inexpensive venture. If you can tell me how we can pay to keep going, then we can consider it. But that's the reality of our situation."

Morris's honest words cut to the heart of the matter. They bantered about a few possibilities but realized each one was a dead end. The group finally dispersed with everyone agreeing to pray for God's guidance.

What he had not told the group was that his financial situation was even more desperate than he let on. Not only had he spent the limited personal funds he had brought with him in order to pay for the theater, the printing and advertising, and his living expenses, but he had also invested the small sum he had saved for his trip to Israel in order to see the meetings succeed. Now he would have to cancel his side trip and return directly home.

After returning to his hotel room very late that evening he was too keyed up to sleep, so he sought God's guidance about what to do.

"Lord, you've heard the cries of the leaders here. You see the huge numbers of people who still need ministry and to embrace the gospel. How can we end it after tomorrow? You know about the stripes on their backs suffered by faithfully serving you. And now they have the freedom to spread the gospel without reprisal during this brief window of opportunity. All we need is more money to extend the meetings and continue to change lives. You know I don't want the meetings to close, and I have to believe you don't want them to stop either. But we don't have the funds, and I don't know what to do."

Before he could continue his earnest plea, God spoke to Morris. The Lord's answer was clear as day—and as unexpected as a snow in July.

"Son, you have the money."

Instantly Morris shouted for joy. Had God just supernaturally produced a satchel of money for them to invest in the meetings? Maybe he had melted the heart of the theater owners, and they would waive the rental fee. Or perhaps there was a wealthy believer who would fund the extension or someone who had been healed who wished to show their gratitude by stepping up to help financially.

"Where is the money, Lord?"

"Son, you have the money at home," came the answer.

Morris fell onto the bed. It was not the answer he expected. In fact, it was not a response that he considered in the realm of possibility. God was telling him that the money he and Theresa had been saving for the house—and had already promised to the builder—was fair game.

Morris pleaded his case. "Lord, you know how hard we have scrimped and saved to put away that small amount of money in order to take care of our family. It's a small sum for a modest home. It would break Theresa's heart to lose that house. No, Lord, forgive me please, but I cannot do that. It would have to be Theresa's choice to do that. And I don't think I could even ask her to consider it."

The young evangelist, who had been so pumped up with enthusiasm over the meetings a few moments earlier, sat on the edge of the bed heartbroken and discouraged. His mind drifted back to his celebration with Theresa when they had placed the deposit on the house. He flashed back on the days and nights when the two of them would take a trip to the property and observe the construction of their future home. He recalled the many conversations they had throughout the past few months regarding buying a house, the interior design they hoped for, the kind of neighborhood in which to raise their children, and how much they could afford to spend.

He pondered how patient Theresa had been ever since they were married. Without complaint she had lived out of suitcases and cheap motel rooms for years, then cramming into a corner of her parents' home upon returning from long ministry trips. She always made the best of carting the children around in cars and trucks, staying in mediocre lodging and eating tasteless meals in forgettable restaurants.

Did she have any idea what she was getting into when she married him?

Probably not. But she was invariably his biggest supporter and cheerleader. She was a tireless prayer warrior. She usually offered to sacrifice whatever was needed before Morris even broached the subject.

So the dilemma facing him now was monumental. He had prayed for years to be sent overseas, to spread the gospel of Christ and see thousands of lives changed. And he had prayed that the Lord would bless them with a comfortable house where their family could have some stability.

Jesus' words in Luke 14 entered his mind: "And if you do not carry your own cross and follow me, you cannot be my disciple. But don't begin until you count the cost. For who would begin construction of a building without first calculating the cost to see if there is enough money to finish it? Otherwise, you might complete only the foundation before running out of money, and then everyone would laugh at you. They would say, 'There's the person who started that building and couldn't afford to finish it!'"

Was that scripture about to be fulfilled in the life of Morris Cerullo?

Morris's two greatest joys in life—ministry and family—had now come in direct conflict. As he lay on the bed staring at the ceiling he knew what he had to do.

He just couldn't muster the heart to do it.

CHAPTER 64

"CAN YOU HEAR me OK, honey?" Morris yelled into the telephone after Theresa had answered the call. International telephone calls were not only very expensive in those days, but it was difficult to get the call through, and there was always a lot of static on the line.

After a minute of pleasantries and reveling in hearing his wife's voice again, Morris coughed and got to the point.

"Yes, dear, the meetings are going spectacularly well, better than anything we ever dreamed of. But it looks like I'll have to end the meetings prematurely," he explained, his voice thick with emotion. "We just don't have the money to keep them going. The locals want the meetings to continue, and we're seeing incredible outcomes—hundreds of salvation decisions and amazing miracles every night—but we have run out of money."

Theresa had been praying day and night during her husband's absence. During her times with the Lord He had revealed the need to her, so she was not surprised by what Morris was telling her. Out of love for her husband she did what she could to make the call easier on him.

"That's so wonderful, sweetheart," she said. "And I know why you're calling."

There was a pause before Morris simply replied, "How?"

"You want me to take the money for the house out of the bank and send it so you can continue the meetings," she said without any trace of disappointment. In fact, to Morris it sounded like she was smiling when she said it.

Morris again coughed and mumbled "I didn't ask you for that."

Now he was sure he could hear a smile behind her words. "You don't have to ask," she said lightly. "I'll wire the money to you today."

Morris paused again before softly thanking her and expressing his love for her yet again. Both of them had tears in their eyes. They were separated by thousands of miles but closer than ever. They said a few more pleasantries before he hung up the phone.

He stood there replaying the conversation in his mind. How incredible was Theresa? All alone at home taking care of their children, not having any contact with him while he was in a foreign country, and then she jumped at the chance to give up something she cherished in favor of fulfilling God's work.

As he reflected on the situation he remembered the story of Barnabas in Acts 4. "For instance, there was Joseph, the one the apostles nicknamed Barnabas (which means "Son of Encouragement"). He was from the tribe of Levi and came from the island of Cyprus. He sold a field he owned and brought the money to the apostles."

That was so much like the sacrifice Theresa was making. Her heart was dedicated to serving God—even if it meant giving up her dream.

With that call everything changed yet again. Morris next called his local ministry associates and informed them that his wife was wiring the money today to continue the events. They needed to make all the arrangements quickly to extend the meetings.

The money arrived the following day, and the events continued, getting bigger every night. Each night God showed up in unmistakable ways.

Morris's initial venture into international ministry couldn't have gone better.

The next step on his journey was Israel.

CHAPTER 65

I F MORRIS WRESTLED with the fear of the unknown when he boarded the plane in New York to fly to Greece, he felt an entirely different emotion as he boarded the plane in Greece to head to Israel.

Morris felt a sense of destiny.

His Jewish heritage had always been a mixed blessing. On one hand he was proud to be Jewish, the heritage of Jesus Christ and God's chosen people. On the other hand, being Jewish in America was not always a benefit. In the 1940s and 1950s there was still a lot of prejudice against the Jewish people. World War II, with Hitler's infamous publicity campaign against the Jews and then murdering more than six million of them, had left a mark in the minds of many people about the alleged inferiority of Jews. After the war, with the Jews fighting to establish their own homeland and Israel becoming an independent nation in 1948, many people were confused about what to think about Jews and their faith.

Morris was not among the confused. The older he got the more determined he was to revel in his Jewish heritage, and he was certain that God intended for him to have a significant ministry to the Jewish people. He recognized that this was not yet the time but that God was preparing him for that day.

The flight from Athens to Tel Aviv gave Morris time to transition from the groundbreaking, exciting ministry that had taken place in Greece to a more reflective few days in Israel.

In 1955 Israel was just beginning to lay the foundation for its national standing. In many ways the region was still as simple as it had been during biblical times. Many roads were still unpaved. Houses were often small edifices made of local stone. The cities were not yet the high-rise, densely populated metropolises they would soon turn into. Israel was still a land of quiet simplicity—and harsh battles for freedom.

He enjoyed his three days of seeing some of the biblical sites and looking over the land from undeveloped mountaintops. Getting to know the people was helpful, as Dr. Cerullo sought to understand the nation and how God might chose to use him in reaching these people.

When the time came to head back home he was eager to see his family but sad to leave the land of his ancestors. He felt as if he connected with the place in a special way. He was excited about someday returning to help the Jewish people.

But that would have to wait. He needed to focus on what God had in store for him next.

CHAPTER 66

W HEN MORRIS STRODE off the airplane in New York City, he was bombarded with whoops of joy from his children.

"There he is! There he is!" yelled three-year-old David at the top of his lungs, excitedly pointing at his tired father moving toward them. "Daddy's home. Daddy's home," he screamed before breaking free from Theresa's hand and making a mad dash for his father. They hugged on the concourse with fellow travelers smiling at the reunion while they rushed toward their own destinations.

Theresa, holding one-year-old Susan in her arms, smiled broadly at her returning hero. Dr. Cerullo stood in front of her, five feet away, with David clinging to his leg. He smiled back and pulled out both of his pants pockets, which had only a few coins in them.

"That's all that's left," he said with a fake frown.

She returned a fake pout while tears trickled down her face. "It doesn't matter," she said, replacing the pout with a grin, "we're together again, and that's all that matters. God will take care of the rest."

And take care of them He did. After investing all of the housing money they had saved for four years into the Athens outreach meetings—including the six-hundred-dollar deposit, which they forfeited—Morris's family was financially depleted. But within a year, thanks to a steady stream of opportunities and a lot of hard work, they managed to save up enough money to go house hunting again. God's generosity toward the young family was monumental.

When the time was right Morris suggested they return to the same housing development where their original house had been built. They loved the neighborhood and thought maybe another lot or home would be available nearby.

They drove up and down the streets near the location of their forfeited house, not quite up to the emotional letdown of passing by their "old house" yet. But after a few passes on the adjoining streets, they mustered their courage and drove to the home they had previously sought to purchase.

To their surprise there was a For Sale sign stuck in the front lawn of the house. They looked at each other, perplexed. How could someone have bought it, moved in, and moved out already? It had only been a year. In those days, people often lived their entire lives in the first—and only—house they purchased.

On a whim they decided to drive over to inquire about the house with their realtor, Jeff Baron, the agent who had sold the house to them. They had enjoyed working with him, and everyone shared in the disappointment when the sale did not go through as expected.

Morris got right to the point. "Listen, Jeff, we were just driving through the development and noticed that our old house is for sale. What happened? And how much is the house going for?"

Jeff laughed and settled back in his chair.

"That house is the worst inventory we've ever carried," he said with a grin. "We have houses selling to the left of it, to the right of it, across the street—it's a hot area, Morris. But for some reason we just can't seem to sell that one. The same builder has been busy constructing houses on every other lot in the neighborhood, and they sell as fast as they go up. But that one, well, it's a different story."

Morris looked the man straight in the eye. "Wait a minute. Are you telling me that after we were unable to complete the deal, nobody has purchased the home?"

"That's exactly what I'm telling you. It's the strangest thing. Everything else goes on the market, and *boom*"—he snapped his fingers—"it's gone. But not that house."

Morris knew a deal when he saw one. He stood up as tall as he could and tried not to keep from laughing. "Well, Jeff, this may be your lucky day. I'm in a magnanimous mood. How much would do want me to pay you to take that lemon off your hands?"

They all laughed but then got down to serious negotiations. Jeff was stuck on the fact that the value of houses in the development had risen by three thousand dollars in the intervening year. Morris was determined not to pay a penny more than he had to since money was still tight for the young family. They were unable to arrive at a price that satisfied both of them. They shook hands, and the Cerullos headed back home.

Morris was very happy. He knew God would do something special for them.

Sure enough, a few days later he received a phone call from Baron.

"Reverend Cerullo, I talked over our discussion with the developers. I can't believe it, but they said that if you'll agree to buy the house for the original price, they'll sell it to you."

Before Morris could say, "Sold!" the realtor continued. "In fact, they have also offered to credit you for the six-hundred-dollar deposit that you lost last year when you were unable to complete the deal."

Clearly, the realtor was amazed by the offer, but Morris and Theresa just nodded knowingly at each other and smiled. God was blessing them for their faithfulness. When the ministry needed funds to complete the work in Greece the Cerullos had devoted the money they had saved without any remorse.

And now God was paying them back—with a premium!

After agreeing to the terms and hanging up the phone Morris and Theresa hugged and celebrated their good fortune.

"We serve an awesome God, honey," he said to his jubilant wife. "No matter how hard you try, you just cannot out-give God!"

CHAPTER 67

————◆————

MORRIS'S FIRST TASTE of international ministry lit a fire under him to return overseas. But that was not the Lord's plan. It would be four years before Morris was called into action overseas again.

Those four years were packed with ministry opportunities throughout the US and Canada. The more he traveled and preached, the more well-known he became. Invitations arrived weekly, and the size of the meetings consistently expanded. The three-thousand-seat tent they had relied upon was no longer adequate. MCWE purchased a tent double that size and within a few months of the purchase found that it too had grown too small to accommodate the masses that were turning out to be touched by God through Morris.

Theresa, who gave birth to their third child, Mark, in 1957, generally stayed behind taking care of the growing duties related to operations and communications. Morris relied heavily upon her to keep everything in order.

Hundreds and then thousands of letters and cards were arriving at their house each week, and Theresa managed to respond personally to all of them. Every day she shared some of the most interesting or exciting letters with her husband. Morris was deeply moved to find that so many people's lives were transformed by their exposure to his ministry and was humbled by the growing number of people who said they were praying for him or wanted to help his ministry financially.

The events continued to produce mighty works of God night after night. Not only did thousands of people accept Jesus as their Savior in each city he visited, but there was a regular parade of miracles in each town as well. People of all ages and backgrounds were healed of diseases, injuries, physical defects, emotional trauma, and disabilities. Even though he was at the center of those miracles every night, Morris never ceased to be astounded by the power and mercy of God.

It was a joy for Morris to be involved in such a great life adventure, but he was never able to predict what would happen in any particular location or during a specific event. God surprised him every night with how He blessed those in attendance.

No matter how open-minded Morris was, though, he was not prepared for what took place in Lima, Ohio, in 1957.

He was ministering for ten days in a high school auditorium that a local church had rented for the meetings. The presence of God was so thick that week that it was palpable. Salvations and miracles abounded.

After returning to his motel room after one of the evenings of ministry Morris fell asleep replaying the night's highlights in his mind.

His reverie was suddenly shattered by a bright light that filled the room. The light was so intense that his eyes had trouble adjusting. He had even more difficulty trying to figure out where the light was coming from. It was pitch dark outside, and none of the room's lights were turned on.

His grogginess disappeared in a flash when he finally realized that the light could only be from a supernatural source.

Morris was used to the presence of God. He never took the stage at any event until he felt the nearness and guidance of God. But his room that night was saturated with a powerful presence of the Holy Spirit. It reminded him of the appearance of God when he received the vision at age fifteen.

By now Morris was lying prostrate on the floor waiting on direction from the Lord. Everything seemed magnified to him. He could hear his heart pounding. His breathing slowed. Time seemed to stand still. His hearing was acute.

And then the Lord graced Morris with yet another magnificent vision.

The walls of his room faded away, replaced by a great horizon that met huge banks of pure white, fluffy clouds that moved lazily toward the center of the horizon. When the clouds were in place they stopped moving, and Morris could see large drops descending downward. But the raindrops did not appear translucent, like drops of water. Instead, they seemed dense and heavy, like drops of oil.

Confused by the vision, Morris spoke out, "Lord, what does the rain mean?"

The answer was received in his spirit. "This rain is an outpouring of my Holy Spirit upon all flesh. It will be poured out upon all nations of the world."

Hearing those words caused the young evangelist to rejoice. It brought to mind the passage relayed by the prophet Joel—the same pronouncement offered by the apostle Peter as a precursor to the Day of Pentecost in Jerusalem, shortly after the resurrection of Jesus: "Then, after doing all those things, I will pour out my Spirit upon all people. Your sons and daughters will prophesy. Your old men will dream dreams, and your young men will see visions. In those days I will pour out my Spirit even on servants—men and women alike."

Morris's mind wandered through various historic manifestations of the Spirit. In particular he was reminded of the famous Azusa Street Revival in Los Angeles in 1907. Morris felt like he believed those saints must have felt when God's Spirit rained down on them after concerted prayer and seeking of God's presence.

As he pondered those things Morris began to wonder with heartfelt longing who would be used by God to usher in the next great outpouring of His Spirit. American society was changing so rapidly, reveling in its postwar capacity and wealth but so often seeming to ignore the greatness and benevolence of God. The nation definitely needed a full-scale revival. Revivals needed men and women who were prepared to devote their lives to moving people into holiness. Who was God preparing for the task?

Hungry to know how revival would come and how he could participate, Morris dared to ask the Lord, "Who will lead this great outpouring of Your Spirit, Father?" Pausing to consider the wisdom of his inclination, he then asked, "Will I be an instrument that You use to bring this to pass?"

Morris did not mean his question to be impertinent or haughty. He sincerely hungered to know who God would use and how he could help. He was feeling frustrated by the absence of clarity at that moment and simply wanted to be of service to His Father in heaven.

"Son, no person will lead this move. The work I am about to do will be without human direction. This outpouring will not be the work of a man but the work of My Holy Spirit."

Those words provided the insight that Morris was seeking. He relaxed as if the words were a soothing balm to his anxious heart. As he continued to meditate on the implications of those words the vision dissipated, and his natural surroundings came back into his field of sight.

Morris took the Lord's words to heart and emerged with a clear direction for his ministry for the rest of his life. It all hinged on a simple, scripturally consistent idea: This will be a work of the Holy Spirit, not the work of a man!

This immediately precipitated a subtle but profound shift in his emphasis. Morris recognized that to experience continued success and impact his ministry would have to be based upon his ever-deepening relationship with and sensitivity to direction from the Holy Spirit, not upon his own personality or abilities. It was, when all was said and done, God's ministry; Morris was merely a privileged servant, called to be useful in whatever ways God wanted.

This vision caused him to reflect more carefully upon Jesus's words to His disciples: "Those who exalt themselves will be humbled, and those who humble themselves will be exalted."

God had thus far chosen to use a Jewish orphan boy to reach many souls, but the success of the ministry was not because of the boy; it was God's ministry. All impact came from His power, and all the glory was due to Him alone. If the Holy Spirit of God was not at the center of the work, that effort would certainly fail to produce spiritual fruit.

In time Morris discovered that the revelation to give all the glory to whom it truly belonged actually took the pressure off of Morris. Ministry outcomes were no longer up to him; they were the providence of God. As long as Morris remained obedient, he had no worries, no fears. He realized that the only way to truly be an instrument for God was to get out of His way, let Him do what He wanted to do, and make sure He received all the glory for it. If He allowed Morris to play a role in the process, so much the better, but the focus had to remain on Him.

"This is not the work of a man, but this is the work of the Holy Spirit" became both a ministry cornerstone and a freeing realization to Morris.

PART FOUR:

—•—

THE MINISTRY GROWS

CHAPTER 68

Tʜᴇ Mᴏʀʀɪs Cᴇʀᴜʟʟᴏ World Evangelism (MCWE) ministry continued to grow, causing Morris and Theresa to begin praying about establishing a more strategic location as a base of operations. Confident that their future included a lot of global travel, they needed a place that was convenient for international flights and where they could host large gatherings of people at any time of year without worries about weather.

Their evaluation of locations was full of starts and stops. Whenever they thought they had found a place with strong potential, obstacles quickly arose. That is, until they encountered San Diego in southern California.

Having spent their lives living in the northeast they were only vaguely aware of the area. In the 1950s the United States was exploding with growth, but most of it was taking place in the eastern portion of the country. Many Americans considered New York City to be the center of the universe. It was home to the nation's most prestigious newspapers and magazines, television networks, radio stations, and premier sports and entertainment options. Its skyscrapers were a marvel, and the city's eight million residents were more than double the population of its closest rival, Chicago. Other major population centers in the northeast corridor included Philadelphia (2 million); Baltimore (1 million); Washington, DC (more than three-quarters of a million); and Boston (700,000).

San Diego, paradise that it was, remained the secret jewel of the west. Tucked in the southwestern corner of California, by 1960 it had barely more than half a million people. The more the Cerullos studied San Diego, the more promising it looked. The weather was as good as it gets. The airport provided a steady stream of flights on multiple airlines to all areas of the world. And being on the West Coast facilitated flights to Asia and the South Pacific nations, such as the Philippines.

After many months of praying and waiting for guidance they chose San Diego and moved there in 1959. They spent their first six months in a motel with their three children before moving into an apartment in the Kearny Mesa region of the San Diego metropolis. Although it was a radical change from living in New York, the family immediately embraced the milder climate and quickly felt at home in the new environs.

Setting up an office for their operations enabled Theresa to expand their communications with the ever-growing list of supporters and partners. The ministry invested in some of the cutting-edge printing and mailing equipment of the day, saving thousands of hours of labor and enabling more frequent and descriptive information to be sent. Most importantly, it enabled the ministry to solidify its relationships with the thousands of people they had met and ministered to around the nation and to receive timely advice and prayer support from that network of friends.

It wasn't long after settling down in San Diego that invitations to minister overseas were received. The West Coast relocation proved to be immediately advantageous, as Morris accepted invitations from churches in Hong Kong and in the Philippines.

But in some ways, the ordeal experienced in Greece was child's play compared to what Morris was about to face while ministering in the Asian countries.

CHAPTER 69

—•—

WHEN MORRIS TRAVELED to Greece for his initial international ministry experience, he had assumed that the church hosting him would put together the necessary logistics to have a smoothly run event. He had been wrong—very wrong.

As he prepared to minister in Hong Kong and the Philippines he was determined to learn a lesson from past mistakes. This time around he would take whatever steps were necessary to ensure that what needed to get done would get done and that the quality he expected would be achieved. He was, after all, serving God, not men; nothing but the best effort would be satisfactory. He had to prove himself to be a worthy steward of God's trust and of the resources—time, money, ability, relationships—that God had allocated to him.

Morris knew it would be foolish to attempt to organize meetings to be held in foreign countries from his base in the United States. So, he and Theresa packed up the kids and flew to Hong Kong to begin the preparations for the crusade in that island nation and the one to follow in the Philippines. He also took with him two superb preachers, Gordon Lindsay and Lester Sumrall, who would help carry the load.

There was a massive learning curve for Morris and his team. Morris knew nothing about the Chinese and Filipino cultures or how business was conducted in those places. While Greece at least had a relatively Western mindset, the Asian ways of thinking and interacting were dramatically different. Pulling off a daunting enterprise like a crusade was a hard task to master in the United States. Trying to pull off such events in foreign lands with a small team operating on a limited budget in the era predating all the technological innovations that had not yet been invented—well, it was a huge challenge.

The team started by renting a stadium in Hong Kong whose seating capacity was more than forty thousand people. Talk about a leap of faith! The cost was staggering, and so were the logistical issues. They needed to build a platform, working within the boundaries allowed both by law and by the stadium's owners. They had to ensure there would be sufficient power piped into the stadium for the kind of sound and lights they would need on stage. Permits, ad design, newspaper space, radio ads, parking, security, ushers, lighting, sound, platform equipment, counselors—the list went on and on, each new item a brain twister of its own.

Another lesson drawn from the past was the importance of following up with people after the event. One of the most common criticisms of crusade-type evangelism was that after an evangelist left town, those who indicated their desire to follow Christ were left hanging. Morris wanted to be sure that those new believers would be adequately connected to partnering churches and ministries after he and his team moved on. In his mind, God used him and MCWE to introduce people to Christ, after which it was the privilege of the churches in the area to build lasting relationships with those people and disciple them. Nonetheless, facilitating that process, especially in a vastly different culture operating with a different language, was a big hurdle.

Managing the personal logistics for the team was complicated enough. Team members coming and going at all hours of the day and night over the course of several weeks was very challenging. Booking the right number of hotel rooms in a decent facility close to the event venue, arranging efficient air and ground transportation, supervising travel documentation, coordinating with the venue suppliers, scheduling each precious minute of the event time, recruiting and training volunteers, applying for the countless permits required—the logistical needs were enormous. All of these activities took time, money, expertise, and precise coordination. No matter how hard they tried, every day seemed to introduce additional, unexpected requirements that demanded immediate attention.

As he soon discovered, such a massive enterprise demanded a chief executive, someone who would be the mastermind with ultimate decision-making authority. A complicated and diversified project like the crusades required someone who had the big picture in mind and could assign every necessary undertaking, from the smallest detail to the most substantial task, to people who were competent enough to do the job right and on time—the first time.

In Hong Kong that job fell on Morris's rapidly sagging shoulders. Early on in the project he realized how completely naïve he had been to think that a handful of young, passionate ministers could invade a foreign country in which he was completely unknown, mount a multi-day event in a gigantic stadium, and pull it off without a hitch.

Managing the crusade in Hong Kong became the ultimate on-the-job training experience for Morris.

Well-intentioned and hardworking as he was, mistakes were made. For example, he radically underestimated how difficult—and expensive—it is to rent and install a sound system that provides clear sound to every portion of a large, open-air stadium. Further, he hadn't even thought about the fact that they rented an open-air stadium for an event in February when the temperatures typically hovered in the single digits. And all of those types of considerations were moot if he could not secure—and maintain—the many government-issued permits for an event promoting a religion that the government did not support.

Perhaps the hardest balancing act for Morris was to be sure to spend enough time in prayer for the people who would be attending the event. The ultimate success of the event was not about the presence of Morris or his fellow speakers or the counseling team. It was about the presence of God. Morris believed that it was imperative for him to spend enough time engaged with God and beseeching His participation in the soul-winning work that God's presence would be as overpowering as it had been in Greece.

The real test would come on the night of the first event. Morris and the team invested themselves fully in the preparations. In the end, it all came down to one key reality: "This is not the work of a man but of the Holy Spirit."

CHAPTER 70

THE MEETINGS IN Hong Kong turned out to be a big victory for the kingdom of God. Night after night thousands of Chinese people braved the frigid weather to hear the American evangelist speak. At the end of each service the aisles were flooded with throngs of people who streamed forward to become followers of Christ.

The tremendous response brought tears to Morris's eyes numerous times during the Hong Kong event. The more he learned about the island, which was still under British rule at the time, the more overwhelmed he was by the spiritual poverty of the densely populated territory and its positive response to the gospel. Despite the obstacles, a substantial share of those who made their way to the front each night were avowed communists—people so touched by God at the events that they were willing to publicly buck their party's teaching and discipline to revolutionize their lives around through the love of God.

During the daytime Morris and his team rented a theater in which they conducted discipleship sessions for the new converts. Before the end of the crusade every seat in the theater was filled by Chinese men and women who were hungry for the Word of God and eager to discover more about the new faith they had adopted.

In fact, the great response created a serious problem for the church in Hong Kong: the existing churches did not have enough capacity to handle the influx of new believers. As Morris and his leaders met to discuss the challenge, they realized the only viable solution was to start a congregation designed for the new believers.

That represented another big step of faith. The team was still reeling from the pressures of pulling off a smooth crusade—and it wasn't done yet. But in order not to allow the enemy to discourage or redirect those new Christ-followers it was necessary that they have a focused and understanding church home to foster their spiritual development. Starting a new church of that size on the spur of the moment in a foreign country was an absurd idea. However, it was a solution that Morris felt led by God to pursue.

Real estate was at a premium on the small island, so finding a viable space for a church—and being able to afford it—was a miracle in itself. After a few days of prayer, searching, and negotiating, they located a building overlooking a harbor that had a vacant floor. It was an outstanding location, and the space met the needs of the soon-to-be church, which became New Life Temple.

Working with the existing Hong Kong churches, Morris's team identified a leadership team for the new church. That group included one of the ladies who had been deeply affected by the meetings. Her name was Nora Lam. She had been abandoned at birth, adopted by a wealthy doctor in Shanghai, was highly educated, and eventually came to receive Jesus as her Savior. The crusade had reinvigorated her faith, and she agreed to work for the new church as its administrator. She proved to be very adept at providing the operational wisdom required. In later years she would become known throughout the world through the book she wrote titled *China Cry* about the struggle of Christians in communist China. The widely acclaimed book eventually became the basis of a popular movie.

Exhilarating as the outcome in Hong Kong was, it was just the first stop on the mini-tour of Asia. The next challenge was awaiting Morris and his tired group in the Philippines.

CHAPTER 71

ONG KONG COULD easily have served as the highlight of any evangelist's life. Starting from scratch, the small team that flew to the crowded island nation managed to cobble together a surprisingly smooth event. Several hundred thousand seats had been filled over the course of the meetings there, and thousands of people had received the miracle of salvation as a result. A new church opened in the nation as a result of the crusade, a megachurch from the day it opened its doors.

Morris was just twenty-eight years old at the time.

But God was just getting started with him. The young man had passed every test the Lord had thrown at him, so He continued to orchestrate bigger and more amazing events through the born-again Jew.

The MCWE team arrived in Manila, the sprawling and impoverished capitol of the Philippine islands, exhausted but awestruck by what God had done through them among the Chinese people. And, as in Hong Kong, they touched down in this next nation ill-informed about its culture and ill-prepared to put together yet another set of massive meetings.

But, by the grace of God, that's exactly what they did. Again.

The miracle that emerged in Hong Kong was the astonishing number of salvation decisions. In the Philippines, a country filled with nominal Catholics, the remarkable result was the number and nature of miracles performed.

As usual, Morris spent hour upon hour praying intensely to God before ever taking the stage. He refused to deviate from his standard practice: praying and waiting for God to inhabit the premises and then lead him in ministry to those who attended. He was not about to change that practice in the Philippines.

Even Morris was struck by the magnitude of the miracles God performed through him in Manila. Much like had happened in Greece, once word circulated that a man of God was doing miracles, poor and crippled people jammed the massive public park that was the site of the crusade. These were people who had no hope. If the man of God could address their pain and suffering, their hope could be restored.

More than thirty thousand people showed up every night praying that this white man from another country, a person whom they had never heard of, could help them.

The drama started when Morris finished his first sermon and implored them to be healed in Jesus's name, by His power alone.

Looking out at the mass of people stretching the length of the park, Morris was blown away by the ocean of dysfunctional bodies waiting for a wave of God's power to transform them. There were untold hundreds of crippled, diseased, blind, deaf, deformed, and otherwise handicapped people staring back at him. Some were in wheelchairs, some had been carried on pallets. Many were bent over canes or walkers, others had been thrown over the back of a friend or relative, and a few had metal braces holding their joints or bones in place. Most of them were adults, but a large number were children, ragged and unkempt.

The man of God looked up to heaven as his heart shattered into a thousand pieces.

The procession of hurting and hopeless people continued to fill the park for three consecutive weeks, seven days and nights each week. On the closing evening of the crusade, lying just a few feet away from his podium was a badly crippled man. His body was grotesquely twisted and deformed. He lay on the ground watching Morris out of the corner of his eye while curled up in a ball on the trampled grass. His family, who had carried him to Roxas Park and pushed their way to the front of the gathering, were pleading with God, their arms stretched high, as if they were striving to touch the hem of Christ and draw healing power from it, as others had done two thousand years earlier.

Dumbstruck, Morris stared in fascination at the man. His legs were wrapped up tight like a pretzel, and his thin arms were nestled in toward his stomach. He was the most hideously deformed human being Morris had ever encountered.

Moved by the magnitude of the man's needs, Morris focused on the debilitated man and began ministering to him from Isaiah 53:1–3:

> Who has believed our message? To whom has the Lord revealed his powerful arm? My servant grew up in the Lord's presence like a tender green shoot, like a root in dry ground. There was nothing beautiful or majestic about his appearance, nothing to attract us to him. He was despised and rejected—a man of sorrows, acquainted with deepest grief. We turned our backs on him and looked the other way. He was despised, and we did not care.

As Morris recited these verses and prayed over the man, with one hand stretched out toward the cripple and the other lifted to God, the motionless life form on the ground started to move.

Morris's eyes widened as he watched the invisible Spirit of God answer the man's silent cry for mercy. Morris looked around at his colleagues on the stage. They, too, were riveted by the scene unraveling before them. Tears of compassion and joy were on Theresa's face.

Then Morris heard the man's bones cracking as God began to reshape and reposition them. As if watching time-lapse photography, Morris saw the man's legs straighten. The women surrounding the man screamed in shock. His arms began to unravel, straightening for the first time in many years. Again, the crackling sound of bones breaking and reconnecting filled Morris's ears.

Suddenly supernatural occurrences spread like wildfire. People all around the front of the park experienced miraculous healings of all sorts.

Morris turned to watch the tumult happening in a section of the park that had dozens of children in braces. The mothers of those children were removing the braces and yelling at their children to "walk, in the name of Jesus."

Morris had never witnessed anything like this. Nobody had!

Watching these youngsters try to walk reminded Morris of footage he had seen of young calves attempting their first steps after birth. The children took a step and would wobble to the ground. Then their parents would pick them up and encourage them to try again. Their mothers kept moving the children forward as they put one, then two, then three, then multiple steps together. After a few minutes several of those children were running and jumping, whooping for joy and swirling their arms in the air. Another little girl pretended to be a ballerina, clasping her hands over her head while leaping and turning in the air. Her mother sat there with tears coursing down her face, gasping for breath at the spectacle she thought she would never see.

A few feet to their left was a group of older people who had hobbled in with the use of crutches and canes. The area looked like a battle zone as their crutches and canes were being hurled to the side and thrown overhead as formerly crippled people now walked without hindrance.

In another part of the crowd a woman shrieked in amazement as she and others watched a man with a shriveled leg gaze in astonishment as his shorter leg grew to the same size as his longer limb.

On the other side of the field another woman cried out as she slowly and agonizingly stood up straight for the first time in decades. Her backbone was now straight, and the large hump that had been so prominent only moments ago was suddenly gone.

Dozens of people could be seen looking skyward and all around them as their previously blind eyes had vision for the first time. People whose hearing was healed were laughing at the plethora of sounds they heard, some even covering their ears from the volume of noise.

While the entire place went wild with excitement and astonishment, Morris stood at the center of the stage sharing in their joy. He had been

privileged to participate in miracles before, but even he had never seen—
or dreamed—of anything like this. Scores of people were simultaneously
being healed by God. The evangelist stood there weeping like a baby at the
spectacle.

As the healings and rejoicing continued Morris didn't know what to do.
God's presence was so powerful and palpable that he felt was not needed. As
emotions swirled through his body, he did the only thing that made sense to
him in that moment.

He ran off the stage and hid behind a huge tree.

CHAPTER 72

————•————

IKE A LITTLE boy hiding from his parents, Morris stood behind the tree and watched the miraculous event unfold. Even for the man who had initiated the event and participated in signs and wonders many times before, watching the awesome power of God was overwhelming.

A while later an Assembly of God missionary named Alford Cawston made his way to Dr. Cerullo's ineffective hiding place.

"Isn't it something, Brother Cerullo?" he asked in wonder. Without taking his eyes off the scene in the park Morris silently shook his head in affirmation. As the two gazed at the activity throughout the park Cawston put his arm around Morris's shoulders and continued, "I think you had better return to the stage and bring the people together before they break out in a riot." When Morris showed no sign of moving from behind the tree, Cawston added, "I think you are the only one who can do that."

Morris did not want to go out front again. Like so many others in the building, he was overwhelmed by the activity and sheer force of God. Who in his right mind would dare to take the spotlight away from God while He was demonstrating that unstoppable and unfathomable power?

But before he could protest, the Lord reminded him of the story in the second chapter of Acts when God had similarly revealed His power to a group of new believers and the apostle Peter had taken charge of the meeting, explaining to everyone what had happened and leading more people to Christ.

Reluctantly, Morris slowly walked to the middle of the stage and took the microphone from its stand. The crowd was still in full fury, oblivious to the person moving about up front. Morris was still weeping as he uttered the first words that came to mind: "God, no one should ever see this much of Your glory and be allowed to live," he began in earnest. "God, take me home. I am ready to die."

As he stood there, speechless, he fully expected God to take him to heaven at that moment. He figured he had seen it all. He had the privilege of being used by God in that tidal wave of miracles. What else could he ever experience that would top that moment? How could he return to doing normal things when he had just seen the most incredible surge of God's power and love that he could imagine?

It was the highest note possible, wasn't it? Who wouldn't want to go to their heavenly reward after witnessing the most glorious moment they were likely to experience?

That's when God pulled another surprise out of His hat.

"Son," the Lord said to Morris, "you haven't seen anything yet."

CHAPTER 73

A ROUND THAT TIME Morris had the chance to minister to the people of Trinidad and Tobago, island nations at the southern end of the Caribbean. Like so many of the events in those days, things started with a very modest gathering of people on the opening night to watch the unknown evangelist from America. As God healed people and individuals heard about the love and power of the living God, large numbers of those in attendance came forward to claim Jesus as their Savior.

Then, after the opening night's event ended, the word would start to spread throughout the city. Those who had witnessed God's power manifested through Morris would tell their friends who in turn would share the news with their friends, and so on. By the fourth or fifth day of a ten-day crusade the grounds would be standing-room only.

After the final meeting in Trinidad, another slow-building but ultimately record-breaking event, Morris was exhausted. The ten-day meetings, which usually incorporated additional meetings in the mornings and afternoons in other locations for specialized groups of people, drained him of energy. People could not see the invisible spiritual battles that were occurring as he spoke and ministered. As exhilarating as the results were, it always depleted Morris of his natural reserves.

Sitting in a chair sapped of strength but grateful for the mighty ways in which God had blessed the island people during the past ten days, one of Morris's team members quietly approached him with a request. A small group of pastors visiting from British Guyana (now known as Guyana), a small nation on the northeastern tip of South America, had appeared outside his door begging for a chance to speak with the man of God. Exhausted as he was, Morris did his best to always accommodate the needs of Christian pastors who were earnestly seeking to advance the gospel.

At that time Guyana had no particular strategic or economic value on the world stage. The population of the entire nation was less than a million people, and its land was mostly wild forest and infertile savannah, best known for producing sugarcane and bauxite ore (used to produce aluminum).

The British government had realigned its intentions over the years and was in the process of moving the small nation toward independence, which required self-government. Accordingly, it gave every citizen twenty-one or older the right to vote, and the political race was on.

To the chagrin of many, one of the leading political figures to emerge was a young, radical communist named Cheddi Jagan. Educated in the United

States, he had returned to his native land and formed a political party known as the PPP (which stood for the People's Progressive Party). Together with his wife, he promoted a left-wing, Marxist worldview, railing against colonialism and capitalist exploitation and manipulation.

The gathered pastors feared the destruction of their reforming nation and believed that only the presence and power of God could truly save the country from utter calamity. After seeing God work through Morris in Trinidad, the pastors felt God urging them to invite Morris to British Guyana—and to not take no for an answer.

Honored as he was, no was indeed the answer they initially received from the evangelist. He explained that he was totally spent from the ten-day effort in Trinidad and that the necessary planning and preparation would need to be done to have a successful crusade in Guyana.

But the pastors were not to be denied. They implored Morris to simply board a plane and "hop across the water" on the short trip from Trinidad to British Guyana and do a simple, bare-bones event that would bring stability and sanity to their country.

God's Spirit softened Morris, and he eventually gave in to their request. He sent a few of his colleagues, including Bishop John Meares, ahead of the rest of the team to do whatever advance work was possible in the short time available.

Their efforts were fruitful. They secured Queen's Park as a venue and received the requisite permits. They quickly had posters and handbills printed and hired a team of locals to plaster the city with the posters. They purchased ad space in the major newspapers—big half-page and full-page ads featuring a big photo of Morris inviting people, with all the event details.

As might have been expected, the typical pattern followed. The first night the crusade launched with a few hundred people sprinkled inside the massive park, showing up out of curiosity or desperation. But God showed up, miracles happened, souls were saved, and the people present were wowed. Word of the incredible event spread rapidly.

Before the end of the week crowds of forty thousand were jamming the park to see what God was doing through the man nobody had ever heard of. And God did not disappoint them.

And He had a couple of surprises in store for Morris too.

CHAPTER 74

AS THE CRUSADE progressed Morris took advantage of whatever moments of rest and solitude he could. One afternoon he joined Bishop John Meares in the restaurant of the hotel in which they were staying. Meares ordered his meal, and Morris requested a glass of water.

Morris was not in the restaurant to share a meal since his normal practice was to abstain from food for the duration of a crusade. Whenever he was on the road his habit was to spend most of his time either on a stage ministering or in his room sleeping and praying. He never went sightseeing, played golf, or engaged in other recreational sports while immersed in a crusade. It was common for him to spend five or six hours in prayer and study every day seeking the glory of God and specific guidance for the day's event.

When Morris left his family and home, it was for one purpose: to serve God in ministry events. Few people were more focused and dedicated to their calling.

While the two American ministers sat in the restaurant in Georgetown, the political turbulence continued outside. With the important national election drawing near, Cheddi Jagan, the communist candidate, was stirring up the masses, and the little country was in a state of general turmoil. In fact, Jagan happened to be in the capital city that day.

Sitting just a few feet from the ministers was a group of seven other Americans, also hotel guests. Their conversation drifted toward Morris and Bishop Meares, who listened with great interest.

"So the network sends us here to cover Jagan and the election," snarled one of the men, smoking his cigarette while describing his plight. "We fly the whole crew down here and show up at these events scheduled here and there with senators and other leaders speaking. No matter where we go around the city only a handful of the public shows up. I keep asking, 'Where is everybody?' and they all give me the same answer."

"What's that?" one of the Americans asked.

"That there's some guy named Cerullo, an American, who's down here, and he's doing some kind of religious event in Queen's Park. Apparently everybody is showing up there instead."

Meares smiled at Morris, held up a single finger, and got up from the table. He took a couple steps to the adjoining table, leaned over, and addressed the American journalists.

"You know, I couldn't help overhearing your conversation. I happen to be

Morris Cerullo's crusade manager. And you're right about the meetings in Queen's Park. Huge crowds. Big stuff. Would you like to meet him?"

The conversation took off, with the journalists expressing interest.

Meares pressed further. "I heard you say something about a network. Who do you guys work for?"

He almost fell over when he heard them say they represented NBC. As they then introduced each other he realized that the men sitting around the table worked for the nationally respected news anchors Chet Huntley and David Brinkley. They talked for a few more minutes before Meares had an inspired idea.

"Hey, you know, would you guys like to come to the crusade itself, and we could allow you to take some footage of the event?"

The newsmen jumped at the chance. The arrangements were made, and that evening NBC News filmed portions of the crusade, where tens of thousands of the Guyanans they'd been looking for were excitedly hearing about and receiving Christ.

The following evening, after a very brief summary of the political unrest and election in British Guyana, NBC Nightly News aired a segment on the evangelistic meetings of Morris Cerullo in the tiny South American nation.

Morris never did much to make a name for himself, but God consistently took care of that for him.

However, not everything was smooth sailing once they got the crusade up and running. A few days before the end of the crusade in British Guyana, a mix-up occurred, and Theresa, who was at home with the three children in San Diego, received a call from Bishop Meares's wife to come join Morris in South America.

CHAPTER 75

THE CALL FROM Mary Lou Meares caught Theresa off guard. She insisted that there must be a mix-up. She explained to Mary Lou that she and Morris had worked out a system that if there was ever to be a change in plans Morris would personally call Theresa to explain the change. She was certain that if Morris wanted her to join him in South America for some reason he would have called her directly.

The bishop's wife remained firm, however, noting that she had been told Morris did not make such a call because they had used all their funds on the crusade and could not afford the expensive international call. Instead he had asked that the request be passed along to her by their ministry friends. Mary Lou eventually convinced Theresa to make the arrangements to meet her in New York City, and they would fly down together.

But for Theresa to join her husband in British Guyana was no simple or easy task. First, she had to figure out how to scrape together the money. Then she needed to make arrangements to have someone take care of their three little children. She was understandably reluctant to simply leave them with neighbors or other people in town, so she decided to leave them with her mother in upstate New York. That, of course, meant bringing them on the cross-country trip to the airport three thousand miles away and getting the kids to grandma's house.

Once she figured out that plan Theresa had to get the affairs of the ministry in order so that everything would continue to run smoothly in her absence, especially since she did not know how long she might be gone.

Travel costs were substantial in those days, especially for international flights. After talking with a travel agent Theresa realized the only way she could afford it all was to take a train across country with the children before catching the flight to British Guyana. She booked the train tickets, packed up her things and then everything the children would need, and boarded the train. It took three days to get to Newburgh, New York.

Once she was in Newburgh she still did not have the funds for the trip south but figured God would provide a way. While she was waiting on the Lord Morris called.

"You're doing what?" he asked in shock. He had never requested her presence in British Guyana. In fact, the political climate was so unstable that he was angry that she was even contemplating the journey. Theresa, who had simply been responding to the information given to her by associates of his ministry colleagues, was miffed by his rebuke. Suddenly they found themselves in a tiff, and Morris hung up after scolding her for abandoning their plan not to change plans without direct communication and then for using poor judgment.

A soon as he hung up Morris knew he'd been wrong to scold Theresa. Feeling disappointed in himself, he immediately sat down and prayed. After a few minutes with the Lord he returned to the telephone and called Theresa back. He apologized and told her to join him as soon as she could, that he'd somehow arrange for a ticket to be waiting for her at the airport.

Later that day Theresa met Mary Lou Meares at LaGuardia Airport in New York City, and the two women travelled south. Upon reaching the immigration desk in Trinidad, their connection point en route to British Guyana, a customs official confronted her.

"Are you related to Morris Cerullo?" the government official casually asked her as he processed her passport.

After indicating that she was his wife, his face softened. "Oh my," he said, starting to softly weep, "I am so sorry. He was a great man."

"What are you talking about?" she demanded, alarms going off in her brain. "What do mean he *was* a great man? What's going on?"

"Oh my gosh. You have not heard?" he replied, now in full crying mode. "Your husband is dead. He was killed by the communists in British Guyana."

There sat Theresa, a young wife in a foreign country, separated from her husband, with three young children staying with her mother. How could this be true? They always knew that his work was dangerous, that Satan was on the lookout for ways to get Morris out of the picture, and that God could take him home at any moment.

But she had just spoken to him on the telephone hours earlier. Had the rebels in the little upstart nation fighting for independence truly murdered her husband?

With Mary Lou consoling her and the two of them praying non-stop, they had a fitful night of sleep in the dingy motel near the airport while they waited for their connecting flight scheduled for the following morning. They boarded the flight, hoping for the best but expecting the worst. After the puddle-jumper landed at Georgetown Airport in British Guyana's the capital city, Theresa weakly descended the exit stairs and reached the tarmac. As she did, she heard her name and looked up.

Morris was standing there smiling and waving to her.

Grateful and relieved, she ran over and hugged and kissed her husband on that tarmac. There was nobody in all of British Guyana happier at that moment than Theresa Cerullo.

CHAPTER 76

WORD SPREAD QUICKLY through the Christian community in the United States about Dr. Cerullo's ministry. He had the opportunity to meet many ministry leaders whom he had heard of but never had a chance to spend time with.

One such ministry leader was Demos Shakarian, who had founded a group called the Full Gospel Businessman's Fellowship International (FGBFI). Based in southern California, it was a growing ministry that reached out to men involved in the business world. Although it had started in America, it developed branches in countries throughout the world.

Shakarian loved tent-based evangelistic crusades. For years he had been sponsoring such events, at first in California and then in an ever-widening area. He personally invited Morris to hold a series of meetings in the impoverished Caribbean island of Haiti.

The motivation behind the crusade was to counteract the darkness of the Haitian Mardi Gras. Americans are familiar with the Mardi Gras in New Orleans every year. The version in Haiti dwarfs it—in duration, participation, and depravity. Every year Haiti's Mardi Gras occurs on seven consecutive Sundays. The revelry features open drunkenness, sexual debauchery, and widespread displays of witchcraft and voodoo that would startle the typical American. The year that Morris was in Haiti more than five thousand women were reportedly raped, yet no police action was taken to address the allegations. Perhaps that was because the real power on the island belonged to its legion of witch doctors.

Although the Cerullo team had substantially improved their international event planning procedures and they were able to enhance the efficiency with which they used their available funds, Morris arrived on the island insufficiently versed in the nuances of the local culture. For instance, he knew next to nothing about voodoo, superstitions, and the related "black magic" practices.

Morris was aware that most Haitians described themselves as Catholic and many regularly attended Catholic church services, but he was ignorant of the power that witch doctors had in Haiti. The people of the island believed deeply in the power of voodoo and witchcraft and feared the witch doctors.

It wasn't long before Morris was confronted with a difficult reality: Haitians were more apt to believe in the power of voodoo than the power of God. They were certainly more apt to follow the instructions of a witch doctor than those provided by a Catholic priest, a Christian minister, or even the Bible.

Morris agreed to lead a five-day crusade scheduled to take place in the large soccer stadium in the center of the capital city, Port-au-Prince, during the middle of the Mardi Gras season in 1960. Once the advertising began for the crusade—churches alerting their congregants to the coming event, posters hung throughout the island, newspaper articles published—the island's witch doctors became upset and began to plot how they would attack Morris, his team, and his event.

With the team having become more sophisticated in its international event planning, Morris was looking forward to the event. His airplane landed in Port-au-Prince, and he was met on the tarmac by a bevy of dignitaries and high-ranking officials. After numerous introductions and greetings, the entire assembly filed into a line of black limousines that were standing by. The motorcade proceeded from the airport toward the center of the city, where a parade down the main streets had been planned. Haiti's president, François Duvalier, also known as Papa Doc, had invited the Businessmen and the MCWE team to the island and wanted to be sure his guests received a royal welcome.

Before even reaching the limo, though, Morris knew something was wrong. He could not identify the problem, but he was sure that something was off. Not wanting to offend his hosts, he agreed to participate in the motorcade. Yet, the closer they got to the center of the city the more physically ill Morris felt.

Finally he asked one of the team members riding in the limo with him and several dignitaries to tell the driver that he had to go to the hotel immediately. He felt a desperate need to be alone with God to pray. After a little fuss, Morris's limo left the motorcade and delivered him to his hotel.

After they escorted him to his room and departed, Morris fell to the floor. He couldn't move. He wondered if he was dying.

Virtually paralyzed on the cold tile floor, Morris did what he always did when anything was not clear to him: he prayed.

"Lord, what is happening? Why do I feel this way? What's wrong?"

Immediately God spoke into the spirit of the stricken evangelist: "Son, this is not a physical sickness. It is a spiritual discernment you are experiencing. I have allowed this to happen for a reason. Listen carefully.

"This evening there is going to be trouble. Many religious leaders here are opposing your meetings. There are hundreds of witch doctors who are angry that you are here and furious about what you have come to do.

"Tonight, they will come to kill you. They intend to stop the meeting."

Morris had never had an attempt like this on his life before—at least not that he was aware of. In spite of the magnitude of the danger, he felt no fear or even anxiety. Oddly, he felt relieved to know the problem—and comforted by the fact that his heavenly Father was sharing the information with him. He did not consider postponing or canceling the event. He felt this would be a serious but exhilarating opportunity to showcase the power of God.

After a few moments of silence, as Morris pondered what he had been told, he responded, "Lord, thank You for telling me. If I'm supposed to die, that's fine. You know I will surely be a martyr for Your sake. If that is Your will, it is alright with me. But what should I do?"

Unknown to him at the time, this was simply the first of numerous times when Morris's life would be threatened due to a pending outreach meeting. In every instance, his response would be the same.

It would be fair to say that God had Morris's attention. He then revealed how He wished Morris to proceed, even describing who would be there to murder him, how to identify them within the massive crowd expected to attend, and how to respond.

"Son, the word that you speak will be exactly as if I had spoken it, and that word will come to pass."

Morris was awed by the depth of trust God was placing in His servant. He did not interpret it to mean that he had earned any special standing but rather that later that day he would have the weighty responsibility of wielding the power of life and death through his words to the crowd.

If there were ever a time when it was paramount to "abide in Him," this was it.

As Morris and the Lord continued their dialogue, he grasped the fact that God's will was for everyone at the event—including those who intended to kill Morris—to know the true God and be saved through the power of Christ's resurrection. But—and this was a big *but*—He made it clear that if a few antagonists were blocking the people from receiving salvation He would not stand for that kind of opposition.

He made it clear that Morris had the right and the power to do what was necessary for the gospel to go forth.

In a short while Morris was physically restored. He began to prepare for the evening's event.

Then there was a knock on his hotel room door.

CHAPTER 77

———◆———

STANDING IN THE doorway was the group of ministers who were part of the host committee for the meetings. One look at their faces revealed that something was of deep concern to them.

Morris knew that look: fear.

Without a word being spoken Morris knew his hosts firmly believed in the power of the witch doctors. Morris needed to know if they believed in the power of black magic more than the power of the living God.

The answer was quickly revealed.

One of the men stepped forward to speak for the group. His brow was creased with worry, and he spoke quickly but softly. He had trouble keeping Morris's gaze. "Brother Cerullo, we don't want to tell you what to do, but we don't think you should have a Sunday night meeting. It will conflict with the Mardi Gras celebration. In Haiti, that is the most important celebration of the year. The witch doctors will not like it if you interrupt that celebration with a gospel meeting. Already they have torn down your posters all over Haiti."

There was a general murmur of agreement from the other men standing beside him. He cleared his throat before sharing the information he found most disturbing.

"Some of your posters they have burned in effigy. The only posters they have left up are the ones where they have poked your picture with their voodoo pins, which they believe will inflict actual harm on you. Already they are calling their evil spirits down on you to keep you from conducting the meetings."

The murmurs from the group rose in both volume and intensity after he said this. A couple of them looked directly at Morris, their eyes opened wide with fear.

"If you decide to have Sunday meetings we will come with you," the minister stated firmly, adding the all-important conclusion, "but we don't think you should."

It was a tense moment for the Haitians as they stood between a rock and a hard place—telling their invited guest that they no longer wanted him to do what he had flown six thousand miles and spent months of time and thousands of dollars preparing to do. They were essentially admitting that they did not have enough faith to trust in the power of God to protect and provide.

Meanwhile, Morris paused to think about how to gently explain that there was no decision to be made. Before he could begin his response, though, one of the two Americans in the group spoke up.

"Friends, let me tell you something about Brother Cerullo," said C C Ford, a friend of Morris's and one of the executive directors of the Full Gospel Businessmen who had flown to Haiti with Demos Shakarian and the MCWE team. His tone was gentle and reassuring. "One thing about him you will come to understand is that he is not consecrated unto life."

Ford paused to allow the Haitians to consider that bold statement. The response was a lineup of puzzled looks on the faces of the ministers. They waited for him to explain what he meant.

"Brother Cerullo is consecrated unto death. He has no fear of death and no fear of your witch doctors."

Morris grinned, both flattered by Ford's insight into his calling and pleased that such a succinct explanation had been given at that tender moment. Morris was prepared to die for the gospel that night, or any night, if that were God's will. It certainly wasn't his preference, but his primary interest was obedience to God. From his conversation with the Lord just minutes earlier Morris knew that he was obliged to hold the meetings regardless of the consequences.

As he stood there watching the Haitians process this information Morris related in a new, profoundly personal way to what the apostle Paul must have been thinking when he wrote in Philippians 1:21, "For to me, living means living for Christ, and dying is even better."

Paul was a man of action, a disciple who pushed for results. He certainly did not have a death wish, but he also understood that physical death was not the end of the road; he would wake up in heaven face to face with the King of all creation.

That was exactly what Morris believed and how he felt. As long as he remained faithful to God's calling he was in a win-win situation: lead a successful evangelistic event or die for the sake of the Cross and spend eternity with God in paradise.

The Haitian group nodded their heads silently to indicate they understood the situation, though they didn't seem convinced it was the right perspective. Nevertheless, they bowed and stated their respect for the decision to hold the meetings.

As they filed out to allow Morris time to finish preparing, several of them were thinking how sad it was that this would be the last day on Earth for this fine young man who had travelled so far to help their country in service to Jesus.

Morris had a bounce in his step as he dressed and gathered his things. This was the real deal. This was where the rubber met the road, the front lines of the spiritual battle that raged for the souls of men. Could his life be any more exciting?

He had a promise from God and a date with destiny!

CHAPTER 78

————•————

THE SPIRITUAL SHOWDOWN was going to be witnessed by every class of people that resided in Haiti.

The stage was packed with nearly two hundred dignitaries and high-ranking military officials, many of them sitting with their wives. The nation's controversial president himself, François Duvalier, had invited them to hold the event, and everyone who was someone wanted to be seen at the spectacle. The military leaders were decked out in their full dress uniforms, complete with the array of medals, ribbons, and other symbols of their skill and courage. The political leaders, not to be outdone, were in their finest evening-gwear and eager to be seen by the crowd.

The stadium was filled with about fifteen thousand people on that opening night. They were by far the loudest and wildest assembly that Morris had ever faced.

What made the crowd so unusual was their constant noise and activity. In the 1950s and early 1960s, church crowds everywhere practiced a reverent silence during religious services and events.

The memo on such behavior apparently never reached Haiti. The crowd was a study of turbulence and chaos. Everywhere you looked people were in motion. Some were laughing and jeering, others were seeking to stir up trouble, and yet others were simply waving their arms to gain attention or making strange noises.

Many of them knew what was coming—or so they thought. They were pointing at Morris as he took his seat on the stage and began shouting and laughing.

They knew the witch doctors were ready to rumble.

There were some three hundred witch doctors wandering slowly and intently through the large crowd. To the untrained eye they were simply Haitians who had shown up for the big event, part of the intrigued masses.

But as Morris sat through the mind-numbing introductions of the seemingly endless number of esteemed people on the stage, he was able to pick out every one of the witch doctors. God showed him each one; they could not hide from his perusal of the audience. It was as if they had been sprayed in an invisible paint that only Morris could see. He watched with interest as they filtered through the crowd and people quickly gave them space to move. Nobody wanted to mess with the witch doctors.

Finally Morris was introduced. The unruliness decreased a notch or two as the main event was poised to begin.

Morris took the microphone at center stage and raised his right hand, holding his Bible, and said, "I greet you tonight in the name that is above every name, Jesus Christ, Son of the living God."

The uproar that ensued was as if he had declared war against Haiti.

An eerie chant rose from every section of the stadium. The witch doctors, who had clearly orchestrated their plan in advance, sang out the same chant from every corner of the arena.

People's eyes grew wide with fear or concern. Heads turned back and forth, watching the man of God on the stage and the closest bevy of witch doctors as they steadily increased the volume of their chant.

A person here, another one there, then small groups of people and eventually larger numbers of onlookers joined in the chanting, giving a massive voice to the cry of the voodoo masters.

The witch doctors began to move about the stadium heading toward the platform where Morris stood watching them.

"Everyone, please be quiet. I have life-changing things to share with you tonight. I ask for your attention please."

For a moment the movement and noise in the stadium came to a halt. For a moment. Then it accelerated in both volume and pace.

Game on!

From the twitching and bodily repositioning taking place among the officials on stage behind him, Morris knew that the nation's leaders were getting nervous. If past events were an indication of what was to come, their concern was well-founded.

Again Morris politely but firmly requested silence so he could proceed.

Again the movement and noise ceased for a moment and then reignited. The volume of the chanting continued to grow as more people joined in and people's sense of security grew. The chanting reached a point at which it was difficult for anyone to hear what Morris was saying into the microphone.

His third call for silence drew a third moment of quiet followed by a more vociferous resumption of the chants.

By now some of the dignitaries on the platform were scoping out their exit route in case the stadium broke out in a riot. Even the host pastors looked frightened and appeared to be calculating ways to escape. To everyone's consternation, there was no escape path, however, because the platform was surrounded by people.

As Morris watched this unruly mob begin to lose control a sense of righteous indignation rose up within him like none he had ever experienced. The Holy Spirit had taken command of his mind and emotions and was about to change the course of Haitian history.

Morris's interpreter for the meeting was a young student from a local

Bible school. With fire in his eyes, Morris turned to the youngster and sternly pointed his index finger at him. "Son," he shouted above the din of the chanting witch doctors and Haitian crowd, "I want you to interpret exactly what I say—every word! Do not dare change a single word. Not one syllable!"

With that, he turned his full attention to the crowd and began his presentation.

Morris's eyes had gone steely, and his voice was hard and unwavering.

"People of Haiti, this is the last time I am going to speak. I have asked for reverence and quiet three times now to be able to give you God's Word.

"I want you to know that it was not my decision to come to Haiti. God sent me here. The true and living God sent me to you.

"He sent me to Haiti to share with you the message of His love. He gave me a message of healing for you. He loves you. He wants to save you. He wants to forgive your sins, to bless you and heal you. That is the message He sent me here to bring to you.

"But that God is also a God of judgment."

Morris paused and took account of the crowd. They were still restless and chanting, but the volume had decreased, and people were beginning to focus on his words.

"Today, in my room, God showed me that there were hundreds of witch doctors who would be here tonight to disrupt this meeting." He pointed to some of the red-shirted witch doctors who were circling the platform. "I am going to be here in this city for some time, so we had better find out tonight—this first night—whether you and your devil have more power than me and my God!"

It was as if a boxer pushed into a corner of the ring had thrown a strong punch back into the face of the aggressor: people's attention was now riveted on the man who was calling out the witch doctors in no uncertain terms. Morris's nostrils flared as God's indignation poured out of him. He turned to look at the dignitaries who were uncomfortably shifting in the seats on the platform.

"I now serve notice that I take no responsibility for what happens from this point on. The *next person in this stadium* who opens their mouth and says one word to hinder or destroy this meeting, I will take no responsibility before all these dignitaries on the platform when they carry you out of this stadium *dead!*"

Immediately the stadium was filled with silence. The chanting stopped. The bodily movement ceased. The air grew still. You couldn't even hear the usual ambient noise, like crickets chirping.

To the amazement of thousands in the crowd, even the witch doctors seemed unwilling to test the fury of God for disrupting His service.

Satisfied, Morris spent the next twenty minutes preaching a powerful message of salvation. He was indisputably under the anointing of God as he spoke to the now-silent throngs.

As he completed his message, a piercing scream from the far end of the stadium cut through the evening air, causing many to gasp in shock—or fear.

CHAPTER 79

————•————

THE BACK OF the stadium suddenly erupted into a mass of commotion that slowly swept its way toward the platform, where Morris passively stood his ground.

A smattering of officials on the stage rose from their seats to get a better look at what was happening. A dozen feet in front of them stood Morris, narrowing his eyes to get a fix on what was coming.

What they witnessed was many people with their hands over their heads passing a little baby over the top of the crowd, one by one, carefully but quickly propelling the prone baby toward the platform.

The stadium once again exploded in yelling and general chaos.

Morris turned to his left and asked his young interpreter what was happening.

"Brother Cerullo," the boy responded without shifting his gaze from the center of the action, "while you were preaching a child back there who was born blind can now see and was grabbing for his parents' eyes, nose, ears, and head. The place is going wild."

They continued to move the child toward the platform, passing her over the heads of the people row after row until the tiny body reached the front of the stadium.

Morris looked down at the baby held aloft in the front row and smiled.

The little girl was gaping in confusion at her unusual journey through the stadium crowd. The poor child had never seen anything before, and suddenly she was being passed through the hands of total strangers amidst shrieks of awe and fear with the bright stadium lights illuminating her path to the platform.

Meanwhile, her startled and unsettled parents were doing their best to push through the humanity that had spilled into the aisles of the stadium during the pandemonium that had broken loose. When they, too, reached the end of the line at the foot of the platform they retrieved their daughter and waved their fingers in front of her eyes. For the first time in her life she followed their fingers everywhere.

Suddenly she changed her focus from the fingers to the closest face, which turned out to be her father's face. A big smile took over her face as noticed her daddy's nose and started grabbing for it. Her father, tears in his eyes, smiled and laughed along with her as she played with his nose. Beside them, the girl's mother was worshiping God in Creole, the Haitian language, while tears of joy drenched her face.

Suddenly, a prestigious official seated in the front row behind Morris jumped to his feet and started yelling in Creole.

"What's he saying?" Morris asked his interpreter.

"He's saying, 'Oh my God! That's my neighbors.'"

Word was circulating throughout the stadium about the miracle the white man's God had performed on the little girl.

So far the witch doctors had managed to do nothing but chant.

But the show wasn't over yet.

In another part of the stadium word started to spread of another supernatural healing. Then from the opposite side of the crowd another miracle was identified. In just a few minutes' time there was no zone in the entire stadium where some miracle had not been discovered.

Healing dozens of people's ailments and diminishing the stature and iron grip of the witch doctors would have been spectacular enough. Such a demonstration of love and power would have driven thousands of those present to their knees with droves seeking forgiveness and salvation.

But God was not done that evening.

The spotlight returned to the witch doctors, but not in the way they had planned.

The black magic practitioners still stood out in the crowd because of the red shirts they had donned. Now, many of them were visibly weeping as they watched the little blind girl receive her sight and bask in the beauty of the world God had created.

Throughout the stadium other witch doctors could be seen falling to their knees with their heads thrown back and their arms lifted high, crying out to Jesus Christ to save their wretched souls. They sought forgiveness for manipulating the people and for holding them in the grip of fear. They sought God's grace for their masquerading as agents of power and for blocking people from the true power source.

The breaking of the witch doctors' stronghold opened the floodgates for revival that evening. Morris seized the microphone again and issued a powerful altar call that was heeded by thousands of people. The stream of converts included a number of the government and military officials who had been sitting behind Morris all night.

CHAPTER 80

ORT-AU-PRINCE WAS ABUZZ the next day as word of the electrifying events in the stadium became the talk of the city.

The following evening the size of the crowd inside the stadium more than doubled, filling the arena to its capacity of thirty-five thousand.

The challenge match, however, was not over. The witch doctors may have been diminished on night one of the crusade, but changing a culture doesn't happen overnight.

On the second evening the sky was menacing, with a thick layer of heavy-looking gray clouds hanging over the stadium. It seemed certain to burst into rain at any moment.

Morris had anticipated an upbeat, high-energy crowd on the second night. He was perplexed when he found the assembled people very reserved. Upon mentioning his surprise to one of the host pastors, the Haitian explained that his countrymen were very superstitious people, and being rained upon was a sign of bad luck.

Just before Morris took the microphone to present the gospel the clouds turned dark and ominous. Without warning, large numbers of people began to run toward the exits, desperate not be rained upon and suffer the consequences of bad luck.

Not even realizing what he was doing, Morris leaped to the microphone and shouted into it, "In the name of Jesus I command you to stop running and stand still!" His interpreter quickly repeated the phrase to the audience.

As soon as Morris's words echoed into every corner of the stadium everyone stood still and looked up at the man on the stage. The result looked like a children's game where the music stops and everyone must freeze in place.

Morris was under a powerful, irresistible anointing from the Lord again that night. Seeing the cessation of the frenetic movement toward the exits, he issued the next command.

"Now, in the name of Jesus, turn around and look at me." When the crowd obeyed in unison he finished his command: "Do you see those dark clouds above our heads?" Nearly every head in the stadium jerked upward and gazed at the clouds pregnant with rain. "Now you are going to know what kind of prophet of God I am. *It will not rain* until this service is over!"

Whether they were curious, scared, or hopeful, nobody else left the arena. They sat down, and Morris began to preach. For the next ninety-plus minutes he held them spellbound with stories about the compassion and love of God and offered a simple but profound understanding of how their lives could be changed forever that evening.

When he finished Morris gave a salvation call and prayed for the sick, the blind, the deaf, and the crippled. As had happened the previous evening, dozens upon dozens of people experienced miraculous healings. Thousands of people prayed to receive Jesus as their Savior.

Before leaving for the evening Dr. Cerullo gave one final instruction. "People of Haiti, this service is over. After I pray, if you don't want to get wet you should leave quickly, because it's going to rain."

He closed the service in prayer and people moved out of the stadium quickly.

Less than fifteen minutes later the clouds burst open, and a torrential rainstorm drenched the stadium.

CHAPTER 81

THE FIVE-DAY COMMITMENT originally made by Morris turned into a three-week marathon of nightly meetings. Morris spent most of his time during the day resting, praying, and studying the Bible. Although the meetings went better than anyone could have expected—dozens of witch doctors and thousands of Haitians gave their lives to Jesus—every day was an epic battle of supernatural forces. The evil one does not give in easily, and despite the early victories God had claimed through Morris's efforts, the intensity of the battle never let up.

On the Wednesday after the crusade had begun several members of the host committee approached Morris.

"Brother Cerullo," one of the men said, "the leading witch doctor in Port-au-Prince wants to speak to you. He is the man whom all the other witch doctors answer to, and they greatly fear him. He has seen what is going on and has requested a private meeting with you."

Morris quickly agreed, and the others dispersed to set up the meeting. Even though Morris had no idea what to expect, he knew that he would enter the get-together with the power of God behind him. It might be his best opportunity to lead the voodoo master to Christ.

The trio of event organizers drove Morris to the witch doctor's house, located in the middle of the city. As they were ushered through the entryway into a meeting room Morris observed the countless voodoo items placed in strategic locations throughout the man's home. Morris had never seen many of the objects before and had no idea what most of them were or how they were used in the dark arts, but he knew they had received plenty of use in keeping Haitians in spiritual bondage.

After the introductions had been made and everyone was seated the voodoo chief told an amazing story. The witch doctor and his entire family had attended the meetings held earlier in the week. He had been among those who planned to kill Morris and had led the chanting and ominous marching around the stadium by the assembled witch doctors. Morris spied the red shirt that had been worn by the voodoo practitioners laying over the back of a chair at the far end of the room.

The voodoo man gave a gentle smile to Morris as he paid the evangelist a compliment. "You were very brave to stand on the stage and challenge us like you did," he began. "We did not expect such boldness. Yes, you certainly surprised us," he repeated, his eyes crinkling into a little chuckle.

Morris and his group still had no idea where this was going. Was he preparing to put a spell on them? Were his fellow magicians surrounding the house, about to pull some evil stunt? Did the chief want to have a private power challenge with the man of God away from the glare of the spotlight?

His next words shocked them all.

"Yes, you really surprised us. We have been controlling the power here for a long time. Your meeting was life changing." He paused, not to be dramatic but as if reliving part of the event in his mind. "The power of God was undeniable and mesmerizing. Your teachings, my friend, about the love and majesty of the Creator God were powerful."

Again he paused and then offered a toothy smile. "My whole family and I have dedicated our lives to Jesus now," he said. Morris and his colleagues joined in his smile, and it seemed as if a wave of relief washed over them. There would be no confrontation of powers in the voodoo man's home, only the joy of victory for the kingdom of God. Another great miracle to celebrate!

"What should I do now?" the man asked Morris.

Without a moment's hesitation the man of God replied, "Let's clean up your house."

The plan was to rid the home of every tool or representation of evil that they could find. The man and his family belonged to the Lord now; there was no reason to display tools of the devil in a house inhabited by disciples of Christ. Those items had now been stripped of their power in the family's life, so it was time to physically destroy them.

Morris and his small crew joined with the former spell master and meticulously went through every room in his house collecting the relics, fetishes, and other charms related to his voodoo practice. The items were placed in a giant pile in the street directly in front of his house. As the pile grew the people in the neighborhood ceased their normal activities and stood around watching this curious episode. Some watched furtively from behind drawn blinds in the home, still fearful of inciting the witch doctor. Others were bolder, standing on the sidewalk or leaning on cars parked by the side of the road, watching the parade of paraphernalia.

It took a while, but finally the men were convinced they had collected the full array of voodoo items. At Morris's suggestion they then doused the pile with gasoline, lit the articles on fire, and marched around the giant bonfire singing, "What can wash away my sins? Nothing but the blood of Jesus!"

Perhaps nobody enjoyed the celebration more than the ex-voodoo chief. People gathered closer to watch his face—one whose scowl had caused shudders of fear and anxieties over supernatural retribution but who now was beaming with joy as he sang the old church song while the tools of his former trade were torched to ashes. Some of the bystanders had no idea what was going on. Others clearly received the message.

The God of Israel was defeating the false gods of Haiti.

The crusade continued to gain momentum, so much so that by the end of the second week the revered Mardi Gras had dwindled in size and energy to become almost irrelevant. So many thousands of people had given their lives to Christ that those who practiced voodoo or reveled in the debauchery of the Mardi Gras celebration felt uncomfortable practicing their lewd ways in public. Police reported that the number of rapes, thefts, and instances of drunkenness dropped to record low levels.

CHAPTER 82

—◆—

A FTER THREE WEEKS of crusades in Port-au-Prince some Haitian pastors converged upon Morris to ask if he would conduct a meeting in Cape Haitian on another part of the island. Exhausted and anxious to return home, he graciously rejected the offer. But the men persisted, not aware that Morris had a soft spot in his heart for pastors. They emphasized that it was the second largest population center on the island but did not have a single Christian church; the people *needed* him to present the gospel. Finally, without fully knowing what he was agreeing to but feeling led by God to accept, he and his team prepared for the journey.

The drive to Cape Haitian was brutal. As usual, the temperature was in triple digits, and the humidity was off the charts. There were no paved roads, so Morris sat in an open Jeep under the blazing sun, bouncing here and there, trying to stay focused on his prayer time with God.

Some eight hours into the journey they saw a hut with a small red box to the left of the front door. The swirling white letters on the box read Coca-Cola. The Jeep slowed down and pulled up next to the hut. Everyone in the caravan followed suit. As the men stretched, a young black boy lumbered through the doorway.

Bishop Meares, who had accompanied Morris on the trip to serve as the crusade director, spied the red box and called out to him, "Brother, would you like a Coke?"

Morris yelled in the affirmative, and the Bishop paid the price to the teenager. He spoke no English, so the trip interpreter explained the desire to the boy. He pulled a longneck bottle from the red box and brought it over to Morris. He jumped when he wrapped his hand around the refreshment; it was burning hot. It had been sitting in the box all day under the scorching sun. There was no electricity available for miles around. The teen from the hut had probably never heard of refrigeration.

The boy pulled a bottle-top opener from his pocket and flipped the aluminum top to the ground. Morris thanked him, a sentiment passed along by the interpreter. He then turned to the interpreter and asked him to pose a question to the young man.

"Please ask him if he knows Jesus."

The interpreter looked at the Haitian pastors for approval. He was taken aback by the simple question. Haitians are not as forward as Americans when it comes to discussing their religious views.

The Haitian pastors looked at each other, and then one of them accepted the challenge. He turned to the boy from the hut and said in their native language, "This white man is from America. He has a question. He wants to know if you know Jesus."

The boy looked at Morris. "Jesus? Is that another soft drink from America, like Coca-Cola?"

Heartbroken, Morris put his bottle of Coke back in the hot, red Coca-Cola box without taking a sip. Returning to the Jeep, he turned his back to them and silently wept. Coca-Cola had managed to penetrate the jungles and plains of Haiti, but the church had not yet figured out how to share the good news of what Jesus had done for these people.

He left that hut more determined than ever to hold a mighty series of meetings in Cap Haitian. He realized he alone could do nothing, but he was willing to do whatever God would allow to bless the Haitians in God's name.

Two hours later Morris and his colleagues arrived in Cape Haitian energized about the possibilities of bringing the good news of the gospel to thousands of spiritually isolated people. His fatigue had been replaced by a God-given zeal to see the shroud of darkness and deception lifted in that region.

Several days of life-changing meetings followed in Cape Haitian.

Haiti, a country wracked by poverty and kept enslaved by the voodoo masters, was given a reprieve by God. The nation was offered a chance to restore its soul.

PART FIVE:

———◆———

A NEW MANDATE

CHAPTER 83

———•———

EVEN AFTER RECEIVING the vision from God to tirelessly preach the gospel and spending years traveling throughout the United States and other countries of the world, Morris still felt humbled by his calling, excited by how God had been using him, awed by the power of God demonstrated through hundreds of miracles every year, and overwhelmed by the need for spiritual insight around the world.

He constantly reminded those around him that even though his ministry had experienced much success it was not the work of a man but that of the Lord. Things were going very well.

And yet he had an uneasy feeling that he couldn't quite explain.

The more he reflected on the mechanics of his ministry, the more things came into focus. He and his team had made the planning and preparation aspects of their outreach efforts quite efficient. The administrative elements of his ministry were run on a shoestring. The thousands of people who accepted Christ at the crusades were personally prayed for and given a printed copy of the Gospel of John to read. They were encouraged to connect with a local church. In many parts of the world the ministry had even started new churches for the many converts, ensuring that they would have a gospel-preaching church to attend. From the home office, MCWE attempted to stay in contact with those who made decisions for Christ, continuing to encourage them in their newfound faith.

But deep in his spirit Morris knew that even those efforts were not enough. He had heard too many stories and seen too many statistics indicating that the excitement about Jesus that was birthed at a crusade simply faded away after the event. Some churches did not do an effective job at following up on the new converts. Sometimes the converts themselves invested little time or energy in their own spiritual growth.

The more he prayed about it, the more Morris knew that meeting that challenge would be the next big step in his ministry.

CHAPTER 84

W ITH THAT CHALLENGE on his heart he prepared for a crusade in a huge complex in Porto Alegre, Brazil, a place called the Exposition Grounds. It was to be the first open-air crusade in their history. The Assemblies of God churches were excited about the event and prayed for a strong turnout.

As usual, the number of people attending grew larger as the ten-day event wore on. God was doing tremendous miracles each night, and the word spread quickly. Newspapers were giving the miracles front-page coverage. By the midpoint of his stay people were streaming into Porto Alegre from the entire region. Many people, especially the poor farmers and plantation workers, walked from their farms or were carried in ox carts. Sick people were waiting by the roadside lying on a couch or mattress hoping to catch a glimpse of God's healer. Thousands of hopeful people lined the streets en route to the stadium.

A team of doctors had been brought in from a local medical college to verify the healings. A person seeking a miracle would be examined before Morris prayed for them and then again afterward. The doctors would then file a report about the healing, and the person blessed by God would give a personal testimony. The process was carried out for the duration of the crusade.

Halfway through the meetings, on the morning before that evening's event, Morris was in an intense prayer time with God. He felt His presence in an especially powerful way and was confident that God would minister in a special manner that day. He remained in that prayer connection until the time the service started, then quickly dressed and was driven to the stadium.

The service was underway by the time he arrived. He watched as the crowd swayed in rhythm with the worship music. Morris sensed an unusually strong presence of God's Spirit in their midst. Even though there were more than fifty thousand people present, the crowd experienced a level of intimacy and unity that fostered an atmosphere of praise and trust. There was a palpable sense of hope that lifted Morris's anticipation of what would take place.

It was a typically hot and sticky Brazilian evening when Claire Hutchins, his crusade director, introduced Morris and invited him to take the microphone. The crowd had gone quiet waiting to hear what words God had for them through His American servant.

The makeshift stage creaked as the evangelist strode to the microphone.

Morris as a young boy.

Morris standing outside the Daughters of Miriam Orphanage where God reached down and brought him the message of salvation.

In a vision, Morris saw the manifested glory of God! During a vision at the young age of 15, God took him into the heavens, where he had a supernatural encounter that forever changed the course of his life and ministry.

Morris and Theresa when they were dating.
"The moment I saw her I knew she was the one!"

Morris and Theresa cutting their
wedding cake at their reception
surrounded by family and friends.

A young Morris during his
Bible School years.

The New York Metropolitan Bible School in Suffern, New York where Morris and Theresa attended Bible School.

Morris and his young bride Theresa ready to reach the world for Jesus!

Morris Cerullo during his early ministry.

Morris holding Mark, David (standing), Theresa and Susan

Young Evangelist Morris Cerullo

In the mid-1950's Morris conducted large tent crusades. The crusades grew so big that he and Theresa bought a tent seating 6,000, and a tractor trailer to put it in. This is the tractor trailer that carried the huge 120' x 240' tent from city to city.

One of the many revival posters used to advertise the crusades.

God's miracle power was released during Morris'
1960 Washington D.C. Crusade in the shadow of
the Washington Monument and U.S. Capitol.

Morris personally visited President Dwight D. Eisenhower during the 1964–
1965 Bibles for the Nations Crusade and presented him a Deeper Life Bible.

When Morris presented the Deeper Life Bible to
General William C. Westmoreland, he said,
"This is the greatest gift I could ever receive."

Morris holds crutches and canes that were no longer
needed as God's miracle power swept through the
audience during the 1965 Fortaleza, Brazil crusade.

1966 Rosario, Argentina—Morris and team stopped from entering the stadium
at gunpoint! Morris, Claire Hutchens, Argemiro Figueiro, and Alex Ness are
stopped and barred from entering the stadium where the crusade was to be held.

Morris and Argemiro Figueiro being escorted by Police in
Corrientes, Argentina. Morris faced a three and one half hour
trial facing accusations brought against him by the College
of Doctors for "practicing medicine without a license"!

"My boy can see! My boy can see!" Morris tests ten-year old Freddy who had lost his eyesight in his left eye in an accident four years prior to this 1966 Morris Cerullo Crusade. On Tuesday night as Morris prayed the miracle prayer for the blind, his eye was healed and he had perfect vision.

1983 Costa Rica—Central America School of Ministry and Crusade: 40,000 pack the stadium, thousands are saved, as a wave of God's miracle power released! 1,300 National leaders trained as part of God's Army.

1998—Guayaquil, Ecuador. Thousands accept Christ during the Morris Cerullo crusade. A miracle explosion took place with wheelchairs and crutches being passed over the heads of the people onto the stage. Morris has always said, "This is not the work of a man, but this is the work of the Holy Spirit"

2007: Manaus, Brazil. Over 45,000 Nationals came to be trained and equipped to reach their cities and bring in a harvest of souls in Brazil.

Like a modern-day Apostle Paul, Dr. Cerullo was used by God to break open the nation of Mexico. During Morris' first meeting in Mexico, over 15,000 people jammed the Tijuana Bull Ring.

During the 1989 Mexico Journey of Love over 200,000 reached with 40,000 decisions for Christ in two weeks of meetings.

Morris joined by his friend, Evangelist Reinhard Bonnke (center), Mexican church leaders, J. Guadalupe Reyes (far left), and Apostle Carlos Quiroa, Chairman of the Mexico City outreach.

1973: Nairobi, Kenya. During the Africa crusade and School of Evangelism, Morris prayed the Sinners' Prayer with over 20,000 Africans. There were 35,000 in the final service, and God's miracle power was released in every service with hundreds of miracles taking place. Three hundred Nationals attended the School of Evangelism.

Liberia 1969—President W. S. Tubman—In 1969, during Morris Cerullo's trip to Liberia, he was privileged to meet with President William S. Tubman, who, for twenty-five years, had successfully governed his people. President Tubman took such an interest in the crusade that he personally went on record as sponsoring the crusade.

1978 Ghana—President Edward Akufo-Addo

GOD HAS USED DR. CERULLO TO IMPACT MANY WORLD LEADERS, INCLUDING THESE SIX AFRICAN PRESIDENTS.

Tanzania—1995 President Ali Hassan Mwinyi—
"I thank God for sending Morris to Tanzania to unite us!"

1997 Ghana—President Jerry Rawlings

1997 Nigeria—President Olusegun Obasajo

1997 Uganda—President Lt. Gen. Yoweri Kaguta Museveni

1997 Ivory Coast—President Laurent Gbagbo

1999 Kenya—President Daniel Arap Moi

Morris on the grounds of the Pan-African National
Training Institute in Nairobi, Kenya, during the
first East African Deeper Life Conference.

1987 Kinshasa, Democratic Republic of the Congo (formerly Zaire),
100,000 saved, 3,500 Nationals trained. In Morris Cerullo's first
major outreach to French-speaking Africa, an estimated 300,000,
nearly 25 percent of the population of the city, attended the crusade.

1969 Taipei, Taiwan: Morris conducts largest Christian meeting in the history of the nation at that time. 80 percent of the audiences each night responded to accept Christ as their Savior. The stadium was packed every night with people hungry to hear the Word. They came expecting to receive their miracles.

In what was the largest religious gathering in the history of Sulawesi Island; Morris leading the people who have come forward to a point of decision.

1974 Medan, Indonesia: God's miracle power penetrates Sumatra Island—crowds estimated as high as 80,000 in a single service. 75 percent of the people accepted Christ!

1979 Jakarta, Indonesia Crusade: The stadium was
packed with an estimated 200,000 people.

Seoul, South Korea: Historic meeting between two generals of the faith! During his 2014
Mission to Southeast Asia and South Korea, Dr. Cerullo met Dr. Yonggi Cho, one of the
greatest church builders in the history of the Church. During this historic meeting, they
prayed and ministered to one another. Dr. Cho stated that when he ministers throughout
the world, Dr. Cerullo's opening of nations once closed to the Gospel is still felt today.

1977 More than 6,000 packed the historic Royal Albert Hall in London, England; 1,000 stood in the gallery; and over 1,000 were turned away during the greater London Crusade and 10th European Deeper Life Conference.

1991—a total of 45,000 packed Moscow's Olympic Stadium during the three-day 1991 Miracle Crusade.

A spiritual first for Russia! 1990: Moscow, Russia—Dr. Cerullo during an interview on Moscow News, leading viewers in the Sinners' Prayer over prime-time television.

Morris with well-known singer, Pearl Bailey, who co-hosted several
HelpLine programs and participated in counseling some of the thousands
who called in on special telephone lines for prayer and help.

2006—New Morris Cerullo prime-time HelpLine program global outreach. Reaching
a potential of over one billions souls around the world. 750,000 calls received
from over 150 nations! Morris on the new HelpLine CBS Studios set greeting and
welcoming the audience and television viewers to the HelpLine program.

The Jerusalem Pavilion. Pastor Wayne Hilsden with
Dr. Cerullo in the beautiful auditorium in the Jerusalem
Pavilion which MCWE helped sponsor.

2010 Mama Theresa's Home Opens! Morris and Theresa Cerullo with Pastor Tommy Barnett, and his son, Matthew, and daughter-in-law Caroline, at the opening of Mama Theresa's Home on September 9, 2010, which MCWE sponsored.

1975–76 prime-time Masada television special reached millions of Americans. Morris on location during the taping of Masada.

Morris and Theresa overlooking Sea of Galilee

Morris and Theresa during an intense prayer under a heavy anointing of the Holy Spirit during the School of Ministry on Prayer and Intercession.

"The Cerullo Family" Morris and Theresa surrounded by their family: David and his wife Barbara, Susan, Dena (Mark Cerullo's wife), and Theresa's sister, Lucille; along with their eight grandchildren and eight great grandchildren.

Morris and Theresa Cerullo have celebrated over six decades of marriage and ministry to the nations of the world.

Dr. Cerullo also received the Lifetime Global Impact Award in May 2015 in recognition of his many years of worldwide ministry. This prestigious award was presented by Oral Roberts University president, Dr. William Wilson, and Assemblies of God general superintendent, Dr. George Wood, at the Empowered21 Global Congress, a gathering of over 4,000 world ministry leaders and pastors in Jerusalem, Israel.

Morris Cerullo's legacy of training, equipping, and mobilizing Nationals will continue through the Worldwide Morris Cerullo Legacy Center in San Diego, California.

He placed his Bible on the tiny, wobbly plywood square that had been nailed to the railing for use as a podium. Morris stood for a silent moment taking in the large crowd of eager listeners, then launched into his message. A Portuguese-speaking interpreter conveyed his every word and move.

The service was flowing beautifully, and Morris could sense God settling over the stadium, moving hearts everywhere. It seemed as if every eye in the place was riveted on him as he led them closer to the heart of God.

Then, barely ten minutes into his presentation, Morris stopped mid-sentence. You could almost feel the audience stop breathing as they waited for him to continue.

But Morris was unable to continue. He felt as if someone had sliced through his chest, directly into his heart. The pain was excruciating. Nothing he had ever experienced—not even the softball that had shattered his jaw and cheekbone—had ever delivered such paralyzing pain.

His mind went blank. His reflexes took over, and he found himself grabbing for the little plywood square that held his Bible, hoping it would hold him up too. He had no realization that he was breaking down in front of fifty thousand spellbound people. He was only conscious of agonizing and intensifying pain.

By this time, uncertain what was happening but sure that there was a serious problem, Claire had rushed forward. Doubling over in pain, Morris thrust his arms out toward Clair, grabbing him to avoid collapsing on the wooden stage floor. While gripping the director with both arms he hoarsely implored him, "Clair, finish the service. Don't ask questions. Finish the teaching and pray for the people. I must get back to my hotel room immediately."

Fifty thousand people watched with open mouths and wide eyes at the bewildering scene unfolding before them.

CHAPTER 85

RESPONDING TO MORRIS'S brusque order, the crusade director whirled around and barked instructions to his nearby ministry colleagues. Two of them jumped forward to help the staggering Morris off the stage while Claire turned to the microphone, calmed the people, and quickly continued the presentation.

Meanwhile, off the stage by now, the men assisting Morris rushed him into the car in which he had arrived and instructed the driver to return Morris to his hotel room post haste. The ride was a blur to Morris as he slumped across the span of the back seat. The driver strained in the mirror to see what the moaning was about.

By the time he entered his room Morris's clothes were completely soaked with sweat. He had regained the ability to move on his own accord, but he was still saturated in pain. He slammed the door shut, staggered to the middle of the room, and fell face down on the carpet.

Still wheezing for breath, he cried out to God, "Are You taking me home now? Is this how it ends for me, Lord? I'm OK with that, but I just want to know."

Because of his special relationship with God many people had asked Morris how God speaks to him. He always explained that it was up to God how He chose to communicate in any particular situation. Sometimes God spoke to him in an audible voice, as clearly as one person talking to another in a common conversation. Other times God would speak to Morris through the Bible, drawing his attention to a specific passage that was meaningful at that moment. In other situations God's voice was revealed through an inaudible impression in his spirit. It wasn't an emotion, as such, but more like a mental leading that was as real and unique to Morris as if he'd heard an audible.

God spoke clearly to Morris in response to the questions he posed while lying in vivid pain on the hotel carpet. First, He informed him that this was not the end of the line and then added that all of this was being done for a special reason.

"Son, I have permitted this to happen to you for a purpose."

Instantly, the pain was gone. It struck Morris that the purpose of the pain was to grab his attention and force him to focus fully on what God was about to reveal.

Feeling relieved at the cessation of the debilitating pain, Morris continued to lie still on the carpet.

"Lord, please teach me."

And He did.

The Lord spoke to Morris and said, "Son, did you know that all truth is parallel?"

Not only did he not know that, but he didn't know what it meant. He asked for an explanation.

The Lord proceeded to describe how people supernaturally live in two worlds, the natural and the supernatural. He then gave Morris mental images of some of those parallels to clarify the concept.

The Lord continued to teach his prone pupil. He explained the concept of a breakthrough, a term not in common usage at the time, describing it as "a sudden burst of advance knowledge." The exchange continued with the Lord showing Morris examples of each new concept.

One of the critical ideas was *divine capability*. God showed Morris what the apostles had experienced in the Upper Room and in specific situations alongside Jesus as examples of divine capability. The Lord imparted a special measure of that divine capability to Morris that night, preparing the evangelist to move to the next stage of his development, thereby capable of adding even greater value to the kingdom of God.

The revelations given to Morris that evening and into the morning were delivered in the context of God teaching him that His people wanted and needed a spiritual breakthrough. He intended to use Morris to help bring such breakthroughs to Christ-followers around the world.

For several years the Lord had been giving Morris prophetic visions and the power to heal. That evening in Brazil, lying on a ratty, grimy carpet covering the cold cement floor in a dark hotel room, the prophet was receiving an advanced course in supernatural phenomena.

And God wasn't done yet.

CHAPTER 86

—◆—

ORRIS'S HEAD WAS spinning with the new insights and the implications of those teachings. He had barely started to consider the radical changes in philosophy and action that this contact with the Lord would have for the remainder of his life.

At that point God again spoke to him.

"Morris, what do you want out of this life?"

For a moment Morris was stunned by the question. Had he somehow gotten off track and the Lord was gently pointing it out? Why would God need to ask such a simplistic question?

Morris's mind instantly replayed some of the sacrifices he had made in order to fully serve God.

He had surrendered time with his wife and children. No one loved his wife more than he loved Theresa, and yet they spent week after week apart from each other every year. He was sensitive about being a great father, wanting to be there for his children, yet he was separated from them a large share of the time in order to carry out the Lord's mandate.

The Cerullos had moved across the country and settled in suburban San Diego, which is a beautiful, temperate area. But they had chosen to live in modest housing so they could avoid the financial pressure of a huge mortgage. They did not feel any need to convey the appearance of wealth, success, or prestige. All they wanted was a home in which to stay dry, safe, and comfortable.

Morris did not spend lavishly on clothing. He wore suits every day, but they were affordable, off-the-rack suits. His shirts and ties were department store items. He was not interested in staying up to date with the latest fashions or flashing the big-name designers. Not only would he never make the annual list of best-dressed men in America, but he didn't even know there was such a list.

He had good relationships with his peers, but his travel commitments made the development of close friendships difficult, if not impossible. Many of his closest friends were ministry associates, and he was reluctant to mix the business of ministry—he was "the boss," after all—and camaraderie. When they had a night off Morris and Theresa usually devoted it to playing with the children and then having a few quiet hours to themselves.

Even his travel arrangements betrayed his simple tastes and modest expectations. When staying outside the home Morris usually registered in whatever lodging the Lord provided, in places often arranged by the local hosts.

He did not arrive with a list of demands, such as many celebrities are known to submit. To him, a hotel room was a place to sleep, shower, study, and pray.

As his ministry colleagues would attest, Morris was a single-minded man: ministry was the heartbeat of his life. Only a person driven by a clear calling from God Himself would persist in his work despite threat after threat upon his life for merely telling people about Jesus.

Wasn't it obvious what he wanted from life?

Morris couched his reply with respect. "God, why would You ask me that? You know my dedication and the commitment I have made to You. Have I somehow displeased You? Why would You ask me what I want out of this life?

"I want to reach souls. Do You have a reason to doubt that?"

A peaceful silence filled the room as Morris laid on the floor turning the Lord's question over in his mind. His statement that his sole desire was to reach lost souls had been what he always told himself and others who asked, yet he had been doing that for several years and still did not feel completely satisfied or fulfilled.

He reflected on the extensive instruction he had been receiving throughout the night. As he pondered his experiences in light of that teaching, the Lord led Morris's mind on a journey. It was almost as if He initiated a slideshow in his mind using pictures of various places where Morris had ministered to bring ideas to the forefront or to drive home a point.

As he considered his various experiences, conversations, dreams for the future, fragments of feedback, and obstacles to greater impact, patterns started to emerge. One of the most significant patterns he regularly encountered was of ministry leaders and individuals who had been led to the Cross in a crusade imploring him to stay for an extended period in order to take them deeper into their newfound faith. Yet, because of limited time or finances he would often leave while people were hungry for more or deeper training.

He was finally identifying his point of frustration. On one hand, he did not have enough time to reach all the souls that needed to be harvested for the kingdom of God. On the other hand, neither did he have the necessary resources to train all the people who accepted Christ as their Lord and Savior. It was a double whammy!

At that point the Lord refocused the revelation on a coming global shift in attitude that would change the possibilities of future ministry. Morris learned how the day of the white missionary traveling thousands of miles to serve a divergent people group in a strange culture—the very thing he had been doing for several years—was coming to an end.

People everywhere were starting to look to their own kind to divulge truth and potential. The practice of God's chosen man flying to foreign countries to do large-scale, short-term evangelistic events would soon be a thing of the past. The era of nationals leading their countrymen to salvation and maturity was unfolding.

"To reach Africans, you must raise up Africans to do the job," the Lord told Morris. "To reach Europeans, you must raise up Europeans to complete the job. To influence Asians, you must prepare Asians to get it done. To reach South Americans, your job is to prepare South Americans to do that task."

It was a stunning impartation from God. It did not negate the groundbreaking evangelistic work he had been doing, but it certainly represented a new direction and a different strategy.

In most cases Morris and his team would travel to another country, share the gospel, see lost souls find new life in Christ, and encourage those new believers to connect with local churches or other indigenous ministries to move them forward in their faith. MCWE would undertake some follow-up from afar but relied upon the local church to build up new believers. That strategy was based on the assumption that the local church was up to the task of discipling new Christians.

But based on the increasing evidence of what he was seeing around the world, it was an assumption that did not settle well in his spirit. It was almost as if, unintentionally, he was leaving before completing the job—or at least before laying the foundation for the job to be completed.

The mental sifting and wrestling went on for an undetermined amount of time. Finally it all made sense to him, and a solution clicked into place for Morris.

Once again Morris responded to the Lord's question about what he really wanted out of life, this time with greater confidence and certainty.

"Lord, there is only one thing that I ask of You in this world—only one thing," he said out loud. "God, please give me the ability to take what You have given me, the power and anointing that is upon my ministry, and give me the ability to give that same power and anointing to others. Enable me to give that divine capability to others to grow your church."

Morris made the request with great humility. He realized that the Lord had provided him with a transcendent, life-changing vision when he was a new believer at age fifteen. From that day forward his passion had been to see people's souls eternally preserved.

He knew that the message God had imparted to him in Lima, Ohio—that his ministry would not be the work of a man but of the Holy Spirit working through a fully surrendered man—was a spiritual cornerstone of his efforts. Accordingly, he consistently reminded people that he, Morris Cerullo, had never healed a single person or wiped out the sins of any person; the spiritual transformations he had been part of were solely attributable to the love and power of God.

Yet as he stayed prone thinking about God's question and the insights it stirred inside him, he realized that he had felt as if he was incapable of completing the job he had been sent to do. However, if the Lord would allow him to impart the same anointing and power he had received to those to whom he ministered, then the burden of completion would no longer be on his shoulders alone but would be shared within the larger church. Armed with the same power and perspective that God had vested in Morris, those believers could then reach and disciple neighbors to whom Morris would never have the chance to minister.

Instead of an American invading a country with the gospel, millions upon millions of people could be led to Christ by their friends and countrymen. Those indigenous ministers would be far more effective and efficient in spreading the gospel. Indeed, the only way to reach all of the people throughout the world who had not yet heard the gospel would be through such an act of duplication leading to multiplication.

It would represent a fundamental change in the way Morris approached his ministry. Many of his most common and proven practices would be dramatically altered.

Morris's ministry purpose was about to be redefined by God. God completed the conversation with Morris with five audible words that would change history.

"Son, build Me an army!"

CHAPTER 87

CHARGED WITH A new mission, Morris emerged from Brazil excited about the limitless possibilities.

His outlook on ministry was revolutionized by the revelation in Porto Alegre. Instead of trying to have larger evangelistic services in every country of the world he was now seeking to build an army of spiritual leaders who would minister with that same passion across their native lands. Instead of expanding the number of new births—converts to the Christian faith—he was to prepare those who had already been saved by Jesus and given a passion for ministry to be more effective in building the church in their own nation. In Morris's mind and heart the three dominant revelations he had received from God were all part of the same message. The original vision was to reach souls, keeping them out of the enemy's control. The Lima message reminded him to stay humble, knowing that the task could be accomplished only in the power of God, not through the cleverness of man. The latest portion refined his strategy such that it was not about a single, godly man doing it all but emphasizing that man passing along the tools God had given him to the other Christian leaders around the world who were eager to immerse themselves in the spiritual battle but lacking in those tools.

This revised ministry thrust made so much sense. If Morris led crusades that reached a quarter of a million people every month of the year for the rest of his life—a feat that no human being had ever come close to accomplishing—how many people would he reach? Maybe 400 million people. That's a mind-boggling number.

But even more astounding was the fact that there were more than 6 *billion* people in the world! Even by reaching more people than had ever been reached by any person in human history, Morris's efforts would still amount to touching the lives of substantially less than one out of every ten people on Earth.

By continuing to do things the way he had been, Morris was losing ground every month. In other words, more people were being born onto the planet each month than he was capable of reaching. Every month, as hard as he worked and as many resources as he was able to raise and invest in his process, he'd fall farther behind.

But, of course, the Lord was not counting on Morris alone to reach the world. What He *was* counting on him to do was conceive and institute a process that developed an army of properly trained spiritual leaders to cumulatively accomplish the task that no single person, no matter how gifted and well-funded, could hope to achieve.

As part of that process, Morris reasoned that if he could train the people already effected by the gospel and identified by God as spiritual leaders and impart to them the same power and divine capability that God had entrusted to him, then the possibilities were staggering!

God's vision was not dependent upon Morris motivating a pool of seminary graduates or even ordained ministers. In fact, just as the apostles and their successors had little if any formal theological training, God had shown Morris that He was ready and willing to expand His kingdom through the work of a remnant of people devoted to kingdom outcomes. They might be educated or they might not. They would likely have full-time jobs to pay their bills and take care of their families, adding a compulsion to make disciples of their world to their daily agenda. The Bible was filled with examples of such "tentmakers"—people who were not relying on a paycheck from a ministry but whose lives were committed to spreading the gospel through any and all means.

Rather than wait for and rely upon the gifting of a single person to lead a nation to Christ, the new strategy would enable tens of thousands of devoted disciples to reach a small segment of his or her culture and add that growth to expansion produced through the efforts of other nationals.

Rather than wait for a single evangelist's schedule to allow him to visit a country to spread the good news, the new strategy would allow an unlimited number of servants of God to be actively and *simultaneously* reaching their communities for Christ.

Morris could barely contain his excitement over the new piece of the puzzle the Lord had given him.

CHAPTER 88

————•————

DURING THE PORTO Alegre encounter the Lord taught Morris about the principle of parallel truths.

God showed him that for every natural truth exists there is a parallel spiritual truth. Similarly, for every spiritual truth that exists there is a parallel natural truth.

With that in mind Morris reflected on the fact that God had called him to build an *army*. Upon his return home from Brazil, Morris spent a lot of time in prayer and study, gearing up to build that army. He talked to his closest ministry colleagues about the broadest possibilities concerning his evolving ministry.

The new strategy provided Morris and his team with a new grid for understanding and developing their ministry plans. Instead of thinking of those attending crusades as sinners given a chance to receive salvation, they were now sinners who could receive salvation as the precursor to gaining the kind of training that every soldier needs before being sent into battle.

And life *is* a spiritual battle.

Critics of crusade-based evangelism had often complained that those who came forward during the altar call were victims of the Matthew 13 dilemma: many would hear the good news and rejoice but then fall away from Christ because they lacked the deep roots to withstand the enemy's attacks and the perspective to understand and pursue God's calling on their life. Preparing them for battle and enlisting them in the growing army of the Lord would be the ideal way of circumventing that problem.

Morris studied the process that great military organizations use to develop their soldiers. He studied the role of basic training. He evaluated the roles of discipline, uniformity, and teamwork. The core values of effective military entities were a crucial foundation, passing along a shared perspective on respect, timeliness, truth and honesty, trust, readiness, reliability, and more.

Those values and the behaviors that spring from them are no different than those required for the kingdom of God to advance. Like new recruits joining the army, new believers must relearn the basic values and behaviors of a follower of Christ in order to be an effective soldier in the war against spiritual darkness.

Morris was excited about the challenge of taking the kingdom's new recruits and whipping them into battle-ready shape. He paid close attention to Paul's exhortations in Ephesians 6:13–17, in which he described what it meant for God's army to be battle-ready.

Therefore, put on every piece of God's armor so you will be able to resist the enemy in the time of evil. Then after the battle you will still be standing firm. Stand your ground, putting on the belt of truth and the body armor of God's righteousness. For shoes, put on the peace that comes from the Good News so that you will be fully prepared. In addition to all of these, hold up the shield of faith to stop the fiery arrows of the devil. Put on salvation as your helmet, and take the sword of the Spirit, which is the word of God. Pray in the Spirit at all times and on every occasion. Stay alert and be persistent in your prayers for all believers everywhere.

But unlike a nation's army, which seeks to protect the population from foreign attack or internal revolution, the army God had charged Morris with developing was commissioned to conquer the works and ways of the devil in a society susceptible to temptation. This was an army designed to foster the restoration of people's souls!

Critics would no longer be able to thwart the spread of the good news by claiming it was based on a foreign gospel spread by professional evangelists from other, more prosperous nations. Indigenous people would reach their own kind. Kingdom growth would come from within the country, facilitated by passionate believers prepared to reach their own countrymen. They would be fluent in the language, customs, and traditions of their people, surpassing all cultural barriers.

The ego of men so often impairs their ability to devise winning strategies, as they are more devoted to getting the glory for their efforts than allowing a more effective strategy to prevail. Morris cared nothing about his own glory or reputation. This revelation—like his entire calling and ministry—belonged to his heavenly Father. And what a brilliant plan God had given to Morris. He praised God for such wisdom and thanked Him constantly for His willingness to use him to implement that plan.

Morris was like a greyhound chasing a rabbit. He couldn't wait to get going.

CHAPTER 89

I T DIDN'T TAKE long for Morris to introduce the changes into his outreach efforts.

One of the most significant of those changes involved the implementation of a means of training ministers around the world to both bring their countrymen to Christ and turn them into lifelong disciples. Initially named National Training Institutes, their intention was to produce kingdom-driven, focused ministers of the gospel who could hold crusades and follow-up events of their own, borrowing from the lessons learned by Morris and his team over the years.

Each Training Institute would be an intensive time of spiritual education and practice, ending with a time of anointing with oil, symbolic of the transfer of God's anointing from Morris to those whom had been trained.

During their training, each national would be given opportunities to preach, give altar calls, and pray for the sick and the lost. They were being taught to minister in the name and power of God rather than worry about their own skills and limitations.

The purpose of the Training Institutes, as one colleague jokingly put it, was to put Morris out of a job—and Morris couldn't have been more excited by the privilege of multiplying the global stable of empowered evangelists and disciplers.

To have a place designed to facilitate the kind of training that Morris envisioned, MCWE needed a suitable facility. As the team scouted San Diego for such a location, they came upon the El Cortez Hotel, a historic landmark in the city. It had fallen upon hard times and was in disrepair. Its dilapidated condition, however, allowed the ministry to buy the building for a very reasonable price and to relocate both the MCWE offices as well as the School of Ministry on the rehabilitated premises.

The hotel was not a typical, one-building lodge. It was actually a five-block complex overlooking the city that encompassed several small motels, a convention center, and the historic and majestic hotel itself. The cumulative space was ideal for large group meetings, housing the hundreds of nationals who would fly to San Diego for the training and serving as the base for the administrative and ministry preparation duties of the MCWE team.

The renovations took time and considerable funding to complete because the buildings had to be redesigned and gutted in order to fit the purposes of the ministry. It was cheaper than starting from scratch, and they had found no other complex that came close to fitting their needs as well, but it was still a big and demanding project.

It demonstrated the commitment MCWE was making to this new component of bringing the gospel to all the world.

CHAPTER 90

———•———

T HE RENOVATIONS WERE a massive undertaking, but the Lord paved the way for the process to move ahead on schedule, on budget, and without much in the way of significant, unforeseen difficulties.

The alterations included converting the top floor of the former hotel into a twenty-four-hour prayer and counseling center. Other parts of the complex were designed to be a state-of-the-art educational facility. A dining hall and kitchen were built that enabled them to feed and turn over one thousand people every thirty minutes. Hundreds of guest rooms were modernized to serve as temporary housing for the nationals to live in during intensive three-month or six-month training sessions.

Each classroom was created to be a state-of-the-art learning environment fitted with technology that was advanced for the year, 1976. For example, each chair had a student response system built in to the armrest. The information entered by students was instantly available on a console that the teacher had at his podium in the front of the classroom. Teachers could track not just attendance but also answers that students entered to questions or challenges raised by the teacher. Based on those answers, teachers could then tailor the training required by each student. The lessons were taught on large projection screens, the kind that would not become common until some thirty years later in churches, classrooms, and boardrooms around the country.

Upon completion of their training, each national would return to their native land and replicate what they had experienced and been taught. If Morris was called to build an army, each of the nationals was being prepared to build an on-location unit of that army, pressed into immediate and permanent active duty.

Morris recognized that most of the nationals who were to receive the ministry preparation delivered by the Training Institutes could not afford the cost of the entire training process. To address that obstacle and prevent the spread of the gospel from being delayed or thwarted, MCWE approached the organization's partners and potential sponsors with a request for help. They caught the vision, and through their generosity funded the Institutes, enabling most of the nationals who attended the Institute to receive a full scholarship that covered tuition, room, and board.

Logistical matters still needed loads of attention, such as assisting nationals in getting the visas they needed to spend a prolonged period in the United States or working within the currency limits some nations place on their citizens who travel abroad. But for every challenge a viable solution was found, and the Institutes moved forward.

CHAPTER 91

OST OF THE students in the training sessions had never been to the United States, so their trip to San Diego was a revelation in many ways. Some had never seen a radiator that produced heat for their room. Others had never taken a shower with hot and cold running water. Many of them had never flown in an airplane before. Stepping in an ocean—the Pacific was close to the El Cortez campus—was a first for a large number of the students. Watching movies or PowerPoint-like presentations on big screens was also a novel experience for a lot of the evangelists-in-training.

Because of Morris's reputation and relationships with other giants of the faith, students in the school were treated to special sessions led by world-known evangelists such as Kenneth Copeland, Dr. Fredrick K C Price, Pat Robertson, and Dr. Walter Martin. The regular teaching staff included men of great wisdom and experience as well, such as Pastors Charles Blair, Alex Ness, Paul Trulin, and Ed Cole. All of the teachers provided keen insight into the advanced spiritual principles the nationals needed to raise the intensity of the spiritual battle in their homeland.

Raymond Mooi was a wide-eyed eighteen year old from Malaysia when he arrived at the school. The elders of his church were big fans of Dr. Cerullo's ministry and believed that young Raymond was exactly the kind of high-potential world-changer who would benefit from accelerated, unique training opportunity.

After his first complete day at the six-month program, Raymond's head was spinning. At two o'clock in the morning, after emerging from several hours of anointed teaching, he made his way into an empty classroom and got on his knees to pray: "Lord, what I am experiencing here is exactly what we need in Asia. Please help me to bring it back with me."

Toward the end of his stay in San Diego Raymond joined his fellow students in spending two weeks on the streets of San Diego ministering to people throughout the metropolis. The miracle service held in the convention center was the culmination of his time in the school. Each graduating student served as a ministry associate in the huge auditorium as Morris presided over the event.

"That experience was something you can never forget," Raymond remembered years later. "People were lined up seeking God's healing, and Dr. Cerullo called me over to lay hands on people and pray for the sick. I went up to a man who had a cataract. His eye was so cloudy he couldn't see out of it. I laid my hands on his head and eye, and I prayed and prayed. And I watched as God removed the cataract. It went away, like a curtain sweeping across his eye. It was my first miracle. After experiencing that, I was never the same again. It gave me the faith and confidence to return home and do powerful ministry."

Today Raymond is a legend in his own right throughout Asia. After working with Dr. Cerullo in countries throughout Asia he began hosting his own crusades, holding some of the largest evangelistic events in the history of many Asian nations. He has led breakthrough events in nations that have resisted the gospel, from Tibet and Myanmar to India and Cambodia, from Vietnam and Thailand to Indonesia and China. He has held the largest crusades ever held in Japan. He has seen Buddhist monks and Muslim imams healed and thousands of Muslims accept Christ.

Following Dr. Cerullo's lead, he has surrendered everything for the privilege of preaching the gospel and bringing healing into tens of thousands of lives. True to the original plan God had given to Dr. Cerullo, Raymond has helped to expand God's army. And like Dr. Cerullo, Raymond has paid a significant price for his efforts, spending many nights in prison for preaching, enduring physical beatings, and being deported because of his ministry efforts.

"Today," he says with great humility, "I am an encouragement to churches in many nations, a voice that rallies them to continue to preach the gospel and raise up followers of Jesus. Dr. Cerullo showed us the spirit of a warrior with a heart of compassion. I learned how to serve God from him. It was a rare opportunity to have a remarkable experience. I praise God for Dr. Cerullo's influence on my life."

———•———

Ayo Oritsejafor was a young man in Nigeria when Dr. Cerullo did his first crusade in Lagos. The teenager had recently accepted Christ as his Savior and heard about a big ministry event that was coming to the city, so he decided to see what it would be like. As usual, Dr. Cerullo gave a stirring presentation of the gospel, resulting in many Nigerians accepting Christ. But Ayo was blown away by the miracles he saw happening right in front of him. It changed his understanding of God—so much so that he immediately decided he needed to attend seminary and prepare for a life of full-time ministry.

While in seminary Ayo spent lots of time in the library reading all he could about effective ministry. In the library he found an archive of the MCWE magazine, *The Deeper Life.* The young man spent hour after hour reading the articles, many of them teachings written by Dr. Cerullo. As Ayo later explained, "Those articles became the basis of my understanding of the Bible and many of my foundational messages. They changed my life."

Not long after graduating from the seminary Ayo attended another MCWE event in Nairobi, Kenya. While there he finagled a personal meeting with Dr. Cerullo. Their conversation impacted him greatly—and led to him being invited to San Diego for the forthcoming inaugural Training Institute.

His six months in San Diego once again redirected his life and ministry. Even though he had already begun a successful pastoral career in Nigeria, the training institute deepened his faith in every dimension. His most memorable experience was a service Dr. Cerullo led one night in which he taught about money. Ayo was so moved that he put one hundred dollars in the offering plate as it passed by—even though it was every penny he had left and he still had months to go before returning home. To this day Ayo has no idea how he made it financially through those final months but speaks intensely about how God took care of every financial need until he returned to Africa. Learning the principle of giving and receiving as taught by Dr. Cerullo was another milestone in his development.

The church Ayo pastored had almost two thousand people regularly attending when he left for San Diego. Within a year of returning from the Training Institute the church was drawing over seven thousand people every weekend. As his church grew, Ayo was chosen to be the president of the Pentecostal Fellowship of Nigeria and later president of the Christian Association of Nigeria, which encompasses all of the Christian churches in the nation.

"By the grace of God," Ayo recently proclaimed, "I have been able to touch thousands of lives, bringing miracles and breakthroughs, and have raised up so many churches that I have lost count. It is all due to the work of Dr. Cerullo in my life. I give God the glory, and I celebrate Morris Cerullo.

"There is no minister of the gospel in the entire continent of Africa," he continued, "particularly in Pentecostal and Charismatic circles, who has not had a direct or indirect impact from Morris Cerullo. There is no village in Africa where you cannot find somebody who knows Dr. Cerullo or his teaching or his impact. He has brought change everywhere. There is no minister of the gospel in Africa who could honestly say he has not had some input from Dr. Cerullo.

"I have met some great men of God around the world, but I have never met anyone who has so much passion and desire to share and impart to others what God has given to him. It is very unique. I have been in crusades when he surprises me, turns around and gives me the microphone, and says, 'Go ahead, you can do it.' And I found myself preaching and healing the sick and bringing deliverance to people, just like he would do. There are so few people of his kind who feel so fulfilled and excited to see other people do what he has done. It is incredible."

————•————

Stories like those of Raymond and Ayo were commonplace among the graduates of the Institute held in San Diego. The future leaders from around the world who descended upon the southern California campus for a life-changing six-month adventure went on to become many of the leading ministers in their nations and regions of the world.

It didn't take long for the Institute to have dramatic influence on the global church. The spiritual fruit born from the process became evident almost as soon as the first graduating class returned to their homelands. Many of the graduates returned to areas where no Christian church had previously existed. They would initiate a modest crusade and begin to pour the life, love, and hope of Christ into the converts that emerged. In a shockingly short time many of those individuals initiated churches that grew to hundreds and even thousands of attenders.

The impact of the training institutes would become more and more spectacular as the years went by. The passion and zeal of those individuals propelled the gospel to people and places that might never have been reached through traditional methods and outside expertise.

But as the school produced new leaders for God's army, Morris felt in his spirit that the Lord was not done innovating with the training process. As he prayed, Morris began to grasp the Lord's next step in the process.

CHAPTER 92

GOD'S ARMY WAS being built!

But the glaring limitation was that despite the scholarships and other assistance provided, thousands of qualified, passionate leaders could not go the United States for extended training. For some the obstacles were legal: they lacked the passport, visa, or other government permissions to make the journey. Some were blocked from coming by the lack of the limited spending money they would need for their time in San Diego. Yet others could not leave their family or job for an extended period of time and hope to survive.

So the Lord gave Morris an expanded vision of how to parse and consolidate some of the core teachings in ways that would allow nationals to use existing facilities in their homeland to host in-country advanced training sessions.

Those lessons would take anywhere from one to three weeks, depending on the capacity of the teachers and students. Students would receive what they needed to launch their own outreach efforts and experience success. Then by offering successive training sessions scheduled months apart they could attend additional, shorter training sessions as time went on without placing an impossible burden on the nascent preachers.

As the process was developed and refined, the National Training Institute (later renamed School of Ministry) became not only an indispensable part of the MCWE global strategy but even more urgent than the crusades themselves. Simple math showed why. Through the crusades, thousands of individuals would give their heart to the Lord. But it was through the Schools of Ministry that hundreds or even thousands of new ministers were prepared for the work of spreading the gospel.

When faced with the decision of having a single man preaching to one nation at a time or thousands of men preaching to dozens of nations at a time, the preference was clear.

If the objective was to preach the gospel to every person in the world, giving them an opportunity to choose to commit their life to God and appropriate the love and power of Jesus Christ, then what was needed was an "all hands on deck" strategy.

Without question, Morris was committed to raising up as big an army of fellow evangelists and disciplers as possible.

But the challenge to Morris was not a simple black-and-white choice of either preaching to save souls or training leaders before sending them into the world. God had called him to continue to preach the gospel while also training and empowering others to do the same.

So, Morris continued his tireless efforts to reach more and more people in nations throughout the world. As exciting as the new training possibilities were, he stayed on his knees thanking God for the privilege of holding the evangelistic crusades, which allowed him to recruit more trainees for the Institutes.

That meant that life on the road—and battling the forces of darkness—remained a central aspect of Morris's life.

CHAPTER 93

MOSCOW WAS A scary place to be in the mid-1960s. It was not a place where Americans were warmly received since it was the era of the Cold War between the world's two superpowers. The USSR was the leading communist power on the globe and was immersed in an arms race with the US.

But when God called Morris to go somewhere, he went, no questions asked, no concerns about personal safety. He trusted that God knew what He was doing.

At that time the Soviet Union was not a churchgoing nation. With the blessing of the KGB, Russia's feared and fearless internal security agency, the Russian Orthodox Church ruled the country denominationally. The only non-Orthodox church of note was a large Baptist church that the KGB allowed in Moscow.

When Morris and his crusade director, Claire Hutchins, arrived in Moscow at the behest of the Lord, they had nothing planned. Morris made contact with a few religious leaders he knew of to inform them of his presence. Through a series of snowballing conversations he was invited to speak at the Baptist church. The KGB approved the plan.

Morris preached at a Sunday service and treated it like a crusade. He gave a simple but powerful gospel presentation. He healed some of the congregants present. He gave an altar call. Everything he said was translated into Russian by his translator, who was a KGB agent.

Some people responded, but the KGB's presence seemed to suppress people's response. They knew they were being watched closely and that too much religious zeal would label them as potential troublemakers—or worse. Regardless, Morris was disappointed that there did not seem to be a breakthrough during that service.

Little did he know that he had planted seeds that day that would blossom into magnificent spiritual fruit a quarter of a century later when the USSR dissolved into various nations, communism fell apart in the region, and the Russian people sought a deeper understanding of and relationship with God.

———◆———

In 1989 Morris was able to return to lead a victorious crusade. Then in subsequent trips to Russia he held crusades that attracted upwards of twenty thousand people night after night for a solid week. Each morning following a crusade a School of Ministry was conducted to train and anoint thousands of new spiritual leaders for the rebuilding country. Those newly saved and trained believers went on to reach out into their own communities and to plant thousands of new churches in the country that for so long had rejected God.

In fact, it was while ministering in Russia that he videotaped a new message titled "Proof Producers." That message became a staple of Morris's outreach efforts for years to come, cited by some as his legacy message. The crux of the teaching was that when a believer appropriates the power of God he can do the works that God intended him to perform, as described in John 6:28. The teaching was made into a two-hour documentary that was then aired across all ten time zones of Russia! The response was so overwhelming that the state-owned television network begged Morris to be able to run it again—twice. The airings produced so much mail that the postal service was delivering numerous, full sacks of letters to Morris's ministry there day after day.

The Russian people were among the first to gain exposure to that-life changing message, but Morris would ultimately share that message with more than three million people across the planet, producing a continually astounding positive response from people.

Morris's simple exercise in faithfulness—showing up in a dangerous country with no invitations to speak—turned into the first domino to fall in a series of mighty outreach events. God used the Russian experience to reinforce to Morris the importance of obedience and trusting God's timing. His energetic ministry in Moscow's Baptist church did not produce immediate, startling results, but neither did God's Word return void from within that cold, dark, reticent congregation that Sunday morning in 1965. Morris's passionate service that morning provided the single ray of light that would later enable him to reach a large body of Christ-followers in a dark and desperate nation.

CHAPTER 94

ARGENTINA WAS ONE of the nations where God was at work in a big way by the early 1970s. A fellow evangelist, Tommy Hicks, had helped to open up the country to the gospel and the power of God. Morris was invited to continue the advance of the gospel in Argentina, receiving a call to come to Buenos Aires. After praying about the possibility he felt called to accept the invitation.

The advance team had a very difficult time getting permits and making the other preparations for the meetings. There was a lot of political opposition to evangelistic events at that time. Some of the opposition came from die-hard Catholics, including some priests and bishops, who interpreted major outreach efforts as an attempt to undermine the Catholic Church. Others were upset that an American was developing such a following in their country. Meanwhile, certain politicians worried that the people might be less controllable if the ministers became too popular or if religious teaching encouraged the public to defy political leaders.

In other words, it was the same kind of multi-pronged opposition that Morris had been facing for years. The powers of darkness continually fought against the warriors of light.

By the grace of God, Morris's team was able to get all the details worked out in the nick of time, and the crusade launched as scheduled. The first night of the meetings went well, with a very large crowd filling the stadium, many miracles occurring, and thousands of nonbelievers coming forward to ask Jesus to save them.

Morris was staying in a beautiful hotel overlooking the coast. He had spent hours and hours in his room praying for God to have His way with the event. Morris had seen the room in a dream, sent his crusade director to find it, and discovered it to be a comforting place in which to prepare for the crusade.

The opening day of the meetings went well. Tens of thousands of people had attended, the energy level was high, and the Lord had done amazing miracles for dozens of people. And, of course, thousands of people streamed forward during the altar call to embrace Jesus as their Savior.

Although it had been a notoriously challenging country in which to minister, the events in Buenos Aries were off to a good start. Morris returned to his hotel room that evening still fasting and praying but enthusiastic about how things had begun.

Such optimism was short-lived. During the morning of the second day the serenity of the hotel was disrupted by the arrival of the police. They demanded to see the proprietor.

"Do you have a man staying here named Morris Cerullo?" demanded the uniformed leader of the policemen clustered around the hotel registration desk.

When the fearful hotel owner admitted that they did, the officer demanded that he lead the police crew to the guest's door, whereupon they banged on it until Morris answered.

Looking up at the towering officer, Morris quietly asked what the fuss was all about.

"You are under arrest!" the officer yelled at him. "You must come with us right now." With that said, one of the junior officers stepped forward, grabbed Morris by the arm, and pulled him toward the elevator. Once they reached the parking lot, they threw the astonished Morris, now handcuffed, into a paddy wagon and slammed the door shut. The police jumped in the vehicle, turned on the siren, and sped through the city streets to the police station.

Inside the police station Morris was booked like a common criminal and led to the jail. While the officers worked out the paperwork and procedures, he sat quietly and unperturbed, silently praying for God's will to be revealed.

Soon thereafter the chief of police marched into the jail area, trailed by several of his men. The chief stood before Morris with his eyes blazing and began yelling at him.

"You call yourself a man of God!" he bellowed derisively. "You are just here to exploit the people. You only want their money. You love the attention, standing on the stage and pretending to be someone special." He went on and on, spitting out epithets at Morris and accusing him of all sorts of skullduggery.

Mid-rant, one of his underlings nudged forward. "May I say something, sir?" he asked evenly. When the chief granted permission, the younger policeman looked Morris in the eye and spoke up. "Sir, last night I was at this man's public meeting. I had my daughter with me. You know her, sir; she is blind. She was standing beside me, and the reverend was speaking, praying for the people. My daughter pulled on my jacket sleeve. I looked down at her and saw she was crying."

The man paused and shifted his gaze from Morris to the chief. "Then she said to me, 'Daddy, I can see. I can see. Something is happening to me.' Indeed, sir, her sight has been restored."

You could have heard a pin drop in the usually boisterous booking room. The chief stared at his assistant, then at Morris. Without taking his eyes off the American he issued a command.

"Take the reverend to the stadium so he doesn't miss the meeting. Do it now."

CHAPTER 95

————•————

BARELY A YEAR after the success in Buenos Aires, Morris was again invited to minister in Argentina, this time in the nation's second-largest city, Rosario.

Once again the atmosphere surrounding the preparations for the event was tense. MCWE was able to rent out a stadium that held eighty thousand and to get a permit for the meetings.

And then it started to get ugly.

The first indication of trouble came from the media. Morris's team, which had successfully printed and distributed the usual flood of handbills and posters, was prevented from buying advertising space in the newspapers and on the local radio and television stations. It took a personal call from a Catholic official on Morris's behalf to get the media outlets to give in.

Unexpectedly, the permit to hold the event was revoked on the day of the first crusade. The reason given: fears that the anticipated crowd would become unruly and the local police would not be able to control them.

That Sunday evening the police sent more than three dozen police to the site of the event arrayed in riot gear and armed for battle. Their instructions included preventing anyone connected with the crusade from speaking with the crowd.

While Morris was preparing for the opening night of the crusade, his team was frantically attempting to find some government or military official who could overturn the last-minute ruling. They had rented a huge stadium and distributed all of the promotional materials and had spent much of their media budget advertising the evening's event. There was no way they would be able to stop the crowd from showing up. Even though many of the police on site were sympathetic to their plight, they informed the crusade team that they were powerless to do anything but carry out their orders.

A couple of hours prior to the scheduled start of that first meeting, crusade director Claire Hutchins visited Morris in his room. At that point Morris knew something was up. His team never disturbed him while he was getting ready to lead an event.

Claire delivered the heartbreaking news. "I'm sorry, Morris," he began, "but there won't be a meeting tonight. They have the streets blocked off around the stadium. There are literally barricades blocking the streets. They are not letting anybody get through."

"Why not? We already paid for the stadium. And we have legitimate permits, don't we?"

"Yes, sir, we do," Claire replied, "but individuals within the government and the police force have decided they don't want the meetings to happen, so the police are enforcing an order to block the crusade from happening."

Morris knew it must be serious if his team seemed so defeated. They encountered such opposition on a regular basis but were usually able to work out a solution and keep the process moving and on schedule. Apparently they had determined that was not possible in Rosario.

Because he had been in prayer all day and the Lord had not given any indication that the meetings were to be cancelled or postponed, Morris knew this opposition was not the work of God. He reached for his suit jacket, then instructed Claire and the team members waiting outside the room to follow him.

They went downstairs and called for a taxi. Within a few minutes the men pulled up in front of the crowd. Sure enough, there were hefty barricades blocking entrance to the stadium. With a grim look on his face Morris sized up the situation and said to his team, "Follow me."

With that, the besuited men climbed over the barricades and purposefully stormed toward the stadium!

People had begun arriving at the stadium at breakfast time earlier that day. By now there were thousands of people waiting around the perimeter of the stadium. Those near Morris saw his bold move, and suddenly thousands of people jumped the barriers as well, anxious to follow God's man.

Before they got far, police ran over to Morris, their rifles and guns drawn and pointed at the small team of Americans. "Who do you think you are? What are you doing? Stop where you are," they cried out in Spanish.

It had the makings of a very bad scene. The first one likely to be shot was Morris.

The situation did not seem to faze him in the least. Without breaking stride, Morris said to his men, "Come on." Turning his head to some of the police trying to block his path, he continued to move forward, saying, "I don't speak Spanish. No speak. No understand."

But the guards prevailed, using sign language and physical resistance to keep Morris from getting to the stadium gate.

The lead officer explained the situation in halting English to the infuriated but calm Morris. He listened politely, then turned to face the crowd behind him.

Because he was not allowed to speak at all—the police feared that he would incite the people to riot—he asked one of the local pastors on the crusade committee to address the crowd. Pastor Andreesen explained to the people that the crusade could not be held that evening but that two nearby churches were open and would be holding services.

That night both churches—as well as the tent that had been prepared for the National Training Institute—were packed with people. Evangelistic messages were offered in each place, and many people received Christ as their Savior. In fact, several dozen people experienced miracle healings as well.

And Morris had yet to speak his first word publicly in Rosario.

The next day Morris's team and other local supporters spent hours attempting to negotiate a way for that evening's meeting to go on as scheduled. But again the efforts were thwarted.

Just like the previous night, on Monday evening thousands of people showed up for the meetings, only to be turned away by the police. And again, the venues featuring local pastors preaching the Word of God and praying for healings and salvations met with great success.

Still, Morris had yet to speak his first word publicly in Rosario. Revival started in Rosario without the featured speaker healing anyone or inviting a single person to accept Christ.

The charade continued the next day. Morris spoke in Pastor Andreesen's church on Tuesday night. The media turned out in full force to hear what the impugned American preacher would say. Would he incite a riot or maybe even an overthrow of the corrupt government? Would he call upon his God to get back at those who had blocked his path, as Elijah had done with the prophets of Baal?

Morris devoted his time to speaking about love and forgiveness. He invited everyone to accept Christ, and he prayed for the healing of many sick and discouraged people. The results were outstanding. Even many of the journalists who had been assigned to cover the event came forward during the call to salvation.

While the negotiators continued their exchange on Wednesday, Morris and his team packed up their things and returned home. They knew that before God was done they'd be back in Rosario now that the revival had been started.

CHAPTER 96

S URE ENOUGH, IN February of 1967—just three months after the initial confrontations—a new crusade was ready to go.

During the intervening months the revival had gained momentum. Churches that had a few dozen listless attenders previously were suddenly filled with expectant worshipers. The local churches joined together to prepare for Morris's return. For the one hundred days prior to the start of the event, Morris and his team were joined by Argentinians who prayed day and night for the event.

But the enemy was not about to roll over and play dead. He had blocked the event before and was intent upon doing so again.

The day of the first scheduled meeting started out as a beautiful, sunny morning. But by midday Thursday there was an unexpected rainstorm turning the local streets to mud. While that depressed the turnout for the event, the skies cleared a couple of hours before the crusade started, and the event proceeded as planned.

Inside the stadium was a different matter. Not everyone was there to praise and worship the Lord. When Morris took the microphone to begin sharing about the glory of God, a few people located near the stage pelted him with rocks and eggs. He continued as if nothing had happened. After a few minutes, they gave up.

As Morris prayed for people's needs, healings were seen.

The opposition continued the next day. A nearby theater had been rented as the site for the Training Institute. When the team arrived on Monday morning they found it to be securely locked and guarded by the police. Despite the permit they had in hand, the police said they were forbidden to open the building.

The local pastors, more confident thanks to the revival that had begun to change the city, converged on City Hall.

Within an hour the ban was rescinded, and the morning meeting took place.

Friday night more than twenty-five thousand people showed up at the stadium. There was a sense of tremendous expectancy in the air. The people were not let down. After a spirited time of praising God in music Morris and his team prayed for dozens of people. Healings were recorded, and the crowd burst into thunderous applause at God's compassion and power.

Off to the side, a small contingency of government officials and medical observers were standing by, looking for ways to close down the meeting.

They listened to every word that was spoken to catch anything that might be considered incendiary. They watched every movement very carefully, waiting for some type of medical chicanery or breaches of local law. They scrutinized each miracle, looking for an opportunity to pounce.

By the end of the night they retreated in disappointment, acknowledging that the healings were real and legitimate.

On Saturday night, though, the enemy decided he had played fair long enough.

The police entered the stadium with a new strategy.

CHAPTER 97

———◆———

T HE STADIUM WAS filling up on Saturday night approaching the 7:30 pm start time.

Little did they know that just before 7:00 pm a judge had given the police an order to turn off the stadium's electricity.

So, just minutes before the scheduled start of the event, everything went dark. And silent. Not only were the lights turned off, but the sound system was useless without power too. There was a bit of pandemonium in the stands as people tried to figure out what was going on.

The legions of police officers who had entered the stadium just before the power was cut disbursed the crowd, sending them home.

Meanwhile, outside the venue another legion of policemen ringed the stadium, preventing those who were still arriving from entering.

One of those arriving was Morris Cerullo.

Upon exiting his car he confidently walked toward the front gate of the stadium, oblivious to the police presence. Word spread among the other people who had been stranded on the outside that it was Morris Cerullo himself, and people ran toward him to enter with the man of God.

However, the police had clearly been forewarned about his boldness and quickly blocked his route. The commander of the unit stepped forward and informed him that he was under arrest and must be taken immediately to the police station for an arraignment.

At the station he was charged with practicing medicine without a license and was placed in custody, pending an appearance before the judge.

Several hours later—early on Sunday morning—Morris was brought before one of the local magistrates. As these things took place there were people in churches throughout Rosario praying for Brother Cerullo.

In the tiny courtroom the city prosecutor explained Morris's trumped-up crime to the judge. When he was done the judge turned toward Morris and asked if he wished to make any comments.

Then Morris rose and shared the gospel with the judge. Despite the tension in the courtroom, Morris was neither perturbed nor hurried. He led the judge through the creation story, the fall of man, the coming of Jesus, the reason for His death, the price He paid for sins, and the salvation He made possible or us.

When he finished he sat down to a quiet courtroom. The judge was the first to break the silence.

"Officer, please release Morris. He has done nothing wrong."

Case dismissed.

CHAPTER 98

—⚬—

THE EFFORT TO build an army had taken off like fire in a field of wheat. Donors in the United States were excited about the process and had been giving generously to help fund crusades undertaken by nationals who had been trained in the National Training Institutes.

The reports that trickled in from those nations showed the wisdom of the strategy—and how anxious God was to bless those efforts.

Theresa and her team accumulated the reports in order to share the exciting developments with their partners via the *Deeper Life* journal. Even the in-house team was floored by the data.

In the first year for which such information was available, MCWE and its partners had sponsored 4,098 evangelistic crusades. From those meetings, 3,060 new churches and evangelistic outposts were established.

But the most staggering number of all was that representing the number of first-time decisions for Christ: 1,692,356! Nearly 1.7 million in just one year!

One of the team members pointed out that due to record keeping and report delivery issues, those were just the decisions that had been officially recorded and successfully delivered to the MCWE offices. Undoubtedly there were many more decisions that did not make the final tally.

Tears came to Morris's eyes when he was shown the numbers. The entire team gathered and worshiped God for His faithfulness in leading them to adopt the multiplication strategies that had facilitated these outcomes.

And then they prayed a pledge to increase their efforts to enable even greater numbers of people to hear the life-changing news of what Jesus had done for them on the cross.

God had commissioned Morris to blaze a new trail on the way to satisfying His command: "Son, build me an army."

The army was coming on strong!

CHAPTER 99

—◆—

MEANWHILE, MORRIS CONTINUED to minister in various countries of the world, as led by God.

The trail was often rugged and challenging. Morris wound up traveling to many places around the world where evangelists typically did not go. For example, India was a country known as a place for evangelists to avoid. Many who had tried to break through that spiritually inhospitable land wound up retreating, including such outreach giants as T L Osborne. When Osborne had attempted to hold crusades in various parts of the Hindu nation he had met with stiff resistance and violence and literally had to run for his life.

On several overseas trips Morris had passed through India and had stayed overnight while waiting for a connecting flight the next day. Those evenings alone pushed any thought of ministering in India out of his mind. He could feel the spiritual oppression and evil spirits all around him. He was rarely able to eat his meals there; the demonic pressure was so fierce that his stomach would be twisted in knots. He invariably left the country feeling spiritually nauseated.

He prayed that the Lord would never send him there.

But, of course, when He felt that Morris was ready for the supernatural conflicts that would confront him there, the Lord did send him to India.

When the Lord placed India in Morris's mind, he fought it. They went back and forth, one of the very few times in his life that Morris dared to resist the will of God. Ultimately, of course, he lost the argument.

His first series of meetings were to be held in Madras. Several team members went to do the advance preparations before Morris's arrival. When he arrived he went directly to his hotel. He could already feel the overwhelming spiritual oppression in the country. Pastors from all over the area had sought a personal meeting with Morris, but he told his team that he was not to be disturbed for the next few days.

He fasted and prayed every waking hour during those days. One of his encounters with the Lord was a seminal moment for Morris's ministry. The Lord provided another core truth on which to build his ministry: To achieve lasting victory in any circumstance, you must deal with the root of the problem, not settle for superficial solutions. This was one of those significant, life-defining moments that further set Morris apart. Each time the Lord blessed him with such a revelation it invariably changed the course of his life and ministry. This new wisdom would prove to have such an effect. Sensing the importance of this new disclosure, Morris devoted the rest of his prayer and study time to meditating on that truth.

On the first night of meetings seventy thousand people jammed the stadium—and the numbers grew from there. Throughout the week amazing miracles happened, stunning the Indian crowds. Because Indians believe in millions of gods and are a very religious and superstitious people, there was widespread interest in Morris's words and works. Several hundred thousand people were ministered to that week. The spiritual fruit from the Indian meetings was unprecedented.

Yet, during the midst of the first meeting the Lord spoke clearly to Morris and told him not to take an offering at any time during the crusade events. India was one of the poorest nations on Earth, without a doubt, but Morris had fronted the money to rent the massive soccer stadium, the complicated sound system, the extensive security force, the airfare and hotel rooms for his team, and so forth. The expense was substantial. Morris was confused by the Lord's command, but he was also determined to be obedient.

For ten days he never mentioned money. When Indian pastors asked if they could take up a collection for him, he adamantly refused to allow it.

At the end of the crusade he had a telling conversation with one of the pastors.

"You know, we pastors were expecting you to take up an offering. If you had done so, the Hindu priests would have come forward to tear apart your platform and beat you and run you out of India. Thank God that you did not take up an offering."

Once again, the miracle-working power of God had intervened to protect Morris and extend the legend.

CHAPTER 100

WHILE MORRIS AND his small team crisscrossed the globe to share the power of God and the grace of Christ, people whose lives had been radically touched at the crusades and Schools of Ministry took upon the baton and carried forth the gospel. Whenever he returned from an overseas trip there were stacks of letters waiting for him. Theresa and her team in San Diego did their best to respond to every note, but some of them either required Morris's attention or contained information they felt he should read.

One such letter came from Juan Soriano, a pastor in the Philippines whose life was changed by Morris's ministry there. Reverend Soriano supervised a growing band of individuals who embraced the call to share God's love with their countrymen. He wrote a letter to Morris that included the following words:

> We heard you say…one of your goals is to reach the unreached. We share this vision and burden for the lost. And so, thru the months, the number of evangelists under my supervision has increased to a total of forty.
>
> We are not educated men…We are not rich men, nor are we considered great in the sight of our fellow men. But we have laid hold of the promises of God, that those who believe in Him shall perform signs and wonders in His name.
>
> Many of us only have one pair of shoes to wear. Whenever we hike over mountain trails to reach the unreached, we walk barefoot in order to preserve our shoes to use when we preach before the people. Some of us have only two or three pairs of pants to use, but because we love God and believe that God can use us, we applied for crusades under the umbrella of Morris Cerullo World Evangelism.
>
> Most of us have turned our eyes to the numerous mountain tribes who for years have been neglected or shunned by civilization. We have looked to the remote regions of our country in an effort to win these people to Christ. The going was rough. Oftentimes we only had our feet to ride on. Many of us almost died on the way, while others were almost killed, but God never leaves us nor forsakes us.

Reverend Soriano added that in a period of less than two years he and his small, under-resourced band of Filipino nationals had conducted one hundred seventy-seven crusades, resulting in the start of one hundred twenty-five new churches.

God's army was on the move!

CHAPTER 101

——— ◆ ———

YEAR AFTER YEAR Morris traveled to nations around the world to continue the Schools of Ministry and to hold occasional crusades. Because of the success of the schools, the crusades were less necessary; those who attended the schools were doing the most effective forms of outreach possible based on the principles and practices they learned from Morris and his team.

To maintain his effectiveness Morris continued to live a life focused on God. Few people realized that when he traveled he rarely left his lodging other than to go to and from an airport or ministry venue. He did not sightsee while in host countries, eschewing the spectacular sights and experiences in favor of staying on his knees in his room to interact with God in preparation for his ministry efforts. He politely turned down the countless interview requests he received from media because he was not present to generate greater exposure for himself or his organization. Fame had no appeal to him.

In order to protect their best interests and safety, Morris's family rarely accompanied him on his excursions. Because the Cerullos were a close-knit family and the children went through periods of extreme sadness because of daddy's absence, each family member had to overcome great bouts of loneliness. Theresa did a remarkable job of taking care of everyone and filling the gaps. When Morris was home he devoted all of his time and energy to the family. It was always a balancing act.

To fill the long days on the road, Morris didn't pursue hobbies or sports. When he read, it was usually the Bible or biographies of great men and women of God. He spent little time watching television. He was a single-minded servant of the living God.

When asked why he remained cooped up in his room while staying in world-class cities that people pay thousands of dollars to visit and enjoy, Morris had a simple answer: "When I come to a city I am often not well-known, but I have a mandate from the Lord. We start in a big venue with a handful of people, and within five days or so the entire city is being shaken and thousands of people are receiving Christ every night. Their lives will never be the same, and because of that the city and nation will never be the same.

"So why don't I leave my hotel room? Because I am under the oppression of the task. I cannot shake a city alone. I remain in my room because of the intensity of the time I have to spend alone with the Lord in prayer. If there is a secret to the success we have experienced, it is praying for hours and hours before the first meeting begins and continuing that prayer commitment throughout the course of the event. Those hours of prayer are times of spiritual warfare where I must confront principalities, powers, spiritual wickedness, and the forces of opposition that Satan musters to combat what we are doing. It takes hours to fight through those battles.

"My time on the road is often unpleasant. I'm not in the room taking a nap or watching TV or reading a novel. I am in prayer fighting with demons and principalities. It is exhausting and all-consuming. It is a direct confrontation with the enemies of God who would have us fail. But failure is not an option. Victory belongs to the Lord, but it does not come without a confrontation and without people paying a price.

"So I guess you could say that the 'secret' to the breakthroughs has been prayer and fasting. That makes the difference between me taking the pulpit to simply give a nice theological lecture versus seizing the moment to usher in a spiritual breakthrough. When we left a city or a country it was changed forever. The influence of the gospel was evident, and the truths of Christ were gaining ground. Believers were multiplied, and great churches were raised up.

"Like many great Christian leaders before me, I had to be willing to pay the price. I was willing, and God has always come through with His supernatural power and glory to transform the people and their city. I have been privileged to be used in the process."

CHAPTER 102

⸻•⸻

THE CONSISTENT IMPACT of the evangelistic meetings and training institutes only seemed to bring increased supernatural persecution against Morris and his team.

When he accepted an invitation to go the Tanzania, the government was controlled by communists. The nationals who were helping put on the crusade informed Morris that it appeared it might be the last chance for the nation to experience an evangelistic outreach event.

As usual, the advance team arrived in the destination city early to begin the massive preparations. The event was going to happen in Dar es Salaam, the country's largest and wealthiest city. Located on the eastern border of the nation along the Indian Ocean, it was the country's most important city for business and government.

As its name implies, it also happened to be a Muslim stronghold.

Lowell Warner, who was one of the longtime MCWE team members, was among the crew that arrived early. He was intrigued by the extensive construction that was taking place in the area. He was especially drawn to the building of the Trans-Zambian Railway, an extensive railroad line that was being laid down by a large number of communist Chinese workers who had been brought into the country to complete the project.

Warner loved photography and decided to take some pictures of the Chinese people working on the railroad terminal. After snapping just a few photos he was accosted by the local chief of police, who demanded to know what he was doing.

After Warner explained that he was merely taking pictures of an interesting process, the police chief said that such behavior was not allowed and that he must confiscate the camera and destroy the roll of film.

Warner was outraged. "How do you think it will look if I return to America and explain that as a journalist I was prevented from taking pictures of the progress taking place in Tanzania?" he ranted at the startled law enforcement official. "What do you think will happen when I report that Tanzanians do not have freedom of the press and that their police obstruct the legitimate sharing of news with the people?"

Spooked by the possible political repercussions, the Police Chief let Warner go with a stern warning. But it was a precursor of the challenges awaiting the team in east Africa.

CHAPTER 103

I**T WAS VIRTUALLY** impossible to spend any time in Dar es Salaam and not know that some guy named Morris Cerullo was coming to town. There were posters plastered everywhere in the city: on pillars, telephone poles, and on the doors and windows of abandoned buildings.

There was plenty of advertising, too, although not as much as the team wanted or had budgeted for. The media were reluctant to sell ad space to the American evangelist, but several media outlets relented because they needed the money. They did insist, however, that the ad copy avoid any language alluding to miracles. Thus, the usual tagline of the ads, which talked about sight restored to the blind, the lame being able to walk, and deaf people hearing, was eliminated.

A permit had been secured for the events, allowing the crusades to take place on the grounds of the military training fields, which spanned the size of three football fields. The MCWE team was ready to roll by the time the opening day of the meetings arrived.

And that's when the government pulled the plug.

Emmanuel Lozzaro, the national director of the Assemblies of God churches and the primary facilitator of the meetings, was being chased by government officials to officially revoke the permit he had been granted. Lozzaro found Warner and explained the dire situation. Warner gave him the best advice he could: "Keep running. Hide someplace where they cannot find you. We will keep working on the preparations here as if nothing has happened. God will prevail. We will pull it off."

It was not exactly what historians would cite as a brilliant strategy, but it seemed to work well enough. By the start of the crusade police estimated that fifty-six thousand people had crammed into the grounds to participate in the heavily anticipated event.

Dozens of military vehicles and hundreds of soldiers lined the perimeter of the field. Everyone who entered the event passed by numerous soldiers who stood at attention, were armed with machine guns, and wore their battle uniforms.

After the music had begun, the car transporting Morris to the event arrived at the main gate. They had strict orders from the head of the military to arrest the American as soon as he arrived so that he would not be able to preach. Morris was completely unaware of the tensions and challenges surrounding his arrival. As was his custom, he had spent the previous three days secluded in prayer, fasting, and study. When he exited the car he was completely unaware of the permit fiasco that was in full swing.

To Morris, it simply seemed as if the military had shown up to honor his presence. When the soldiers formed a box around him, he mistook the formation as a military drill designed to protect him. Moved by their thoughtfulness, he smiled, stood erect, and saluted the men.

This was not what the military captain was expecting. Dutifully, he led his men in returning Morris's salute and watched in confusion as the American strode right through them toward the nearby platform.

Within minutes he began to preach.

Word was relayed to the police headquarters about the incident. That triggered the dispatch of a small armada of black sedans, with lights flashing and flags mounted on the front of the vehicles that went screeching through the city streets and skidded to a stop just behind the platform. A couple dozen top police officials charged from the cars toward the steps at the back of the platform.

One of the ministry team members approached the man in front, who had exited from the lead car. He asked them what was going on.

"We are here to arrest Morris Cerullo," the chief of police said, pushing the team member aside. "He is holding an illegal meeting."

And with that, he and his imposing cadre, fully armed and in riot gear, moved rapidly toward the platform steps behind Morris.

CHAPTER 104

B EFORE THEY COULD climb the first step, however, a large black African jumped in their way. Mac Nwulu, a Nigerian pastor who had traveled for several days to be part of the crusade, blocked the stairs and eyed the leader of the military brass.

"I am sorry, but you cannot go onto the platform," he said with great indignation, full of spiritual authority. "That space is for ministers only." He folded his arms across his chest and stood his ground with a determined look.

He was a graduate of a National Training Institute. He had learned the power of spiritual authority well from his mentor, Morris Cerullo.

In the background, they could hear Dr. Cerullo preaching up a storm. The police chief, used to getting his way but feeling out of his league in the situation, argued for a few seconds but to no avail. Mac informed him that the service would be done soon. They would have to wait.

Glaring at Nwulu, the police chief then held up his right arm with an open hand, signaling his men to wait.

Unaware of the turbulence playing out just twenty feet behind him, Morris continued to forcefully preach the gospel. People in the stands were in the grip of God's Spirit. Many were crying as they heard about the sacrificial love of Jesus Christ for the first time, feeling a sense of hope for their lives.

By the time Morris finished and asked people to raise their hand if they wanted to receive Christ as their Savior and lead a transformed life, more than 90 percent of the military officials waiting behind the platform to arrest him had their hands in the air!

After leading the assembly in a prayer, Morris then asked if anyone needed to be healed, informing them that God would demonstrate His love through the miracle of healing. Soon the aisles were clogged with people seeking a touch from this powerful God.

Morris moved through the throng praying for dozens and dozens of people and asking God to be merciful and gracious. As was the case at every meeting he led, many people were healed and gave verified testimonies as to what God had just done for them.

The military officials, moved by the blessings that God was bestowing on their people through Morris's guidance, waited respectfully backstage. They would arrest the man of God when he was finished and climbed down the stairs to leave.

Morris, still unaware of the drama unfolding in his midst, moved back and forth on the grounds praying for people and reveling in the glorious healings provided by the Lord. As usual, he was in no hurry; God would reveal when it was time to close the meeting, and Morris would not rush to conclude the proceedings a second earlier—even if he *had* known who was waiting for him.

When he felt God moving him to end the time of prayer and healing, the music team took control of the stage and led the crowd in a spirited time of worship. Morris unobtrusively moved toward a side exit close to where he had just prayed for someone. A pair of team members had come alongside of him to guide him toward that exit, where a car was waiting to bring him back to his hotel.

It was the typical way that Morris left the premises of a public meeting. He did not want to be the focus of people's attention. The glory should be directed to God, not a man. They were now immersed in praise and worship. The crowd had no idea that Morris had discreetly left the arena.

Neither did the military men waiting patiently for him behind the platform.

CHAPTER 105

L ATER THAT EVENING the police and military officials caught up with Morris. He had no idea what they had been through during the day and evening while he had been doing the Lord's work. They were stern toward him. He was very cordial to them.

The chief of police was furious with Morris, feeling as if he had duped the police.

"Your meetings are over, sir," the chief said crisply. "The government will allow no more of your gatherings."

"Why not?" Morris asked gently, evincing the confusion that he felt. "Everything was peaceful. Thousands of people were blessed. We paid the fees that were requested. We have a permit to hold those meetings."

"Sir, Tanzania is beset by a terrible famine," the chief explained smugly. "Every citizen has been instructed to return home by four o'clock each day and work on their plot of land in order to increase its productivity and grow more vegetables. Your meetings are interfering with the national program to provide food for the nation. Your meetings are hereby terminated."

Morris looked up at the man without a trace of emotion. After a pause, he responded.

"Well, I'm sorry, but that just won't do," he began. "Why don't we work out a compromise? You can let us hold tomorrow's evangelistic meeting in the same place where we are holding our school of evangelism. That way you will have your military training grounds back, and we will be limited to the less central space that we were already using."

There was a bit of haggling, but then the chief reluctantly agreed to the compromise.

The meeting was held at the auditorium where the School of Ministry had been scheduled, some two miles from the crusade grounds. The building filled up hours before the crusade was scheduled to start, with thousands more gathered outside the auditorium straining to see and hear the proceedings.

The Assemblies of God hastily arranged for the remainder of the events that week to move to a church twelve miles away where there was ample land for a decent sized crowd to assemble. Thousands more showed up at those meetings, learning of the location by word of mouth.

In the end the meetings produced the spark of inspiration that the Christian church needed in Tanzania. The region grew from one hundred Christian churches to over a thousand in just a few years. The leaders of those churches were people whose lives had been changed at the MCWE events. God used Morris to bring a powerful revival to that spiritually lethargic nation.

CHAPTER 106

A
NOTHER ADVENTURE IN Africa broke significant ground as well. South Africa was still in the throes of apartheid when Morris was invited by a group of white pastors to minister there. When he asked if black pastors would be invited, he was told that they would not.

Morris replied that he would decline the invitation unless black pastors would also be invited and treated as equals.

A few days later he was informed that the invitation committee had entertained some intense discussions about Morris's request and decided that blacks would be invited but would have to sit in a segregated section of the auditorium.

It wasn't ideal, but Morris figured it was a start. After all, blacks and whites never did anything together in South Africa during the apartheid years. At least showing that churches were willing to have the two groups together was progress.

When Morris arrived to lead a week-long School of Ministry, some two thousand pastors showed up: roughly one thousand nine hundred and fifty whites and about fifty blacks. Sure enough, the black pastors sat together in a separate section of the auditorium, but they were there, and they were treated respectfully by their white colleagues.

While he was in Johannesburg for the School of Ministry, Morris conferred with the black pastors and arranged to lead a two-night crusade in Soweto, the all-black township that had produced Nelson Mandela, who was jailed at that time. Whites were not allowed in Soweto. Morris was taking his life into his hands simply driving into the township, much less attempting to teach the people. But he knew God was calling him to do this.

With the help of several of the black pastors he met at the School of Ministry, he rented out the big soccer stadium in Soweto. At the School of Ministry he informed everyone the day before the Soweto crusade that he was going there, and he invited every white pastor in the building to join him to help him teach and minister to the people of Soweto.

Not a single white pastor showed up for either night of the Soweto crusade.

Each night in excess of eighty thousand people showed up to listen to the white man from America preach the gospel. What began as a scary evening became one of the most holy and unified ministry experiences of Morris's career. Great miracles happened, and the people were ecstatic over the presence of God.

The newspaper reports the following day mentioned the miracles but emphasized the fact that when Morris was speaking the large, boisterous crowd was completely silent and attentive.

What the newspapers did not know was that when Morris was finished speaking he, Theresa, and their driver ran back to their tiny car to leave before the massive crowd dispersed.

They were unprepared for what they discovered.

Cars were parked everywhere, in total disarray. There were no aisles, no order, and no security—just cars left wherever the driver had given up seeking a better spot. Because Morris's car was close to the stage exit, they were as far from the stadium exit road as possible with no available path to get there.

They had to wait for the entire parking lot to clear out, which wound up taking several hours.

But it was the wait that was scary. While eighty thousand people departed from the stadium, they were bumping against cars. Some were bouncing the cars or jostling them from side to side. Theresa was deathly frightened. Morris instructed her to put her jacket against her window to keep people from seeing the white woman inside the tiny vehicle. Morris did the same on his side of the car, hoping to block out people's view of who was inside the auto.

"Mama," he said to her forcefully, "you sit there and pray with all the energy you have!"

The trio sat silently watching as the people continued to bump against cars as they wandered around trying to find their own. Some groups of men simply stopped at random cars, repeatedly pushing up and down on the trunk or engine, jerking it up and down for fun.

How scary was it, sitting there in the midst of the chaos and disruption? The Cerullos' young driver, eyes wide with fear, sat petrified behind the wheel of the car—and peed in his pants.

Finally, spared from recognition and with enough cars gone to enable them to escape, they drove out of Soweto to safety in the neighboring township.

Morris returned the next night for the final crusade. Theresa waited at the hotel.

In the end, though, Morris's efforts shook the white churches and initiated some important changes in the mentality of the white Christian leaders. It took a few more years and many courageous acts, but apartheid was eventually dismantled, and the church became a positive force in the move to facilitate racial reconciliation.

God's army was being built. South Africa was never the same.

CHAPTER 107

————•————

T HE PHILIPPINES IS a nation comprised of more than seven thousand islands clustered together in the Pacific Ocean in the Southeastern Asia region. It has a history of political unrest. That unrest was particularly evident during the final years of the Marcos regime.

Ferdinand Marcos was the heavy-handed ruler of the Philippines for many years. He was known for corruption, political repression, and constant human rights violations during his two decades in power. His downfall began in earnest when one of his most effective political opponents, Benigno Aquino, was assassinated at the airport in Manila. That killing, suspected to have been ordered by Marcos, set off riots and demonstrations that resulted in the election that removed Marcos from power.

A few months after Aquino was murdered and the nation was in turmoil, Morris landed in Manila to hold a School of Ministry. MCWE rented a large hall in the city with a seating capacity of four thousand two hundred and fifty. To his surprise, more than five thousand five hundred spiritual leaders from throughout the Philippines showed up for the week of spiritual training.

Even though the auditorium was overflowing on the first day, even more pastors and church leaders arrived each subsequent day. Hundreds of spiritually hungry Christian leaders, unable to squeeze their way into the overcrowded hall, sat on the lawn outside the convention center listening in rapt attention to Morris's teaching through remote speakers placed on the lawn. The Filipinos ignored the conditions: blazing sun, temperatures exceeding one hundred degrees, and humidity above 90 percent.

Keenly aware of their social situation, Morris spoke plainly and directly to those who had come to see him. He taught them that all truth is parallel and that this particular principle was crucial for the Philippines at that time. He opened the meetings with a moving story drawn from the pages of history.

"Shortly after World War II, General Douglas MacArthur sent letters to dozens of missions boards of various church denominations around the world. He pleaded with them to send him ten thousand missionaries, and he would deliver to them a new Christian nation: Japan," Dr. Cerullo explained. "The Japanese had viewed their leader, Emperor Hirohito, as invincible. He was a god in their eyes.

"But when MacArthur's forces defeated Japan, the Japanese people lost their faith in their stone Buddhas and in their emperor. The nation's temples were empty. MacArthur realized this and sent letters to all those missionary boards imploring them to send him missionaries for Japan.

"Out of the dozens of request letters that he sent, only three missionaries were eventually sent to Japan," Morris continued, his voice breaking as the pain of the sad reality stabbed at his heart. "Three! All of those mission boards, representing tens of thousands of churches and millions of Christians around the world, and all together they sent three missionaries. MacArthur received excuses like, 'We're not ready,' and, 'We don't have the money.'"

The auditorium was as quiet as a morgue as the pastors listened to the heartbreaking story.

"Today," Morris whispered into the microphone, with his head hanging low, "less than one-half of one percent of the Japanese people are Christian. Why? Because we failed to respond in God's spiritual timing."

Pausing to collect himself, Morris then lifted his head and roared at the audience.

"Today is God's spiritual time for the Philippines! We ignored God's timing for a spiritual harvest in Japan, and they slowly returned to their temples and worshiped their stone Buddhas and their pagan gods.

"But today we will not fail the Philippines. Today we will not rely upon missionaries sent from North America. Today we will train you, Filipino pastors and leaders, to go to your countrymen and win this nation for Christ!"

All five thousand five hundred people inside the hall instantly jumped to their feet cheering, clapping, and raising their arms in a victory salute. At the same time the crowd that had been sitting in the scorching sun outside the hall followed suit. Some started to sing a popular Filipino worship song, while others lifted their voices heavenward in prayer.

God's army in the Philippines had been called to battle!

The spontaneous celebration lasted for more than five minutes before Morris was able to get their attention so he could continue.

"The time has come for the Philippines to stop looking to America for help. Keep your eyes off politics and turn them on the Lord. Stop worrying about the next move of the communists. When you know the truth about your God and practice the truths that He teaches you, then your hostile environment and your enemies will crumble. If God is for you, who can be against you?

"God is building His own army here in the Philippines, and you can be part of it. Your time is now!"

Again the leaders erupted in applause and shouts of excitement. They were ready to fight the good fight of faith.

Morris and his team spent the week pouring truth and spiritual power into those leaders. He taught them how to hold their own crusades. He taught them how to disciple people. He taught them how to deal with spiritual lethargy in a nominally religious nation. Dr. Cerullo imparted the decades of spiritual wisdom he had gleaned from hard-won experience and from his countless hours of prayer and study.

As the meetings drew to a close, Morris's team was already busily engaged in preparing for a one-day public event to be held in Luneta National Park. Not even the foot of rain that fell the day before the event would stop it. God was doing something special in the Philippines.

On the day of the event more than fifty thousand people braved the inclement weather to be part of the Manila Miracle Rally. God showed up in irrefutable ways. Morris preached on Isaiah 53:1–6, challenging the people to recognize the power and love of God exemplified through the miracles performed that day and the offer of eternal salvation through Jesus's death and resurrection.

Thousands of emotional Filipinos streamed to the altar to invite Jesus to be their Lord and Savior.

Toward the end of the event Morris uttered a prophecy that people would not think about much until two years later: "I will return to the Philippines on February 7, 1986."

He said nothing more than that. It was just a simple statement, with no accompanying warning or explanation. In a couple of years' time, Morris apparently would be back in the Philippines.

Morris's team members looked at each other in surprise. They had no trip to the Philippines scheduled for that time. Morris had not alerted them in advance about this new event. Most likely, the Lord spoke through Morris without warning, as was wont to happen. They shrugged and wrote it down in their calendars. Such was life with a prophet of God.

CHAPTER 108

────◆────

S URE ENOUGH, FEBRUARY 7, 1986, rolled around, and Morris was serving the Lord in the Philippines.

It was not just a random date, as things turned out. It was the very day that an emergency election was held in the Philippines in an effort to quell the foment that had been building since the assassination of Benigno Aquino just prior to Morris's earlier excursion to the island nation.

Aquino's widow, Corazon "Rose" Aquino, a political novice and a woman of God who had no interest in being at the center of the political storm brewing in the nation, had finally acquiesced and run as the primary opposition to the ruling dictator, Ferdinand Marcos.

On that very day Morris was scheduled to hold a School of Ministry meeting with forty-five hundred pastors, booked into a large hall in the Philippines International Convention Center.

But that morning President Marcos took over the same space to be used to house the computers that he said would be tabulating the national votes. His associates moved Morris's meeting into the meeting space next door.

There was no greater example of the principle that "all truth is parallel" than what transpired that day.

In the room to the east, Marcos and his minions were plotting to steal the election from Rose Aquino. Marcos's computer scientists sat in the room rigging the computers to produce vote totals showing that the general had won re-election.

In the room to the west sat Morris and several thousand Filipino pastors prepared to do God's bidding and learning about spiritual warfare.

After the initial night of vote tallying, thirty of the computer specialists who had worked in that sealed auditorium fled under the cover of night and sought refuge in a local church. They told the media about the voting scandal that was underway and that they refused to be part of the plan to throw the election in favor of their corrupt president.

As additional reports of irregularities filtered out during the second day of the vote count, the forty-two hundred pastors on the other side of the wall from those computers joined together in hours of intense prayer, interceding on behalf of their nation.

When Marcos eventually emerged and declared victory, Morris stood before his pastors and challenged them to be spiritual warriors.

"This is your hour," he began. "This is not the hour of defeat. God has revealed to me that Jesus is praying for the Philippines. What we face as a challenge here in the Philippine islands is what we face as a challenge throughout the world today. There is a great shaking coming. Everything that can be shaken will be shaken: governments, economies, families, relationships, religious systems. That shaking has now started."

With that, the pastors returned to prayer for their country.

Within two weeks, Corazon Aquino had been installed as the eleventh president of the nation, and Ferdinand Marcos and his wife, Imelda, fled the country in exile. His declarations of victory notwithstanding, the people refused to recognize that claim and accused him and his team of election fraud. In his place they embraced the self-proclaimed "plain housewife" who would seek to reform the nation's corrupt government and return it to democracy.

And there were forty-five hundred pastors who had learned firsthand the power of the supernatural as they watched their prayers get answered in a most spectacular way.

CHAPTER 109

THINGS DON'T ALWAYS go smoothly for those serving the Lord. One year when Morris was scheduled to do a series of events in six Mexican states he had invited Theresa to accompany him on the trip. The children were older and on their own at that point, and it seemed like an ideal time for them to travel together. But shortly before they were to leave, while Morris was in prayer, the Lord instructed him not to take Theresa along. Before he finished praying and went to tell her of the change in plans, the Lord also asked Morris an unusual question.

"Son, what would you do if I took Theresa home?"

Startled by the question, Morris replied, "You know how much I love her, Lord, but if you want to take her, I'll give her up to you."

Theresa was upset when Morris told her that she could not come on the trip. He did not mention the question the Lord had posed about taking her to heaven, nor did he offer much of an explanation for the cancellation.

Already stressed by some of the difficulties their youngest son, Mark, was enduring at the time, she had been looking forward to the trip and became agitated when Morris told her about the change. He stood firm though and left soon thereafter for his two-week journey.

Toward the middle of Morris's trip Mark came by their house to see his mom. While there, she was paying some bills and collapsed. Frightened, Mark called for an ambulance and rushed to the hospital to be with her.

In the emergency ward the doctors checked Theresa and soon discovered that she was suffering from bleeding ulcers. They had to give her seven pints of blood, meaning she only had one pint of her own left by the time she reached the hospital! The doctors were not optimistic about her condition.

Understandably, Mark freaked out. He called his siblings, David and Susan, and told them they needed to join him at her bedside. David flew in from North Carolina. The three of them took turns calling Morris, who was in a hard-to-reach area of Mexico.

When David finally reached his father he explained the situation and stated that his father needed to leave the crusades and Schools of Ministry immediately to be with his wife. The doctors had said they did not think Theresa was going to make it through the ordeal and that there was not much more they could do to save her.

Morris was heartbroken by the news but suddenly understood why the Lord had asked him about taking Theresa home. He felt he could not tell his son about that exchange with God but also knew that he could not fly home to join his family in the hospital. Morris simply explained that he was in the midst of a ministry trip the Lord had called him on, and it was not possible for him to leave Mexico.

David was livid. In no uncertain terms he told his father how wrong his priorities were, that family must always come first. From two thousand miles away Morris gently tried to explain that as much as he cherished his wife, his highest priority was God, the only One who could keep him from his family. The pair argued for a brief time before David hung up the phone in anger.

Meanwhile, Theresa was having her own conversations with God while she lay in the hospital bed with tubes and probes hooked up to her failing body. She was aware of her children's presence and understood her husband's absence but was concerned about the state of the family. As she neared what she felt might be her final hours, she prayed earnestly to God, "Dear God, I understand if you want to take me home. I'm ready. But if it means my family will be broken up or badly divided because their dad is gone serving you, then please keep me here for all of them. I do not want to leave knowing that the children will harbor resentment against their father."

As Theresa's condition declined and she lost consciousness the children stayed by her bedside throughout the night, expecting the end to come any moment.

Theresa, though, entered a peaceful state in which she was able to sense everyone's presence in her room and able to hear their thoughts. She was especially perturbed by David's thoughts. He remained furious toward his dad for refusing to return to be wife his wife and children.

During the course of that day, while Morris was in prayer, the Lord spoke to him about Theresa and told him he could leave the ministry events to his associates and fly home to be with his wife and children. He had been expectantly waiting for such a release and hurriedly packed and left. Because he was deep in the heart of the less populated areas of Mexico it took almost a full day for him to get back.

He finally landed at the San Diego airport around midnight and immediately drove to the hospital, where he joined Theresa. He kissed her gently, took her hand, and kneeled beside her bed and prayed for her throughout the night. As sunrise approached Morris fell asleep for a short time.

When he woke up in the morning Theresa was fully conscious—and completely healed! The doctor making his morning rounds was astonished. He double-checked the medical records and ran an extra test. Once he was convinced that the recovery was real he explained his perplexity to Morris and Theresa.

"I've never seen anything like this in my life. Frankly, I expected you to pass away during the night. But I cannot find anything wrong with you at this point, Mrs. Cerullo. This is the kind of wonderful news we don't get to see often enough. I'm happy to pronounce you fit and ready to discharge. Mr. Cerullo, since you're here now, why don't you take your wife home?"

David joined his dad in rejoicing over his mother's miraculous healing, and they praised God for His graciousness.

Time after time, Morris experienced the supernatural power of God to do things that were beyond explanation. Theresa's condition and recovery joined a long list of adventures in which God superseded the laws of reality. In this case, he was deeply thankful for that intervention.

CHAPTER 110

THE DREAMS OF a prophet never die.

The most significant portion of Morris's formative years were spent in the Jewish orphanage, where his cultural education was rooted in their traditions and practices. When he accepted Christ and was given God's vision of souls being ravaged in the fires of hell, that call to serve Christ did nothing to remove his sense of heritage. He retained a passion for Jews and prayed continually over the years for God to empower him to reach Jews around with world with the good news of how Jesus Christ was the long-awaited Messiah.

When Morris had the opportunity to take his brief post-Greece excursion to Jerusalem, the adventure merely stirred his soul more deeply.

After he wrote a tract about his conversion from Judaism to Christianity in 1959, he had the pamphlet translated into Hebrew and was able to pull some strings and lean on some personal contacts to get one hundred thousand copies of his testimony distributed to Jews living in Israel. He wanted desperately to journey to Israel to follow-up on that effort but did not feel that God was releasing him to do so.

So Morris waited.

The call from God came while he leading crusades in Argentina in 1967. The Lord called him to return to Israel and to deploy an unconventional but strategic plan.

Jews did not want a Christian to preach at them. Neither would they respond to street-corner evangelism or tracts passed out in public places. In response to his prayers the Lord gave Morris a strategy of using literature and events to expand His kingdom in the Holy Land. He would start by launching an ongoing, strategically crafted literature campaign that shared truths about Christ. Then he would hold training events in Jerusalem for Jews who had received Yeshua as their Messiah, to prepare them to reach unsaved Jews through their personal relationships with those people. Eventually he would expand the media used to reach an ever-widening band of people.

Early in Morris's tenure in Israel he was able to publish his first messianic booklet in Hebrew, titled *Besorat Shalom*, which means "the good news of peace." He mailed the booklet to twelve thousand Jewish homes. Although it was a risky venture in many ways, the response was phenomenal and positive. More than two thousand Jews responded, either accepting Jesus as the Messiah or seeking more information as they contemplated the possibilities.

That effort led to him getting the name of a mailing house in Tel Aviv that had a reputation for reaching a large segment of the nation's population.

After negotiations the company offered to rent Morris the coveted voter registration list for all of Israel, which contained the name and address of every registered voter in the country! The broker secured permission for Morris to use the list, eliminating months of bureaucratic red tape and scrutiny. And, as an unexpected bonus from the Lord, the broker inexplicably allowed Morris to use the list for free!

That was another great miracle that Morris experienced in a life of great miracles done by the Lord.

As the plan to reach Israel with the gospel continued to roll out, the timing could not have been better. Israel had recently been attacked on all sides by neighboring countries with larger and better equipped armies but managed to defeat all of its foes and protect its borders. The victory was a military triumph but not an emotional advance. The people of Israel, proud of their military, nevertheless realized that the hostilities meant they were still at odds with their neighbors and vulnerable to attack at any time. Israelis lived with an uneasiness that caused them to question the foundations of life and liberty.

As a result, when Morris's booklet describing "the good news of peace" arrived in people's mailboxes Jews all over the nation read it with interest, looking for answers to the deep life questions that plagued them. Thousands upon thousands of Jews responded to MCWE indicating that after reading the booklet they had accepted Jesus as their Messiah.

That swell of new believers gave Morris the traction needed to launch a Deeper Life Conference in Israel to raise up an army of Jewish nationals who would carry the gospel throughout the nation.

Again, through another series of miracles Morris was able to rent a prestigious hotel in the heart of Jerusalem as the site for the event. But, it is one thing to rent a hotel and promote an event; it is something else to actually have anyone show up at the event, especially in a country protective of its religious heritage and suspicious of Christians.

After some marketing and a lot of prayer the day of the event arrived, and people showed up. However, the first one-hundred-plus people to arrive were not the ones Morris and his team had expected. Dozens of Orthodox Jews had assembled in front of the building carrying placards and yelling protest slogans over the presence of the Christian event in the very center of the Jewish nation.

But then the people Morris and his team had been praying for slowly trickled into the building, pushing past the protesters to register for the event. When the conference started some one hundred and fifty Jews had made their way into the large meeting room—a standing-room only crowd.

Grateful and humbled, Morris taught the group from Isaiah 53. When he was done he did what everyone he spoke to in Israel said could not be successfully done: he gave an altar call.

Every person there came forward!

Unknown to Morris at the time, God would use him to undertake at least one significant outreach project to the people of Israel each year for the coming forty years! Those included breakthroughs such as the distribution of a Bible correspondence course, offering every registered voter a free Bible, and sending at least one mailing to every Israeli voter's household each year. Many of those mailings included free copies of unique ministry publications, such as Morris's book *Two Men from Eden* and the Book of Daniel. In fact, that was the first time that portion of the Bible had ever been published in modern Hebrew.

God opened doors for Morris to be able to send a copy of his book *The Messiah*—re-titled *The Peace* for Israelis—to every household in the entire nation. The gospel penetrated the nation through the airwaves too, as MCWE was able to broadcast a thirty-minute evangelistic program into Israel every week from stations located in nearby nations. Israeli-based television networks, like radio stations, were also banned from carrying Christian programming, but Morris struck deals with satellite providers to beam his programming into Israeli homes once the technology was available. School of Ministry training programs ran successfully every year, raising up thousands of Jewish Christians to share the gospel in culturally appropriate ways.

In 2004 MCWE held three healing festivals, one each in Tel Aviv, Haifa, and Jerusalem. The results exceeded all expectations. The team followed up with a series of Schools of Ministry to develop the faith and hone the outreach skills of the increasing number of Jewish believers.

Various outreach meetings were held over the years, culminating in the historic Israel Outreach of 2010, which drew both Jews and Arabs. That event was held in Hangar 11, the world-renowned, cutting-edge performance venue featuring video, sound, and lighting systems that are among the most advanced in the world.

How can one explain such an abundance of impactful Christian ministry taking place in the homeland of the Jewish people, all of it instigated by one Jewish Christian living nearly eight thousand miles away? Only by the supernatural guidance, protection, and provision of God. Laws were legally circumvented, millions of dollars accessed and invested, and impossible transactions completed only because this was the will of God—and because one man dared to follow God's commands and pursue the impossible. It is the stuff of legend, the legend of Morris Cerullo.

CHAPTER 111

A S MUCH AS the Jews in Israel were always on Morris's heart, a majority of the world's Jews lived outside of Israel. In fact, there are about as many Jews living in the United States as live in Israel. (The two nations together encompass more than 12 million of the world's 14 million Jews.) Morris never lost sight of the need to reach the millions of Jews living outside Israel's borders as well.

Toward that end, his efforts in Israel stoked his interest in reaching American Jews. However, he knew the strategies that enabled him to reach them in Israel were not the same strategies that would allow him to reach American Jews. So, he prayed and he waited.

The Lord gave him the ideal vehicle.

Recognizing that the world was changing and people's minds were being shaped by various forms of communication, Morris was led to create entertainment content that could be broadcast into every Jewish home in America. He raised the money to create a full-length video presentation of the gospel produced on location in Israel and purchased airtime during prime time hours, when people were most likely to view the broadcast. The dramatic special, *Masada*, garnered positive responses from more than two hundred thousand Jews across North America. Tens of thousands of them accepted Christ as their Lord and Savior as a result of seeing that broadcast.

Morris followed that up by sending a copy of a book he had written, *Two Men from Eden*, to every identifiable Jewish household in the country. The book compared the lives of the first and second Adam—Adam, the first man whom God created, and Jesus, the Man who redeemed all of mankind. The book received an enthusiastic welcome by many American Jews, resulting in more than ten thousand of them embracing Jesus as their Messiah.

The resounding success of *Masada* led Morris to produce yet another television special aimed at North American Jews. This one, titled *The Sound of Trumpets*, was also filmed in Israel at historic sites. It detailed the ministry, miracles, and prophetic fulfillments of Jesus Christ. In addition to filming scenes at important biblical sites such as the garden of Gethsemane and the sites of various miracles, the program included an interview with former Israeli Prime Minister Yitzhak Rabin. Again, the critical reaction was overwhelmingly affirmative, and many Jewish people turned their lives over to Christ.

Encouraged by these successes in reaching American Jews, MCWE produced a full-length motion picture titled *The Rabbi*. The movie was broadcast in every city of North America during prime time, as well as shown in theaters and via television channels in various nations of the world.

Throughout forty-plus years of efforts to reach the Jewish people, Morris never stopped praying for God's direction regarding how else he might be used by God to influence those people to consider Jesus. His efforts drew ire and flak from Zionists and others who resented his efforts to convert Jews. He shrugged his shoulders and accepted the criticism and resistance, realizing that it was part of the price he must pay to be obedient to God's call.

PART SIX:

—◆—

THE ARMY
MARCHES ON

CHAPTER 112

———◆———

ORRIS RECOGNIZED THAT because the successes he had witnessed were not about him it was important to continually embrace the new tools that the Lord made available for life transformation.

The Bible, first printed mechanically by Gutenberg in 1455, was a technological breakthrough that changed the church forever. It allowed for the more rapid and accurate reproduction of the Bible, which made it possible to put God's Word in the hands of common folks everywhere.

Radio was a technological breakthrough that allowed the gospel to be heard in every home around the world. From the 1920s forward, gospel preaching, music, and counseling have been a staple in radio programming.

Airplane travel allowed evangelists like Morris to travel to every country anywhere on the planet in a matter of hours and to ship in enormous quantities of equipment and training materials safely and quickly.

Television and movies proved to be powerful tools for communicating the gospel to a broad audience with emotional impact and compelling imagery.

For centuries church leaders had been able to exploit these and other new technologies for the advance of the gospel. As those breakthroughs became second nature to subsequent generations of ministers, cutting-edge leaders were always on the lookout for the latest applications science and engineering had to offer. Despite the tension between faith and science, men of faith consistently appropriated the tools of science to expand the church.

During the 1970s and 1980s one of the most successful religious television broadcasts in the US was called *The PTL Club*, which stood for Praise the Lord. The program was hosted by two Assemblies of God ministers, Jim and Tammy Faye Bakker. Jim had worked for years with Pat Robertson, another Assemblies minister, on Robertson's popular program, *The 700 Club*.

Bakker's broadcast and related fundraising efforts were so successful that the ministry eventually bought a huge parcel of land (3.6 square miles—2,300 acres) in Fort Mill, South Carolina, to create a Christian theme park and related activities. He named it Heritage USA. The complex would include rides, a water park, a residential community, a hotel, an indoor shopping mall, a skating rink, a 400-site campground, and other recreational facilities. The property also encompassed the broadcasting facilities and administrative offices for the Bakkers' ministry, a conference center, a retreat center, and prayer and counseling services.

It was as ambitious an undertaking as any Christian ministry had ever adopted. And, for a while, it worked well. However, after Jim Bakker's affair with a former secretary was revealed, the PTL ministry crashed and burned, taking Heritage USA down with it. After a series of legal and financial maneuvers, Heritage USA went into bankruptcy before Hurricane Hugo came along and ravaged the property, damaging many of the buildings. By 1990, the once-glamorous facility was closed and in disrepair.

A year later, while buyers were being sought for the property, the Lord spoke to Morris about buying out the assets. Purchasing any kind of assets out of bankruptcy—especially with many investors and creditors still searching for ways to get paid what they felt they were owed—was messy at best. But Morris diligently followed the Lord's leading and became increasingly intrigued by the possibilities that the PTL holdings represented.

Through a series of divine encounters Morris partnered with an international investment group and became part of the purchase team. After some time as a minority owner, chairman of the board, and chief executive managing the enterprise, the relationship turned sour, and Morris decided it was no longer a good use of his time. After a lot of prayer and personal reflection, Morris realized his best option was to sell out to the investment group, which he did.

And then he turned his attention to the little jewel that had been carved out from the main deal—the remains of the former PTL Television Network.

CHAPTER 113

——·——

B Y THE TIME the final transaction was completed, the PTL Network had plummeted from more than five million viewers each day to less than five hundred thousand viewers per day. It was a shambles.

But as Morris's track record over the years had shown, a man who follows God's vision can do anything. And someone with his business acumen and willingness to blaze new technological trails could see great outcomes emerge from an otherwise daunting mess.

Knowing that his oldest son, David, was a very wise businessman and understood the foundations of broadcasting, Morris asked David if he would be willing to move his family to Charlotte, North Carolina, to run the network.

That represented a great opportunity but also a huge sacrifice for David and his family. They loved living in San Diego. Morris and Theresa hated to see their son and his young family move cross country. In the end, though, David accepted the offer, and he and his family moved to Charlotte and began the long, difficult restoration of the network.

One of the first major alterations that he and David agreed upon was to change the name from PTL Network to The Inspirational Network (known as INSP).

David continued to make major changes to bring the network back to life. He completely rearranged the programming. He altered the look of the network. Even the financial model was reconfigured to facilitate a more efficient operation. Many of the changes were expensive, but Morris believed in the network, and he believed in his son, so the ministry made the necessary investments.

In the end those investments paid off. Within a few years the network was running smoothly, and the finances were solid.

After several years of growth David expressed his desire to see the network become an independent ministry under his leadership. After a period of intense negotiations Morris convened the MCWE board and David to discuss such a transition. By the end of the meeting a separation strategy had been laid out and agreed upon through which INSP would become an independent non-profit organization and ministry beacon.

INSP has continued to broadcast thousands of hours of classic preaching and teaching, along with original family programming and many of Morris's presentations. David continued to lead the network into new opportunities, expanding its reach and increasing its value into the tens of millions of dollars.

All of this took place because Morris listened to the Lord direct him to get involved in the acquisition of the remains of the PTL holdings. Even in the business of ministry God performed great miracles through Morris and his family.

CHAPTER 114

———•———

A CENTURY AGO ENGLAND had a vibrant Christian population. But as secularization and immigration altered its population, the nation lost its connection with Christ. It was not uncommon as the new millennium approached to see beautifully designed and crafted churches with hundreds of years of history turned into bed-and-breakfast inns or theaters.

In 1992 Morris heard the Lord call him to London. As was becoming a pattern, when he first visited the city he had no idea where he would hold his meetings or how to reach the people.

Upon arriving in the British capital Morris and his crusade director, Greg Mauro, were driving through the streets of London marveling at the historic beauty of the city and the cosmopolitan nature of the people. At one point they were slowed by traffic in front of Earls Court. Morris was intrigued by what he saw happening outside his window and asked their driver to pull over.

Greg and Morris walked into Earls Court and ran into a display of military hardware that happens there each year. There were tanks, armored vehicles, a variety of weapons, and an array of uniforms, among other things. Brits were wandering from item to item inspecting everything with great interest. Military personnel were on hand to explain things and answer people's questions.

Morris stood in the middle of the activity for a minute, quietly observing the people and examining the space in which the display was housed. He slowly turned around to capture the full panoramic view in his mind. When he finished his intelligence gathering he turned to Greg.

"This is it. We should have our meetings here. Let's find the director of Earls Court." Fifteen minutes later they were talking to the man who managed Earls Court. Not surprisingly, he had never been asked to rent his site for an evangelistic meeting but was open to the possibility and agreed to have a more detailed meeting in the next day. When that next encounter was concluded Morris had the location for his London meetings.

Reaching the people of London would be no small challenge. Since London is one of the busiest, most expensive, and most cosmopolitan cities in the world, MCWE's marketing budget for the crusade was, at best, completely inadequate for grabbing the attention of the busy Brits.

When Greg met with the advertising agency that had been recommended to them they acknowledged that limitation. Nick Alford, their account executive, was not a Christian, but he was a capable professional. Neither he nor the agency, which was part of one of the largest ad agencies in the world at the time, had ever worked with such a client.

After listening to Greg describe Morris's ministry and expectations, Nick and his creative team were captivated by the challenge. They asked for a day or two to bat around ideas before suggesting a creative direction. They knew that their challenge was to create an instant buzz throughout the city, somehow penetrating people's consciousness with a startling campaign that moved people to talk to their friends about the campaign's content—and to do so with a very limited budget.

Morris and Greg arrived two days later to find an excited creative team eagerly awaiting their return.

"What we are proposing is three different ads that will be posted on billboards in the high traffic areas of London," Nick explained. "We will locate them so that everyone will hopefully be exposed to all three of the ads. Here we've mocked up what we think will get people talking."

He then uncovered large design mock-ups of each of the proposed ads. They were simple but striking, with a picture and only three brief lines of text.

The first pictured a wheelchair laying in the gutter, discarded. The text next to it said, "Some will be moved by the power of God for the first time." The text across the bottom of the ad simply said, "June 6–10, Earls Court."

The second showed a hearing aid that had been discarded. The accompanying text read, "Some will hear the message of the Bible clearly for the first time." Again, the text across the bottom of the ad said, "June 6–10, Earls Court."

The third ad portrayed the white walking stick used by a blind person discarded on the sidewalk. The text alongside the photo read, "Some will see miracles for the first time." The text at the bottom once again stated, "June 6–10, Earls Court."

Neither Morris nor Greg were enthusiastic about the proposed campaign. They agreed that it was interesting that no ministries had previously used a billboard campaign to arrest the public's attention, and they liked the simplicity of the messages sent.

But it was certainly a risk. Should they invest their limited advertising funds in such a bare-bones, minimalist communications effort? Would it really cut through the clutter and succeed?

After some discussion they agreed to trust the professionals and approved the campaign.

They were not prepared for what happened when the billboards went live the week before the first meeting.

CHAPTER 115

GREG'S CELL PHONE would not stop ringing. As the first sign of the potential effectiveness of the billboard campaign, media from all over Europe was aware of the campaign the morning it launched, instigating the calls. Greg fielded inquiries from every major London-based media outlet you could think of: BBC, ITV, Sky News, CNN, *The Times*, *Evening Standard*, *London Mirror*, BBC Radio News, and more. They all called to get the scoop on what was planned in Earls Court for June 6 through 10.

Once reporters heard the basic outline of the event—which included prayer for miracles—they all wanted to speak directly to Morris.

Churches from across the metropolitan area caught on quickly and agreed to help generate additional interest in the events. By the time of the first event more than three hundred Christian congregations were partnering with MCWE in developing the Mission to London.

Some people stirred public interest in the meetings without meaning to do so. One example was a medical doctor named Peter May. He did what he could to contradict everything Morris said about miracles, arguing that there is no such thing as a miracle. There were a few times when Dr. Cerullo and Dr. May were featured in a mini-debate on-air, along with some people who had been healed through prayer.

After making his usual derogatory comments about Morris's ministry, May would then try to convince individuals who testified to their healing that they had not been healed or to attribute their improvement to some other medical reason. The doctor did not make a credible impression, but he did produce more controversy and curiosity about the June event—exactly what the team needed in order to attract people to the crusade.

In the period between the billboard launch and the event, the media attention spawned additional speaking opportunities for Morris. One of those was an invitation to speak to the students and faculty at renowned Oxford University. Not only was their large auditorium packed with curious people, but major media followed Morris to the site hoping to catch a sneak preview of what the London events would provide. The resulting reports raised further public awareness and intrigue.

When the London crusade began the arena was packed to the rafters. Morris preached a stirring series of messages, person after person was prayed for and healed, and thousands of British adults came forward to accept Christ.

In retrospect, those meetings provided a much-needed spark for the Christian church in England. The crusades influenced many of the pastors who would go on to plant megachurches, which were uncommon in England at that time. The response was so positive that Morris returned to England year after year harvesting souls and then developing them through the Schools of Ministry held around the country.

CHAPTER 116

————•————

Aftee twenty-plus years of ministry to London since his initial crusades at Earls Court, the Lord spoke to Morris and instructed him to conduct one last week of crusades in the bustling city.

The year 2014 provided an opportunity to bring Morris's ministry in London full circle. Celebrating the more than one million people who had experienced God's power through Morris's ministry in the big city over the years, the event was promoted as Dr. Cerullo's final full-scale crusade there.

Adding a slightly nostalgic feel, the gatherings again took place in the historic Earls Court Exhibition Centre, one of the last events held there before it was demolished and replaced by luxury condominiums.

Between his first and last London appearances in that place, Morris's efforts had birthed hundreds of new churches and parachurch ministries and raised up numerous widely recognized and effective ministry leaders.

Before the start of the highly anticipated week Morris had shared his vision: "I expect this to be the greatest week of harvest, of miracles, of souls, and of destiny ever experienced in London."

By the end of the week it was clear that the Lord had fulfilled those expectations.

The large hall was jammed each night of the crusade, with another three thousand believers attending the School of Ministry sessions each afternoon. Reflecting the significance of the event, more than five hundred churches from the metropolitan area joined forces to pray for and participate in the week of activity. Some speculated that it was the greatest show of unity among the area's churches in memory. It certainly reflected Morris's undeniable impact on the spiritual health of London.

Day after day special ministry moments added to an unforgettable week. A stellar array of international teachers, prophets, and evangelists were on hand to minister alongside Morris at the events. The list of fellow leaders, drawn from three continents, read like a Who's Who of twenty-first-century ministry. Among the American ministry leaders who flew to London to help Dr. Cerullo share the gospel and God's healing power were Tommy Barnett, Kenneth Copeland, Creflo Dollar, Steve Munsey, and Bill Winston. More than a dozen gifted musical artists took turns leading the crowds in worship.

But it was the team of British pastors whose presence highlighted the historic influence of Dr. Cerullo in England. Among the hometown pastors who spoke to the audience were Alex Omokudu, who testified that his life and ministry had been "massively impacted" by his time under Dr.

Cerullo's teaching and leadership. Pastor Matthew Ashimolowo of Kingsway Christian Centre had attended Mission to London events in the 1990s when his struggling church had just two hundred adults meeting in a cafeteria. His church now numbered more than twelve thousand people worshiping and serving God each week. He, too, offered gushing praise and gratitude to Morris.

Perhaps it was Bishop John Francis, an early disciple of Dr. Cerullo who had risen to become one of the leading spiritual lights in England and beyond, who summed it up best during one of the evening assemblies. Francis spoke movingly about attending his first MCWE crusade with his mother when he was just five years old. Those meetings had been held in the majestic Royal Albert Hall in London. As he grew up and pursued his own call to ministry he was motivated by Morris's passion and the biblical wisdom he had gleaned from the great man of God, and he was anxious to put the ministry perspectives and strategies taught in the schools of ministry into action.

And he did—so successfully that he rose to become a bishop in his denomination, pastored one of the largest and best-known churches in London, and had speaking invitations from countries around the world.

"All of the great churches that are happening in our city can be traced back to the gift God has given to us," Francis told the standing-room-only crowd, pointing to Morris at the side of the platform. "Would you celebrate really loud for Dr. Morris Cerullo? I give God thanks for him."

The auditorium exploded in applause and shouts of joy, recognizing the man who acknowledged that none of this was the work of a man but instead a testimony to the miracle-working power of God. Morris gave all the glory to God and marveled along with everyone else at the great signs and wonders and miracles that were done by their loving God through his willing servant.

As Morris stood on the platform and observed the proceedings, he could not help but feel joyful about what the Lord had done through him all those years. He had been charged with building an army for the Lord. He scanned the stage and saw some of the generals and other officers that had been raised up as part of that army.

God's army was advancing.

CHAPTER 117

I N 2009, IMMERSED in his seventh decade of ministry, Morris continued to travel around the world to teach, prophesy, and heal, according to God's agenda. One of his journeys took him to Chicago to spend an evening with a banquet room full of invited guests. These were some of the MCWE partners who lived in the area. As had been his practice for more than a half century, he met with such groups regularly to keep them informed and involved in the MCWE ministry.

Little did he know that before the evening was over the Lord would deliver what would likely be Morris's last major assignment.

When he stepped onto the platform to address his supporters, Morris felt overwhelmed by God's presence. While awaiting his turn at the microphone, he literally heard God's voice—the same voice he had heard sixty-three years ago in New Jersey when the Lord took him to heaven and gave him a vision. At that time the Lord spoke words that altered the course of his life: "Arise and shine, for your light has come. The glory of the Lord is upon you. When you feel this presence, know that I am there in your midst to do great things for My people."

Sixteen years afterward, while ministering in Brazil, the Lord handed Morris another life-altering commission when He said, "Son, build me an army."

This time the voice said, "Son, do you know prophets never retire?" Almost eighty years old at the time, Morris was constantly besieged by close friends who suggested that he retire and enjoy his remaining years on Earth. Having been solely focused on ministry for so many years, he had been thinking seriously about what such a transition might be like.

It sounded as if the Lord had a different plan in mind. Morris wanted to be sure he understood the message so he could fulfill the Lord's wishes.

After the meeting Morris returned to his hotel room, got on his knees, and entered a time of intense prayer. "God, what are you trying to say to me?"

When the Lord replied, His words were even more significant than those delivered earlier in the evening.

"Morris, make plans for continuing the ministry I have given you after I have called you home. Son, I do not want the ministry that I have given you to ever die."

On his knees, his mind flashed to the ministry giants who had preceded him—Kathryn Kuhlman, Aimee Semple McPherson, Charles Blair, and others—all of whose ministries had long since faded into the history books. He felt compelled to ask the Lord the questions that troubled him.

"So many great giants of the faith came before me, Lord, and their influence has waned. What is different about my ministry? Why would I expect my ministry to thrive long after I am home with you, Lord?"

God's response moved Morris to tears. "You have built an army propelled by the same anointing that has been on your life. They will continue to heal the sick and break open the nations for Me. They will carry on your legacy for generations to come until my Son returns to Earth."

As the Lord continued to reveal His plans to Morris, He reminded His servant that nothing Morris had ever accomplished was of his own doing; it was always the work of the Holy Spirit. And he reminded Morris that his ministry could be extended beyond his time on Earth because the hallmark of his ministry had been passing on the anointing of God to others.

And then the Lord shared a vision for what would later be named the Morris Cerullo Legacy International Center. It would be a resource center from which millions of lives around the world would be touched by the truths and power of God, saving many and training many to serve the God of creation—even after Morris was in the heavens with God.

God's plan shook him to the core. Something that had not entered his scope of consideration—leaving behind a means of extending his ministry legacy beyond his earthly presence—was suddenly front and center in his mind and heart.

CHAPTER 118

——— • ———

ORRIS'S EMOTIONAL REACTION to the Lord's new commission was intense. He felt a burden from that day forward to transition from globetrotting to lead ministry events to creating a legacy through which his ministry would be preserved and perpetuated.

As excited as he was by the concept, Morris also felt somewhat overwhelmed. No man could possibly complete such a task based on his own ideas and skills and expect the venture to receive God's full blessing. This new venture would have to be done in steadfast cooperation with God. Morris felt a trace of anxiety churning within himself as he set about to make this latest vision a reality.

The challenge was to build a unique ministry center that would appeal to the general public. It would be a place where thousands of people every day could learn, worship, rest, pray, and experience healing.

Just as He once commanded Morris, "Build me an army," now He added another element to the mission: "Build me a place." It was to be a place where God's glory—past, present, and future—could be experienced in various ways.

Morris and his team met to pray about and discuss the possibilities. Before long they had a plan that they felt was anointed by God and would reveal His majesty and faithfulness to all who would visit the legacy center.

The first step in carrying out that plan was to find the right location. By the grace of God, within a short time they identified a prime eighteen-acre hillside plot in San Diego's prestigious Mission Valley. Located right off of a major freeway, the site was just a few miles from other highly-trafficked destination points, such as the world-famous San Diego Zoo, Sea World, beautiful Balboa Park, and, of course, the sandy beaches and sparkling water of the Pacific Ocean.

The negotiations for the property were completed, and MCWE prepared to close the deal. But, as happens with so many significant undertakings pursued by God's people, God's enemy did what he could to block the path of progress. Just days before the scheduled closing the bank that owned the property declared bankruptcy. After some delays while the legal ramifications were worked out, the property was taken over by the FDIC and eventually assigned to another bank.

Morris and his team stayed on the trail of the property, confident that the Lord would allow them to acquire the land. But, of course, it wasn't quite that quick or easy. The bank that now owned the property did not want to sell it to MCWE, thinking that if they held on to the parcel for a couple of years its value would increase and they would benefit. After two years of pestering the bank, MCWE was informed that the bank was ready to put the property up for sale—via public auction! They also informed Morris's team that the bank itself would be bidding for the property. To make matters even more stressful, both Morris and the ministry's CFO were ministering out of the country on the day scheduled for the auction.

After prayer, Morris asked the organization's CEO, Lynn Hodge, to represent MCWE at the auction and gave him specific instructions as to how much money he could bid. When he arrived at the auction Lynn was the only person there. The auctioneer told him the bank had given her written instructions as to what their starting, middle, and highest bids would be. After Lynn agreed to exceed the starting and middle bids, the auctioneer read aloud the bank's final offer. She then explained that if MCWE was willing to pay more than the bank's highest bid—even one penny more—then the property would be theirs. With a smile and a sigh of relief, Lynn submitted the highest bid, topping the bank's offer by one penny!

At last the property belonged to MCWE—and for slightly less than the highest amount that Dr. Cerullo had authorized Lynn to spend. The ministry team came to know that transaction as the one-penny miracle.

There were plenty more miracles related to the development of the Mission Valley property yet to come.

CHAPTER 119

————•————

With the property in hand, Morris and the development team got busy. Dr. Cerullo laid out the vision the Lord had supplied. The property would eventually contain a multitude of ministry, educational, historical, and entertainment opportunities for visitors. Among the highlights to be developed were the following:

+ Walk Through the Bible Experience—Conceived as a multi-media presentation using sights, scents, sound, lighting, and movement to guide people through the dramatic and captivating stories embedded in the Bible from Genesis to Revelation

+ March of Prophecy—Designed to provide a dramatic representation of numerous biblical prophecies, some that have been realized (such as Moses descending from Mt. Sinai with tablets containing the Ten Commandments and various messianic prophecies) and others yet to come (e.g., the Rapture, Battle of Armageddon, the Tribulation, and the establishment of the new heavens and earth)

+ Wings Over Israel—With motion-controlled seats and a spectacular forty-foot dome theater screen visitors would have an unforgettable experience of soaring over the magnificent and historic sights of Israel, such as Masada, the Dead Sea, Megiddo (where the Battle of Armageddon will be fought), Bethlehem, Jericho, Nazareth, Mt. Carmel, the garden of Gethsemane, and the empty tomb of Christ. Also included will be spectacular views of the Temple Mount, the Wailing Wall, and the Dome of the Rock in Jerusalem.

+ Jewish Pavilion—This sophisticated exhibition hall would provide people of all faiths with an introduction to the highlights and artifacts collected during Dr. Cerullo's many years of ministry.

+ A variety of other magnificent experiences such as an interactive, holographic experience with Dr. Cerullo and Theresa, a full-scale replica of the catacombs from ancient Rome to provide a sense of what it was like to be a Christian in the early days of the church, a realistic Mediterranean shopping bazaar, and the Wailing Wall Plaza.

+ Shekinah Prayer Center—A non-stop prayer and worship venue complete with healing rooms and prayer gardens. Schools of Prayer would be offered in that location, along with intercession teams and a 24/7 telephone prayer ministry.

+ Legacy Village Luxury Hotel and Timeshares—Providing first-class lodging opportunities for those who wished to spend extended periods of time on the grounds immersed in the beauty and the spiritual atmosphere of the Legacy Center. With a lobby featuring decorative water works, a massive crystal chandelier, cascading stairways, and an impressive, crowning dome, the facilities were designed to offer the kind of world-class amenities that facilitate a time of refreshment and restoration.

The scope of the undertaking took their breath away. And Morris wasn't done laying out the vision.

He then outlined a plan for an online School of Ministry that would provide students from around the world with a world-class distance learning experience accessible through the Internet. Students would receive training in a wide range of subjects, such as healing; miracles, signs, and wonders; prayer, praise, and worship; evangelism; prophecy; the Holy Spirit; and global missions and ministry.

All of the courses would be taught from a Spirit-filled perspective and be designed to enable students to experience God's power and anointing. The training would continue the preparation of nationals to extend the whole message of Jesus Christ to every person on Earth for generations to come.

The teaching would be provided by many of the best teachers the Western world had seen. MCWE immediately began culling its archives to prepare thousands of hours of the anointed teachings delivered by Dr. Cerullo over the duration of his ministry. The team also began to collect teachings available from many world-class Christian leaders, prophets, and apostles, both living and deceased. That roster included historic giants of the faith, such as Smith Wigglesworth, Charles Spurgeon, Dwight Moody, Aimee Semple McPherson, and Kathryn Kuhlman. It also included contemporary leaders and prophets like Oral Roberts, Kenneth Copeland, Tommy Barnett, Jentezen Franklin, Marilyn Hickey, John Avanzini, and many others. No place on Earth could claim such an anointed and gifted faculty. The school would capably serve the young and old, leaders and laymen, pastors and parishioners.

The Training Center itself would be located in a massive, one-hundred-square-foot edifice where nationals and visitors could come for teaching and equipping in the language of their choice. Students and visitors would have access to classes and presentations in a state-of-the-art auditorium and theater, special technology-equipped classrooms, and a library with a multitude of ministry resources.

It was a mind-blowing portrait of a resource that would do justice to Dr.

Cerullo's legacy and that of his peers. To say that the team was enthusiastic was an understatement.

But one lingering question rumbled through people's minds as they envisioned the pioneering center. Who would be able to build such a spectacular but unique place?

CHAPTER 120

———•———

NOTHING THWARTS THE will of God—and the development of the Morris Cerullo Legacy International Center was clearly in His will. He proved that through the continual series of miracles He performed to get the center on track.

First He led Mike Harrah to get back in touch with the Cerullos. A superb contractor and architect, Mike had been a business partner in some real estate ventures with Dr. Cerullo nearly twenty years earlier. During their time together Morris led Mike to the Lord, and they had always maintained a good relationship. They lost contact with each other after they sold off the properties they had developed. In the intervening years Mike had become one of the most successful contractors and real estate developers in southern California.

As soon as he heard Dr. Cerullo's modest description of the Legacy Center, Mike immediately expressed his desire to be the architect and contractor for the project. His motivation? "I really want to be part of the team that sees the vision come to fulfillment." Although MCWE had viable proposals from other world-class contractors, it was clear that Mike was God's man for the job. He immediately got the project on the fast track.

As Dr. Cerullo talked to his team about specific needs for the Center, he asked Don Mandell, the vice president of international ministries, to find an original Torah for display on the grounds. (The Torah is the first five books of the Old Testament, also called the Pentateuch, and serves as the foundational narrative of the Jewish people.) Don had served with Dr. Cerullo for several decades and had an unparalleled network of ministry contacts around the world. But after several months of resourceful searching he reported back to Dr. Cerullo that all of the known Torahs that had been copied by rabbinical scribes were either in museums or owned by wealthy families that did not want to part with them.

Disappointed but undaunted, Morris kept praying about the situation.

Just a few weeks later Morris and Theresa were in Florida helping to officiate an ordination ceremony with their friends Christian and Robin Harfouche. During the course of the service, out of the blue, Robin revealed a fresh adventure with God.

"I could not sleep at all last night. The Lord was telling me to present Dr. and Mrs. Cerullo with a gift of the three-hundred-and-fifty-year-old Torah that we had purchased for our ministry. At breakfast this morning I told my family what the Lord was saying to me. To my surprise they all responded by saying they could not sleep last night either because the Holy Spirit was speaking the same thing to them."

No one was more caught off guard than Morris. He had not mentioned anything about his quest for an authentic Torah to Robin or her husband. As he stood on the platform with them, moved by the provision of God, the Harfouche family presented the Torah to Dr. Cerullo and Theresa.

A miracle? Absolutely! The copy gifted to Dr. Cerullo is one of just twenty still known to exist. It was written on deerskin by a rabbinical scribe who had been specially trained to translate and transcribe the Torah. In keeping with Hebrew tradition, the scribe had to perform the ancient rituals for cleanliness and holiness during the transcription process. By the time he completed the task the scroll itself was twelve feet long.

And now it was ready to travel to San Diego for eventual display at the Legacy Center.

God wasn't done yet.

A friend of Dr. Cerullo's had introduced him to Mel McGowan, a design engineer at the renowned Wald Disney Imagineering, the group that designs the theme park rides, large-scale attractions, and other innovative presentation technologies for the world's most successful entertainment company.

Knowing that the Legacy Center needed the best in the business to satisfy the technological demands of the development plan, Morris got in touch with Mel, who had since left Walt Disney Imagineering to initiate his own company, Visioneering Studios. A believer himself, and working with his in-house team, who were also followers of Christ, Mel was excited to be back in contact with Dr. Cerullo and especially stoked about the plan for the Legacy Center. His company was hired to create the most challenging technology aspects for the center. Their expertise and insight added a valuable dimension to the development of the center in its critical formative stages.

With as competent and committed a team of developers as could have been hoped for, the development process moved faster than expected. Through miraculous and anointed meetings with city officials and development experts, the Legacy Center received unusually rapid turnaround on plans and approvals from the city. The site plan moved through the city bureaucracy in just fourteen days—almost unheard of for a building plan as large and complex as that of the Legacy Center.

But why would anyone be surprised by all the inexplicable, positive turns of events that kept happening in relation to the Legacy Center? It was God's idea, and His chosen servant was leading the process. Perhaps it would take a continuing series of miracles to complete the amazing center, but nothing can stop God's from accomplishing His will.

If anyone has ever understood the supernatural, miracle-working power of God—and cooperated with Him in such miracles—it has been Morris Cerullo.

CHAPTER 121

——◆——

A T AGE FIFTEEN God had supernaturally granted Morris Cerullo a vision of himself standing in one place and reaching the entire world. Now, in his twilight years, the Lord had commissioned him to fulfill that vision through the construction of the Legacy Center. It would provide a mechanism for reaching everyone in the world with the life-changing story of God's love and miraculous power.

Throughout his seven decades of full-time ministry Morris had been a man living in two worlds. He was a citizen of heaven, a servant of the God of Israel, spending his days on loan to Earth. Through his fixation on the call and commands of God he experienced and accomplished things that none before him had been able to. And yet, Morris maintained that every one of those tremendous results was the work of the Holy Spirit, not the work of a man.

As the Legacy Center was being built the elder statesman of the faith continued to obediently log more frequent flyer miles than all but the most peripatetic corporate executives. His schedule remained a jumble of crusades and teaching. His pace would give many a younger leader heart failure. He shrugged off the intensity of the demands, reminding people that prophets never retire.

As he looked back on his ministry years he marveled at how God had chosen a young, rough, rebellious Jew and turned him into a surrendered and devoted disciple, a preacher of the gospel of Christ, a conduit for God's miracles, and a servant chosen by his heavenly Father to impart the anointing of the Lord to millions who thirsted for the privilege of serving the living God.

That brash youngster about whom the Lord said, "I see something in that boy that I will use for My glory," was a trusted and beloved son of the holy Father and a general in the Lord's army—one who had recruited millions of souls for service to the Lord and built that army into a mighty global force.

That ever-expanding army, present on the six continents on which he had faithfully ministered, continues to aggressively seek and restore lost souls today and to bring God's healing power to the lives of people who are suffering and incomplete.

It is a testament to the steadfastness, the creativity, the love, and the power of our almighty God.

It is also the stuff of legend, the legend of Morris Cerullo.

WISDOM FROM THE LEGEND

---◆---

OVER THE COURSE of his many years in ministry Morris Cerullo has spent literally thousands of hours teaching people biblical principles and applications. Here is a sampling of some of the statements he has made while teaching God's truths to millions of people around the world.

---◆---

God Himself has called you and ordained you to be a full-time minister in your sphere of influence. The term "full-time minister" has been redefined!

Beloved, it is harvest time, and God is going to have a people of destiny.

God does not depend on anything we possess. However, God never calls or uses anyone without first giving them an experience.

Remember that the key to victory is spiritual timing. This is your time!

To work the works of God we need the same power that enabled the early church to reach its known world in three hundred years without radio, without television, without airplanes—without Bibles! They had a unique characteristic, a unique ingredient.

Revelation is the stripping away of a veil of darkness, just as a breakthrough is a sudden burst of advanced knowledge that takes us past a line of defense.

You have heard that it's alright to lose some battles as long as you win the war. But I say that we need total victory, to give the devil not one battle—nothing!

We do not deal with the surface. We go past the surface in prayer, to the root cause, and lay the ax to the root of the tree.

A powerful spiritual force is being released in the body of Christ to bring about the greatest manifestation of the power of God the world has ever seen.

Remember the "eleventh commandment," that we love one another. We will never come to unity through our methodologies. But we can have unity in the Spirit.

Beloved, if you love one another, show that love now. Don't wait for your brother or sister to be in the casket and then come by weeping and saying, "They were so wonderful."

Many quote the verse, "Even so, come, Lord Jesus," but how many are actually praying for His return?

Do you want Him to return, or is there something in you that has not died yet?

Don't be a "sideline compromiser." You are part of God's end-time plan, and God has not planned any defeats for you.

The Word of God is alive and powerful. However, the way to faith is not to go around making vain repetitions. The way to peace is not to take a verse on peace and walk about saying, "I've got peace. I've got peace." Faith is a gift! Adam and Eve originally did not need it, as the Lord came and fellowshiped with them. We are not saved by faith but by grace; it is a gift.

Do you think that God looks like me? Do you think that He has my eyes, my nose, or my face? Where is the image of God? It is in our free moral will. That is all we have to give Him—to come before Him and surrender our will back to Him.

Jesus opens the way for us to declare war on the devil's war. "For this purpose the Son of God was manifested, that he might destroy the works of the devil" (1 John 3:8).

Do not look to the bigness of your need but to the bigness of your God. Do not let your circumstances hinder you from seeing His abilities. At the same time, inspect what you expect. Never put your destiny in another man's hands.

When God told me He was going to reveal to me His heartbeat, He said it was "souls." He also said that power does not travel in words but in relationship. This took me back to my vision, as a fifteen-year-old boy, of souls in hell. This also took me back to the moment when God asked me what I wanted out of this life, and I asked for the ability to take the same power and anointing from my life and to pass it on to others.

The mantle must continue to be passed on continually from Elijah to Elisha to millions throughout the world to reach billions who have never one time heard the name of Jesus.

It is harvest time, and God is going to have Himself a people. In the name of Jesus, receive your miracle! Receive the anointing! What is unlawful in heaven, declare unlawful on Earth. What is lawful in heaven, declare lawful on Earth. Beloved, do not stop at the point of blessing. Go on to the point of power. Be truly baptized with the Holy Spirit.

The greatest miracle is not the healing of blind eyes. It is not the restoration of crippled legs. It is not the opening of deaf ears. The greatest miracle is when God saves a sinner's soul from hell. It's called the miracle of salvation.

Epilogue B

ACCLAIM FOR THE LEGEND

———•———

THE WORLD TODAY is literally filled with churches and spiritual leaders that exist because of the faithful ministry of Morris Cerullo. The celebratory remarks of those whose lives have been dramatically altered through their exposure to his efforts would fill another book (or two). But here are a few examples of the esteem in which Christian leaders around the world hold Dr. Cerullo.

———•———

I was first introduced to Morris Cerullo at a revival in 1989. He is a prophet to our nation and many countries in Latin America. In his conferences there were miracles, signs, deliverances, and many unique healings. Witnessing this had a huge impact on me. Seeing people I knew getting miraculously transformed before my eyes was very powerful. The vision of my ministry was born in Morris's meetings.

—FERNANDO PEREZ
TOPILEJO, MEXICO

I would hate to think of where Africa would be today if Morris Cerullo was not faithful to build God an army, hold crusades, and Schools of Ministry. The continent would be 90 percent Islam instead of 50 percent Christian.

—BISHOP ROBERT KAYANJA
NAIROBI, KENYA

You cannot write the history of the spiritual life or climate of Africa without including Brother Cerullo, because he has played such a significant role. I came to the School of Ministry in Lagos, Nigeria, as a new convert. Dr. Cerullo's coming was like the beginning of my Christian life. He is like a spiritual father. At least 60 percent of what God has done in my life has happened through Brother Cerullo's ministry. Most of the ministers preaching across Africa have been directly or indirectly influenced by Dr. Cerullo's ministry. Like me, many of them look to him as a spiritual father.

—PASTOR AYO ORITSEJAFOR
WARRI, NIGERIA

When Dr. Cerullo visited Costa Rica I heard him and was so touched by the power of Almighty God. His teachings and anointing transformed my ministry. This incredible experience turned me into one of the most recognized Latin American ministers all around the world. I attribute much of my success to my relationship with Dr. Cerullo, who has unleashed my growth and has been my mentor, my apostle, and my ministerial father.

—APOSTLE RONY CHAVEZ
COSTA RICA

I will never forget my first trip to India. I saw a little blind Indian girl receive the gift of sight. Jesus put eyeballs in her sockets as she stood at the foot of the platform while Morris was praying for a half a million people during the crusade in Shivaji Park in Bombay.

—BECKYE CHINNADURAI
INDIA

I come from a staunch Hindu background. I got radically saved, and soon thereafter Brother Cerullo came to Calcutta. God used him to do mighty miracles there. I went to his crusade meeting. Nobody had come to India in such a dramatic way. No true pioneers had come to India. There was no major stir. Morris Cerullo caused a major stir in the entire nation.

—MINNY LAL
DELHI, INDIA

I remember a little boy in the Philippines who had a growth behind his ear. As dad prayed the prayer of faith and healing I watched that growth literally shrink into nothing. It was completely healed! That was one of the first miracles I had ever experienced in my life.

—BARBARA CERULLO, DR. CERULLO'S DAUGHTER-IN-LAW

I attended Morris Cerullo's School of Ministry. My life was totally changed. After receiving training I committed myself to return to my province to do the work of the ministry. I began conducting meetings, holding crusades, and open-air meetings. Miracle after miracle took place. I established a church that reaches out to the many tribes in the Philippines. We hold three-day crusades for a tribe, then establish a church with the tribe. We have established more than forty churches in the tribal area of Mindanao.

—PASTOR EUFEMIO MONTEJO
TALISAY, PHILIPPINES

I first came in contact with Brother Cerullo's ministry when I attended his crusade in Manila. During the crusade I saw miracles happening while I assisted as an usher. Later, when I got more involved in the ministry of Morris Cerullo, our church grew. I began prophesying and acting on the teaching of Brother Cerullo. I know this is why my church has increased. Because of Brother Cerullo's ministry here, we concentrated on going into the local tribes in the Philippines. We now have more than a thousand cell churches all over the Philippines.

—Reverend Rolly Blas
Philippines

The School of Ministry is one of the best—if not the best—meeting Japan has ever had in the history of Christianity in Japan.

—Reverend Nobuyoshi Nagai
Bible College President, Japan

During the crusade in Singapore I saw miracles such as I had never seen before in my life. I was totally overwhelmed. When the meeting was over I just stood before the fountain outside the theater and cried and cried my heart out. I was never the same man again. I lost interest in ordinary pursuits. I wanted the same ministry as Morris Cerullo. I attended the School of Ministry and learned how to go into the world and preach the gospel with the same signs and wonders following—and I did!

—Pastor Rony Tan
Singapore

When I was in high school I attended a crusade Dr. Cerullo held in Jakarta. The police arrested Dr. Cerullo and tried to stop the crusade, but the people prayed because we were so hungry for God. Miraculously, the government allowed him to continue the service. That meeting greatly impacted my life and opened my eyes to the reality of God's anointing. My walk with Jesus was never again the same because the power of God was so real in my life. Now God is using me in ministry the same way as Morris Cerullo. I have conducted healing crusades in many cities throughout Indonesia and other nations, and He has demonstrated His healing power. I began a church with twenty-five members, and today, just fourteen years later, we have eight thousand members. I am grateful for Dr. Cerullo's faithfulness to come year after year to Indonesia and to help us prepare and reap the harvest.

—Pastor Petrus Agung Purnomo
Semarang, Indonesia

I watched Dr. Cerullo's television program, *Victory Today!*, and followed his ministry after that. My life was never the same. I received deliverance from depression and developed peace, love, and patience—the characteristics of Christ. Since then, more and more power has been released through my ministry. Miracles, signs, and wonders are resulting in continual growth in the church I lead and in our outreaches.

—Pastor Elisabeth Lindenthaler
Graz, Austria

I attended the Central America School of Ministry. After one week of intensive training from Dr. Cerullo my life was turned upside down. Life took on a whole new purpose, meaning, and destiny. I experienced indescribable personal and ministerial growth. I have not stopped running ever since the day I met Dr. Cerullo. I was asked at one point to accompany Dr. Cerullo as his personal interpreter. I have seen all types of miracles happen right before my eyes. I have seen presidents and high-ranking officials kneel before him, pleading for God's blessings. I have seen crowds of over one hundred thousand people weep profusely in the presence of God, a presence released every single time he ministers.

—PASTOR SYDNEY STAIR
GUAYNABO, PUERTO RICO

ABOUT THE AUTHOR

———•———

Who Is Morris Cerullo?

D R. MORRIS CERULLO is a world-renowned evangelist and the president of Morris Cerullo World Evangelism, which was founded in 1961.

The 85-year-old Christian statesman has been traveling to the developing nations of the world for 69 years. He has ministered in 93 nations, in over 400 cities, on 6 continents, where he has personally trained 5 million Christian leaders and ministered to millions more. He has dedicated his life to helping hurting people and continues to travel more than 250,000 miles every year to minister healing and salvation to the world.

Morris and his wife, Theresa, have been married for 65 years, and are affectionately referred to as "Papa" and "Mama" by the multitudes that have been affected by their love and generosity.

Morris Cerullo – The Early Days

Dr. Morris Cerullo was raised in a Jewish Orthodox orphanage in New Jersey until the age of 14 1/2 when he gave his life to Christ. Because of his faith, he was persecuted and eventually had to leave the orphanage.

Morris attended Hebrew school while in the orphanage and attended public school until age 15. At that time, Morris began preaching three to four times per week in local churches, with invitations growing steadily.

At age 17, with no money to pay for tuition, he received a scholarship to the New York Metropolitan Bible School in Suffern, New York, from where he graduated. Morris later received two honorary doctorates from Florida Beacon College and Oral Roberts University.

By the time he was 20, he was pastoring his own 15-member church, and due to limited funds, he served as the pastor, janitor, maintenance man, and landscaper all rolled into one. His hard work paid off, though. Within eight months, his once tiny church became one of the largest in New England.

At the age of 23, he went on his first overseas missions trip to Greece. Many more overseas trips followed, and an international ministry quickly developed.

THE VISION TO REACH THE WORLD

Morris soon realized that the key to reaching the world was to train Nationals to reach their own people—Africans reaching Africans, Asians reaching Asians, and South Americans reaching South Americans.

This vision and specific call from God has resulted in millions of Christian ministers being raised up to reach their nations.

He has accomplished this goal by conducting Schools of Ministry around the world. Nationals with a heart to learn and lead come to be trained so that they can then go on to impact the lives of others through the ministering of the Gospel of Jesus Christ.

The global impact of Dr. Cerullo and MCWE is staggering:

+ Dr. Cerullo has ministered to innumerable multitudes of people face to face.

+ Miracle Crusades in which the lame walk, the blind see, the deaf hear, and the Gospel is preached have reached up to 500,000 people in one service.

+ Dr. Cerullo has personally ministered to presidents, prime ministers, and heads of state in many nations.

+ Dr. Cerullo has written over 200 classic Christian books, unique study Bibles, and devotionals.

+ Dr. Cerullo has produced an abundance of teaching and training materials on audio and video.

+ Dr. Cerullo has established many organizations and facilities around the world to teach and train new Christians.

+ Dr. Cerullo has been impacting the nation of Israel since 1968 through books, Bible correspondence courses, radio ministries, TV specials, crusades, and even a full-length, prime time movie, which was broadcast to 14 million Jewish households.

THE FRUIT OF HIS LABOR

Few people have put as much effort to help those in need, over such a long period of time, as Dr. Cerullo. The fruit of his efforts has circulated the globe and will forever be cherished by the millions of lives he has touched. Just ask the mother of the little Brazilian boy who had been crippled since birth, healed as Morris prayed for him; or the young Mexican girl whose hearing was restored; or Happiness, the young Nigerian girl who had been born deaf and mute, completely healed by God as Morris ministered during a meeting.

Over 69 years of ministry, Dr. Cerullo has sacrificially done more to help others than could possibly be listed, but here is a brief list of some of his notable ministry outreaches:

In 1974, *Helpline TV* program was developed and telecast to 80 of America's largest cities. It was not uncommon for celebrities, such as Dale Evans and Pat Boone, to help answer the phone lines and pray for those in need. In the years that followed, other television programs were launched that reached global audiences.

In 1976, during the height of Apartheid, Dr. Cerullo was the only white minister who would dare to step foot on the platform for a meeting in which 80,000 (mostly black South Africans) showed up to witness the miracle-working power of God. Countless people were physically healed, and there was a supernatural blending that took place between the blacks and whites.

In 1977 in Cochin, India, approximately 30 percent of the entire population of 500,000, poured onto the field, where countless people were healed and saved by the all-powerful Word of God.

In 1987, and estimated 300,000 French-speaking Africans attended a crusade where more than 50 deaf people were healed and 3,500 Nationals were trained. (A National is a Christian who is trained to teach, preach, and train disciples in his/her own country.)

In 1999, Dr. Cerullo trained 40,000 Nationals from over 32 African nations who attended a meeting in Lagos, Nigeria. Approximately 85 percent of the Nationals were pastors who took the teachings back to their churches, where they trained thousands more.

In 2002, Dr. Cerullo established the World Prayer Center in San Diego. This prayer hotline is staffed with a trained team that prays for thousands of people every year. Reports flood the ministry every week with tremendous answers to prayer.

In 2011, *Victory Today* television program was launched. Responses come in daily reporting alcohol and drug addictions broken, marriages healed, supernatural financial provisions, and many more wonderful testimonies. This cutting-edge television program can be seen worldwide, six days a week, by millions of viewers. The programs offer practical information on topics such as finances, as well as various Bible lessons and healing ministry.

In 2014, Dr. Cerullo embarked on a 20-day journey to 6 European countries where he conducted 20 meetings, mobilized 2,000 churches, and trained 18,000 Nationals.

Over the decades, Dr. Cerullo has trained millions of Nationals all over the world, who have gone on to teach and train millions more. There is a domino effect that takes place. When the Nationals are trained, they establish churches, ministries, and other businesses and organizations that help the poor, care for orphans and the homeless, and provide jobs to countless numbers of people, oftentimes in impoverished areas where jobs, and even basic provisions, are hard to come by. Through his ministry, Dr. Cerullo has seen the Gospel transform nations.

Dr. Morris Cerullo has personally mentored many worldwide Christian leaders. As a result of his decades of personal, face-to-face teaching, these leaders have been equipped to reach millions more. Here is a brief list of some of their accomplishments:

+ **Pastor Ayo Oritsejafor, Nigeria** (trained in 1979) – Currently pastors a 35,000-seat church, founded the African Broadcasting Network, serves as president of the Christian Association of Nigeria, and ministers at conferences all over the world.

+ **Bishop Eliudi Issangya, Tanzania** (trained in 1979) – Opened a 14-acre Christian training compound. To date, over 3,500 have graduated and gone on to establish 900 churches throughout Africa.

+ **Bishop Adebayo Adedimeji, Ivory Coast** (trained in 1986) – Now operates a 400-member church and Bible Institute where thousands have been trained and have gone on to establish dozens of churches throughout Africa.

+ **Apostle Jorge Marquez, Uruguay** (trained in 1996) – Pastors an 11,500-member church and heads a project directed at reaching the entire country of Uruguay via church plants and radio and television broadcasts.

+ **Pastor Omar Cabrera, Paraguay** (trained in 1966) – Has impacted the entire country of Paraguay through crusades, church plants, and prison ministries.

+ **Apostle Rony Chavez, Costa Rica** (trained in 1983) – Has written over 60 books and has preached in more than 70 countries on 5 continents.

+ **Rajan and Beckye Chinnadurai, India** (trained in 1987) – Have trained over 18,000 in their Christian schools and preach the Gospel to thousands more via a daily cable TV program.

+ **Pastor Mohan Babu, India** (trained in 1997) – Has established 300 Christian churches in various parts of India.

+ **Samuel Browne, India** (trained in 1992) – Has ministered to more than 60,000 people living in remote villages in Tibet.

+ **Bishop Eddie Villanueva, the Philippines** (trained in 1979) – Now has more than 5 million members in his ministry, from 42 countries.

+ **Rev. Rolly Blas, the Philippines** (trained in 1982) – Pastors a 10,000-member church, and has planted 1,000 more throughout the Philippines.

LOVE FOR ISRAEL

For over 58 consecutive years, Dr. Cerullo has traveled to the Holy Land with a passion for God's chosen people. As a young, Messianic Jewish man, God laid a tremendous burden on Dr. Cerullo's heart to reach the Jews.

In 1967, God spoke to Dr. Cerullo and said, "Son, now is the time to turn your eyes to the Middle East and begin to work for My people, Israel."

In 1968, Dr. Cerullo began his first campaign of reaching out to the Jewish population in Israel. His first mass mailing was 400,000 books, followed by a Bible correspondence course that was distributed six times per year for 12 years. In 1970, he launched a radio ministry that reached millions in nine surrounding nations. In 1975, he developed a TV special, *Masada*, which won three Golden Globe awards and generated 200,000 responses. In the early 1980s, Dr. Cerullo produced and aired three television specials from historic sites in Israel. Some of Israel's government leaders appeared on the shows, and response was phenomenal—60,000 people wrote or called the ministry with sentiments of gratitude or to report healings, salvations, or freedom from the bondage of sin. In 1992, Dr. Cerullo launched a new television program that reached a potential 110,000 homes in Israel. A full-length, prime time movie, Rabbi, also aired. It was broadcast to 14 million Jewish households and won two awards.

Dr. Cerullo travels to Israel every year, ministering the Good News of Jesus to large crowds that have grown considerably over the years. He also provides assistance to churches and ministries so that they can expand their reach and continue ministering to those in Israel that are hungry for the truth of God's Word.

HUMANITARIAN CARE

MCWE has assisted many organizations and facilities around the world to teach and train new Christians. MCWE is also known for its humanitarian support and has provided aid to Ethiopia, medical assistance in East Africa, and helped build multiple orphanages in Mexico.

The ministry also provides many scholarships every year to up-and-coming Christian students around the world to attend ministry training classes.

Most recently, Morris and his wife, Theresa Cerullo, partnered with Tommy and Matthew Barnett to build several floors of the Los Angeles Dream Center that houses 200 women who have come off the streets of Los

Angeles, out of drugs, human trafficking, and prostitution. The floor is called Mama Theresa's Place in honor of Theresa Cerullo.

COMMENDATIONS

Dr. Cerullo has been presented with the key to San Diego and other cities in America, as well as having received letters of recognition for the work he has done in America and foreign countries, from mayors, presidents, and other governmental leaders.

Dr. Cerullo also received the Lifetime Global Impact Award in May 2015 in recognition of his many years of worldwide ministry. This prestigious award was presented by Oral Roberts University president, Dr. William Wilson, and Assemblies of God general superintendent, Dr. George Wood, at the Empowered21 Global Congress, a gathering of over 4,000 world ministry leaders and pastors in Jerusalem, Israel.

LOCATIONS

MCWE has offices in San Diego, Dallas, London, Ontario, and Paris and employs over 100 staff members. For more information visit www.mcwe.com.

NOTES

NOTES

NOTES

NOTES